Awakening the Creative Spirit

A SPIRITUAL DIRECTORS INTERNATIONAL BOOK

Awakening the Creative Spirit

Bringing the Arts to Spiritual Direction

CHRISTINE VALTERS PAINTNER
BETSEY BECKMAN

Morehouse Publishing
NEW YORK · HARRISBURG · DENVER

Morehouse Publishing, 4775 Linglestown Road, Harrisburg, PA 17112
Morehouse Publishing, 445 Fifth Avenue, New York, NY 10016
Morehouse Publishing is an imprint of Church Publishing Incorporated.

Cover design by Laurie Klein Westhafer
Interior design and typesetting by Beth Oberholtzer

Library of Congress Cataloging-in-Publication Data

Paintner, Christine Valters.
    Awakening the creative spirit : bringing the arts to spiritual direction / Christine Valters Paintner and Betsey Beckman.
        p.   cm.
    Includes bibliographical references.
    ISBN 978-0-8192-2371-5 (pbk.)
    1. Christianity and the arts. 2. Spiritual direction—Christianity. I. Beckman, Betsey. II. Title.
BR115.A8P34   2010
253.5'3—dc22

                                                                                    2009044024

Printed in the United States of America

11 12 13 14 15   10 9 8 7 6 5 4 3

We dedicate this book to our first spiritual directors:
Sister Rosemarie Carvalho, RSM and Sister Mary Kay Liston, CSJ.

Their witness as strong and compassionate women helped
to awaken our own creative spirits.

Contents

Acknowledgments

This book is the fruit of so many amazing and wonderful people whom we've had the privilege of encountering through our lives and ministries.

Our first debt of gratitude goes to Jane Comerford, CSJ. Jane created and led an initial form of the expressive arts program for spiritual directors in the Northwest. She helped co-create and co-teach our first year of Awakening the Creative Spirit and her wisdom shines through our continued work. We are so very grateful for her friendship and support.

We want to thank the following people for reading through the manuscript in an earlier version and offering us essential feedback and input: Kayce Stevens Hughlett, Jane Klassen, Rachelle Oppenhuizen, Lois Perron, Carol Scott Kassner, and Sr. Lucy Wynkoop, OSB. Their keen eyes and wise hearts have helped to make this a better book.

We were blessed with the contributions of many stories and poems from previous participants in our Awakening the Creative Spirit Program, as well as other spiritual directors who engage the arts. Their reflections add richness and depth to this book and we are tremendously grateful to Judy Bartels, Kathy Bence, Sharie Bowman, Constance Bouvier, Claudia Campbell, Trish Bruxvoort Colligan, Maureen Fowler, Cynthia Gayle, Barbara Gibson, Robert Gilroy, SJ, Karen Haddon, Kayce Stevens Hughlett, Rebecca Johnson, Carol Scott Kassner, Marilyn Marston, Suzie Massey, Billie Mazzei, Pam McCauley, Paula McCutcheon, Wes McIntyre, Delores Montpetit, Stacy Nagel, Karin Ogren, Marilyn Peot, CSJ, Lois Perron,

Cathy Rhoads, Lisa Sadleir-Hart, Freya Secrest, Cheryl Shay, Connie Pwll Walck Tyler, Patricia Doheny Tyllia, and Dianna Woolley.

There were also a number of spiritual direction colleagues who contributed an exercise or new way of looking at the engagement of the arts in spiritual direction. We want to thank the following people for being willing to share their expertise with us: Sharie Bowman, Trish Bruxvoort Colligan, Jane Comerford, CSJ, Roy DeLeon, Carol Flake, Marianne Hieb, Mary Lou Weaver Houser, Kayce Stevens Hughlett, Ann Keller, Pam McCauley, Diana McKendree, Debra McMaster, Sally O'Neil, Rachelle Oppenhuizen, Eunice Schroeder, April Sotura, Jennifer Steil, and Maggie Yowell.

An extra special dose of gratitude goes to Kayce Stevens Hughlett for her significant contributions to the supervision chapter. Kayce and Christine lead arts-centered supervision groups together and this chapter is the result of a fully collaborative effort between them. Kayce's generous sharing of her gifts and her enthusiastic support for this project have been invaluable to its successful completion.

We offer heartfelt thanks to Liz Ellman, Executive Director of Spiritual Directors International, who has consistently extended valuable support for and belief in our work with the arts. Thank you to Nancy Fitzgerald, our original editor at Morehouse, who believed in the importance of this project, and Frank Tedeschi, Senior Executive Editor at Church Publishing, the parent company of Morehouse, who has been wonderful to work with in the process of bringing this book to publication.

Betsey would also like to thank mentors and friends, Cynthia Winton-Henry and Phil Porter, co-creators of InterPlay®, whose playful wisdom is sprinkled so generously throughout this book. She also thanks J. Michael Sparough, SJ for ongoing friendship and artistry, as well as teachers Greg Reynolds and Peter Geiler, whose dancing spirits continue to guide from the other side. She warmly applauds Charlie and Chaz, for filling her heart and house with music, and finally, gratitude goes to her creative partner Christine, for continuing to propose audacious adventures!

Christine thanks her beloved husband John who supports her in all of her heart's longings, all of her mentors and teachers in the fields of both spiritual direction and the arts, her sweet and faithful hound Tune, who was an inspiring muse during the writing process, and Betsey, her cherished teaching and writing partner.

Introduction

The book you are holding in your hands has been a labor of passion and love, and the fruit of many years of combined experience. In the most immediate sense it comes directly from our teaching of a program called Awakening the Creative Spirit: Experiential Education for Spiritual Directors offered each year on the beautiful Hood Canal in the Pacific Northwest. But its roots extend much deeper into the background and experience that we (Betsey and Christine) each bring to this unique and growing ministry of integrating the arts and spiritual direction.

Christine's Story

After engaging the arts for several years in creating retreats, in 1998 I began doctoral studies in Christian Spirituality at the Graduate Theological Union in Berkeley. In the Bay Area I encountered the therapeutic field of the expressive arts and a whole language for what I had discovered previously on my own—the healing and enlivening power of the arts. I continued my studies in theology and at the same time began to take a variety of workshops that incorporated multiple modalities including visual art, poetry, movement, and voice.

With my new language and framework for engaging the arts in the service of healing and my deepened skills, I was empowered to continue integrating the arts into contexts of spiritual formation, direction, and retreats. I began teaching a summer course at the Graduate Theological Union in Berkeley called "Arts as Spiritual Practice." Each year ministers from different denominations gathered together for a week of intensive exploration into the gifts of the arts for revealing the sacred dimension of our lives.

After completing my PhD in 2003, I moved to Seattle and founded a non-profit organization called Abbey of the Arts[1] and I dedicate much of my professional work to supporting the arts in various ministry contexts through teaching, retreats, spiritual direction, and supervision. I have continued my personal and professional development in the expressive arts through attending various conferences and programs with a particular love of dreamwork. In 2008, the International Expressive Arts Therapy Association, the governing body of the expressive arts field, began to offer professional status as a Registered Expressive Arts Consultant and Educator. I applied and was approved based on my education, experience, and extensive integration of the expressive arts into spiritual formation contexts. It is an honor to have my work with the arts validated by the expressive arts community in this way.

Spiritually, I root myself in the Benedictine monastic tradition as an Oblate. This means I have made a commitment as a lay person to live out my contemplative practice while living in the heart of Seattle, with my husband and dog whom we call "the Abbess" because of her wise mentoring in balanced rhythms of life. I continue to nurture my own artistic life through the media that I have found myself most drawn to since childhood: photography, writing, and poetry.

Betsey's Story

Mine is a call to dance, in its many aspects. I was first awakened to the art of dance as a young girl studying classical ballet, and in my 20s I eventually embraced the grounded expressive qualities of modern dance while performing with the Greg Reynolds Dance Quintet in Washington, D.C.

What deepened my call was discovering the prayer of dance, which happened spontaneously for me as a five-year-old. In high school and beyond, this led me to a passion for liturgical dance combined with story-theater, which I embraced in the company of the Fountain Square Fools, under the direction of J. Michael Sparough, SJ. I was also drawn to the theology of dance at Georgetown University, during which time I formed and directed the Georgetown University Liturgical Dance Ensemble. Later, I explored the ministry of dance through a Masters in Ministry at Seattle University.

Not long after, I was called to the therapy of dance, which I probed deeply during my training at the Institute for Transformational Movement in Seattle in the 80s, under the guidance of Peter Geiler. I then taught on staff there and developed my own private practice for the following six years.

Most recently, I have been called into the ecstatic play of dance, through the delightful practice of InterPlay® that has become my primary creative community and modality for the past ten years. This intermodal improvisational practice has allowed for music, story, and song to playfully infuse my artistry and teaching as well.

As I integrate the skills of art, prayer, performance, liturgy, spirituality, ministry, play, and therapy, I have created a practice called "Dancing Spiritual Direction," and have produced DVDs, books, meditations, and a repertory of Biblical Storydances that I perform at conferences and churches both locally and nationally under the title of The Dancing Word.[2] I am delighted to bring all of these skills and modalities to bear in the field of spiritual direction.

The Awakening the Creative Spirit Program

From 1997–2000 Jane Comerford, CSJ founded the original incarnation of the expressive arts program for spiritual directors and taught it in Tacoma, Washington, and Portland, Oregon, with Betsey Beckman assisting. We are indebted to Jane for her pioneering spirit.

Soon after I (Christine) moved to Seattle, I had the good fortune of meeting Jane and Betsey. Together we developed Awakening the Creative Spirit, an experiential education program for spiritual directors to learn to engage the arts in their ministry offered in Seattle over a six-month period. After that first year teaching together (2004–2005) Jane decided to focus her energy on other work and Betsey and I continued to develop the material and offer it to others. I have always been most strongly drawn to artistic expression through guided imagination, writing, poetry, and visual arts, especially photography and collage. This was the perfect complement to Betsey's skills in dance, movement, storytelling, song, and music. We both are rooted in Roman Catholic tradition, but work actively to make the material inclusive for people from any faith tradition. The language of art and spirit is universal and we have been blessed by a diversity of participants in our program.

We decided to offer our Awakening the Creative Spirit Program in a week-long intensive format in a retreat center on the Hood Canal as a way to open up the experience to those farther afield and beyond commuting distance. So far we have been blessed with participants from Alberta, British Columbia, California, Michigan, Minnesota, Missouri, Oregon, and Washington.

After teaching our program for four years and developing a body of material we took the next step of compiling it into book form to reach out and encourage others to explore arts in service of enlivening and deepening their relationships of spiritual care. Our training program is designed for spiritual directors in particular, but chaplains, pastoral counselors, pastors, retreat directors, therapists, and educators have participated in our program. Essentially, the tools presented in both the program and this book can help support anyone who works in a context of offering spiritual care to an individual or a group. The foundations and exercises can easily be applied to include the arts on retreats, in hospital settings, in counseling sessions, or in classroom settings. Those who are the recipients of spiritual care, and who want to explore the arts further as a way of praying and encountering the holy, will also find value here. We invite you to read these pages and begin experimenting on your own and then encourage your spiritual director to make space for these modes of expression in a session.

Many of you will bring a higher level of ease or skill in one art form over another. We offer you the opportunity here to deepen this experience while growing in your comfort with other art forms. There is a great joy to be discovered in experiencing the various art forms together.

How to Use This Book

Part One offers a foundational exploration of the role of the arts in spiritual practice and prayer. We give our readers a brief history of the arts in sacred contexts, an explanation of the philosophy underlying the field of the expressive arts, and some practical guidelines for beginning this journey.

In Part Two, we explore each modality individually—storytelling, imagination, movement, visual art, music, and poetry—to understand the particular gifts each form has to offer us. The suggested exercises begin with simple forms so that you have an accessible way to begin your exploration, and can then move into more complex experiences.

In Part Three, we explore different life contexts and themes that arise in spiritual care, including breaking open images of God, discernment, grief, dreamwork, the seasons of our lives, and spiritual direction supervision. Each chapter then offers a series of multimodal approaches to support your exploration of these themes.

We also use a variety of symbols to help indicate which kind of art form a particular exercise engages:

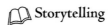 Storytelling

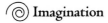 Imagination

 Movement

 Visual Art

 Music

 Poetry

Most of the exercises we suggest can be used in individual "one-with-one"[3] spiritual direction sessions, group spiritual direction, or in retreat contexts. Our sincere hope is that the following pages inspire you to begin exploring the arts in your ministry, or if you are already integrating them, that they help deepen the ways you can imagine them supporting the ministry of spiritual direction and the care of souls.

Contribution Process

Throughout the text we have included reflections and stories from participants in our Awakening the Creative Spirit Programs and others on how a particular exercise impacted them or how they have engaged it in their own ministries of spiritual care. Our hope is that these flesh out and make "real" the work we are suggesting, helping the reader to imagine how the exercises might work in practical ways and their potential impact on a directee.

We also recognize that we are part of a much larger network of spiritual directors who engage the arts in their practices, and we invited contributions of specific exercises from colleagues in the field. These other voices bring a sense of richness and diversity of possibility to the process. You can find brief bios for these contributors at the end of this book.

Spiritual Direction

It is worth adding a brief note about our choice to use the language of "spiritual direction," "director," and "directee." We recognize and honor that there is a lively debate about whether "direction" is really the most appropriate description of what we do in this ministry. In many ways, the language of "soul companioning" or "soul care" feels more appropriate. However, because spiritual direction is a widely accepted term, we use it primarily for our descriptions in this book.

We offer the inspirations in the pages that follow in the hope that your creative spirit will be awakened and enlivened. Whichever ministry of soul care you find yourself in, we are delighted to offer you tools and gifts for a deepening of the journey. When creativity is unleashed, we tap into a sacred power where the newness of life is always possible. We pray that the journey ahead is filled with both confirmations of your essential self and new discoveries of God's invitation to you and to the directees with whom you minister.

PART I

Spiritual Direction and the Arts

1

Art as Mediator of the Sacred

Betsey Beckman

Creativity constitutes the ultimate intimacy for it is the place where the Divine and the human are most destined to interact.
—MATTHEW FOX

Art and God

As spiritual directors, we support others in opening to the sacred, living deeply with mystery, and awakening to an ongoing encounter with the Divine. But, we might ask ourselves a fundamental question: how does one actually nurture an encounter with mystery? In other words, how do we—and those we work with—come to know God? Traditionally, we might suggest that our encounters with the holy can be deepened through scripture, study, prayer, relationship, church, nature, and meditation, but what if we consider the possibility that a primary way we can experience the revelation of God's mystery is through the process of our own creative expression?

Gifts of the Arts

When we engage in the arts, we dip into our souls to discover deep pools of wonder, breath-taking gifts of beauty, and quiet revelation. As we create, we

3

are invited into playfulness, poignancy, and surprise—energies that renew us and revitalize our sense of purpose. Along the way we may encounter archetypal symbols, depth of emotion, and ecstatic expressions that lead us beyond self-consciousness to oneness with community, revealing "intimations of immortality."[4] The arts are the language of the soul. If we become "linguists" looking back on the development of this language through the journey of time, we recognize that God has been inviting us into this sacred dialogue since the earliest awakenings of humanity.

Imagine this . . .

> You are traveling back in time, hundreds of centuries, thousands of cycles, back 30,000 years to a make-shift "village" at the dawn of humanity—a tribe of your own ancestors. The sun is emerging over the edge of the world, and you see a child being carried, a sick child upheld in loving arms. Now imagine yourself as that child—for after all, this is blood of your blood, your own ancestor—and so you feel yourself being carried from the morning light through a crevice deep into the darkness of an ancient cave. Strong arms bear you through ever thinning passages to the heart of the cavern. There, the drums and rattles begin their foundational rhythms, connecting to your own heartbeat, resonating within your inner chambers. Not long after, vocal chords open and chant coalesces around you as you are enfolded in a circular repetitious sound, reverberating to the marrow of your bones. When voices tire, a bone flute picks up the melody and carries it on. A small, sturdy feminine figurine, sculpted from ivory, is placed on your chest.
>
> Then, by the light of flickering oil lamps, you open your dazed eyes to see images being stroked in rust colors onto the walls of the cave; bison and stag curve up the arching chamber. After a time, the group's singing quiets and the Shaman's voice rises up, and the ancient stories begin their recounting in voice and song. For hours, you are drawn into a dream-time telling of myths you have heard before and yet not heard, of animal-spirits and voyages of great courage, of raucous birds and whispers arriving on the wind. At one point, the Shaman lifts a feather and begins dancing over your body, calling, breathing, at times wailing, at times leaping, chanting, drawing energy to you, away from you. After a time, two elders cover their hands with mud and begin smearing it on your body—and you become one with the earth.
>
> After many hours, you awaken to find yourself being washed in waters and emerging into the light. At the cave entrance you are greeted

by your tribe-family wafting flower petals over you and singing with exuberance. Other villagers in masks greet you with their painted faces and bodies. A great feast is assembled and the sound of laughter rises up and your strength is returning now. You have traveled to the under-world, and you are emerging into new life.

By engaging in an imaginative, yet historically based, exercise such as this, we begin to get a picture and kinesthetic sensation of how art, as a lan-guage of the soul, rises up out of our collective human memory, our inner creative fire, and our ancient sacred impulses. Art-making is somehow all at once a journey, a communication, a modality, a healing, and a prayer. Art is a distinctly (though perhaps not exclusively) human activity. Through the arts we connect with the mystery of Creative Spirit beyond us, moving in us and through us. Through the arts we open ourselves to dialogue with the Divine.

Art as the Language of Intimacy

This imaginative journey took us back in time to the Paleolithic Period, where numerous archeological discoveries indicate the prolific artistry of our ancestors from that time. Perhaps even more striking is the fact that engraved blocks of red ochre, traditionally used for decorative or body painting, have been found in South Africa dating from as early as 75,000 BCE.[5] Far from being a secondary activity, these findings verify that throughout time, the expressions of our souls through the arts have been integral to the survival and development of our human race. To this day, we can marvel that whenever we pick up a paintbrush, sing a song in the shower, or even create a slide show on our computers, we are engaging in an ancient practice, a practice once intricately linked to a way of honoring and communicating with the sacred origins of all creation.

In addition to studying our artistic origins in our earliest ancestors, art philosopher and anthropologist Ellen Dissanayake draws attention to another place of recognizing our innate capacity for artistry. In her book *Art and Intimacy: How the Arts Began*, she suggests that the origin of art can also be observed in our most intimate encounters, beginning with the expressive language of love between mother and child. She describes how the original

modes and rhythms of communication between parent and infant are also
the foundations for all of our art-making. These include "moving together
in synchrony, matching vocalizations and gestures, [and] handling or manip-
ulating the physical world."[6]

Picture a mother and her baby spellbound with each other. See their
dance of connection, communicating through song, breath, rocking, coos,
lifting of eyebrows, comforting touch, sounds and words, laughter and
nourishment. See her introducing objects to explore through touch, taste,
smell, and sound. Here is a language of deep intimacy that becomes the
foundation for all of our life experiences, and develops our capacity for
making and receiving both love and art. How we dip and sway, sing and call,
touch and create can all be traced back to our earliest pre-verbal commu-
nicative language. Irish poet John O'Donohue suggests that our very orien-
tation to beauty is fashioned by our gazing up at our mother's faces—our
first imprint of symmetry as an organizing principle for making sense,
meaning, and art of our world.[7]

Contemplating the origins of artistry and intimacy as languages of the
soul, I am reminded of a poem I wrote not long after the birth of my son.
I offer it as meditation on awakening to mystery:

The Ancient Dance
Tonight I hold you.
The dreams I have held in my heart
take on flesh and form,
breath and body and bone
in the shape of you—new one,
egg cracked open in our nest
opening your mouth unabashedly
to drink in life.

I hold you now
against the drum of my chest,
our hearts beating, rocking,
repeating some ancient dance
older than any posture or pose.
This is the sacred dance

where I become mother
and you become child.
Tonight I am not ready
to lay you in your crib . . .
pausing instead to savor this moment
revealing itself, ripe
in our seven weeks of
studying each other's
faces, moods and many movements
that mesmerize and
make our duet.

You squawk and I croon
and together
we sing as we find
our synchrony:
one leads, one follows,
decisions dance between us
like the smiles
newly flashing on your face.

Oh Child—
though it is impossible to do so—
tonight, I hold mystery in my arms:
you, settling against my shoulder,
weight giving in to
my breast and bone.

Finally, I lay you down to
the dream of sleep.
You rest now unawares,
and I linger longer than I need to,
sitting in your presence,
hushed as a sanctuary.
I, the wide-eyed child,
creeping in
to your darkened church.

You rustle and ruffle—
sigh and sniffle,
speaking an original language.

I listen
and this night . . .
in your muffled music,
ancient far-flung mystery
becomes tangible,
breathable,
revealed.
—*Betsey Beckman*

If our deep language of intimacy is also the language of art, then what better language with which to express our intimacy with our Creator? Likewise, if our souls speak in this language to our Creator, we might also anticipate listening to divine messages through the arts as well. As a dialogue, we can expect God to be revealing deep truths, invitations, mysteries, and surprises to us through this language. If art is, in its essence, mediator of the sacred and window to the ultimate mystery, then as spiritual directors, we might invite ourselves (and directees) to become fluent in this language of the soul.

Right and Left Brain

Besides looking at the origins of art as the language of the soul within human evolution and human intimacy, we can also gain meaningful insights from brain research. Much new scientific information has been gleaned in recent years detailing the relative capacities of each hemisphere of the bi-lobed cortex of our brain. Through time, the two halves of the human cortex have differentiated so that each fulfills a critically different function in our everyday usage and in evolutionary development. The right brain (which controls the functions of the left side of our bodies) is responsible for holistic states of being: music, dance, aesthetics, nurturing, and heightened attunement to emotions and images. In contrast, the left side of our brain (which controls the right side of our body's functioning) is responsible for linear thinking: definition, speech, language, mathematical skills, logic, strategy, and focus.

Brain scientist Jill Bolte Taylor's recent book, *My Stroke of Insight* is a detailed documentation of her debilitating stroke that paralyzed her left-brain. While barely able to decipher how to dial a telephone to call for emergency help, she describes the mystical, holistic awareness and sense of deep peace that flooded her, directed by her right brain. Her capacity to be fully at one with the entire world expanded while her boundaries of ego dissolved, giving her a felt experience of radical bliss, enveloping timelessness and oneness with the Divine. She explained how her mind functioned in that time: "Communication with the external world was out. Language with linear processing was out. But thinking in pictures was in."[8] It took her eight years to fully recover dual brain access in order to tell her remarkable story, and to give witness to the evocative blissful insights and awareness that came through her right brain's direct, artistic way of knowing.

One of our Awakening the Creative Spirit Program participants describes a similar right-brain holistic state of being:

During the making of the soul portrait collage, I was instantly taken back to the feelings I had while doing art in high school. And I loved it! That sense of peace, centeredness and an altered state of being was truly re-awakened. I learned that it was the process that fed my soul, a process that took me into Holy Presence and an encounter with the sacred. I did not know as a teen that it was the meditation of doing art that I desired, a spiritual practice available to me and anyone else regardless of commercial talent. The quality of the product and the level of talent to produce it are irrelevant to Divine encounter. I finally understood my love of art was because of my love for Divine encounter. —*Cynthia Gayle*

Holy Balance

Carl Jung also believed that our symbolic, pictorial way of knowing comes before rational thought. He suggests that only after first experiencing symbolic images are we able to then claim them, express them verbally, and come to understand them. There is also much evidence that dreams occur primarily through activity in the right brain. As spiritual directors, a scientific understanding of the functions of our right and left brain can help us to provide a framework for integrating the arts as tools for creating a holy balance in the spiritual journey. For directees who are skeptical about using the arts in spiritual direction, it may also be handy to be able to address their left-brain concerns with clear scientific research.

To further explore this concept in his book, *The Goddess and the Alphabet: The Conflict Between Word and Image*, Leonard Schlain explains that the right side of our brain was the first to develop in humanity's evolutionary journey.[9] Being non-verbal, the right brain synthesizes meaning through a holistic awareness of space, emotion, image, and sound. Schlain explains that in early evolution these traits were especially utilized by women in their gathering and nurturing activities. Through time, the left brain gradually developed detailed linear clarity, and became highly useful for men who were responsible for the tribe's focused hunting duties. Even though the early differentiated role of men and women in our ancestry emphasized uses of the different brains along gender lines, evolution created access to both forms of brain functioning in both sexes. The high degree of refinement and coordination between our two brain halves has made our human brain the most complex on the planet. Schlain goes on to explain that for millennia in human history, a balanced blend of both masculine and feminine modalities existed and is evident from archeological findings.

Approximately 5,000 years ago, however, the culture of our ancestors radically shifted to an emphasis on left-brain functioning. Simultaneously, history reveals a shift to patriarchal values, which included a growing dominance of men over women, as well as use of force to control. There are various theories about why this major shift towards the masculine modality occurred. Schlain's theory suggests that a primary reason for emphasis on left-brain came through the development of the abstract alphabet. He proposes that this key to literature, philosophy, and law also radically altered the balance between feminine and masculine characteristics in the development of culture, even shifting religious perceptions away from icons and images to a new emphasis on the written word and patriarchal dominance.

Schlain also notes that in our present age a new revolution is occurring through technology: the television, computer, and camera are re-introducing visual images as a primary modality of communication. Simultaneously, recognition of the gifts of women is re-awakening. Indeed this gives us a framework for understanding why the modalities of image, sound, story, and music are reemerging in modern culture as language of the soul, not to replace the analytical, but to be integrated with critical thinking on the path of the spiritual journey.

One spiritual director describes a retreat she led which provided possibilities for both right and left-brain wisdom:

I led a workshop about finding holy balance in our lives. Most of the workshop was left-brained work, thinking about our time, values, and priorities. But at one point I invited the group to do some art to open up new channels for hearing God's call. One woman told me later that she took her artwork home, posted it on her wall and used it for the next six months to help her pray. This was a new way of contemplation for her and new understandings came from this form of prayer. —Karin Ogren

Invoking the Creative Spirit

As presenters leading the Awakening the Creative Spirit Program for Spiritual Directors, after a circle of introductions, we invite participants into a meditation on Creation. Engaging the arts of dance, poetry, and storytelling, we offer an embodied imaginative portrayal of God as artist and creative Spirit. To do so, we call upon "The Creation," a poetic retelling of Genesis by African American poet James Weldon Johnson.[10] As dancer and storyteller, I embody and enact the poem. Imagine this . . .

> "And God stepped out on space,"
>   The dancer enters with long slow steps, her form, voice, and breath becoming an image of God at the foundation of the universe. Now stretching her arms into the emptiness of infinity she pronounces:
>   "And [God] looked around and said,
>   'I'm lonely—
>   I'll make me a world.'"
>   With God's decision to bring forth life, the dancer leaps into the boundless energy of creation: she flings the stars across the universe, "spangling the night"; she gives birth to the world and declares, "That's

good!" God's footsteps hollow out the valleys; she swirls with abandon to spit out the seven seas and throws herself to the floor, sliding across it like the waves of the surf. God's spine arcs to feel the curve of the rainbow; her toes become the blades of green grass sprouting. Then God lifts his arms to call out *"Bring forth! Bring forth!"* and she becomes the antelope bounding, the salmon coursing, and the eagle soaring across the sky. With all of life teeming around him, God proclaims with profound pleasure, *"That's good! That's good! That is so good!"* But finally, when God surveys all that has come forth from his very being, God slows down to listen inside again. In that moment of stillness, God discovers, *"I'm lonely still."*

Then, we see God sit down by the side of a river to think. Here, even God honors the rhythms of the cycles of creation, where some moments are replete with abundance and fullness, while others are spacious and quiet. In God's own surrender to the unknown, a new possibility awakens in the mind of God—*"I'll make me a [human.]"*

Now God leans over to scoop up clay from the riverbed, curving and shaping and fashioning a human. "Like a mammy bending over her baby," God toils. We see God working . . . and we are reminded that the process of creation is not always easy: it takes care, detail, and loving attention. In the end, what we create is a reflection of ourselves. And so, God shapes us, humanity, into God's own image. As the dancer embodies this moment, she holds in her hands an imaginary figure of the first human, the first living being that looked up in the heavens to contemplate the origins of the universe. And into this lump of clay, God breathes the breath of life.

As humans we awaken to the breath of life; we awaken with the breath of life. *Ruah*, Great Spirit, Holy Spirit is breathing in us from our moment of waking to our last gasp of embodiment. God's Spirit is our in-spiration. As the dancer breathes, she turns and recognizes all those seated before her. There she sees God's handiwork, fourteen billion years in the making. She takes a deep inhalation, then blows a long stream of breath out on to her audience, her witnesses to prayer. Three times she inhales, and gives forth, passing from one end of the audience to the other, in a holy trinity of breath, before ending the prayer— "Amen. Amen."

During the retreat, Betsey told the story of the Creation using her whole body. When she got to the part about God blowing the breath of life into humanity, she used her whole being to blow the "breath of life" into us, the audience. A radically new awareness broke through for me in that moment: I began to real-

ize that God was not a distant entity that I needed to please, but was in my every breath. As long as I was breathing, I could not separate myself from God! This realization was not a cognitive process; it was a knowing that came through my whole body. I realized that not one of the countless books that I had read in my search for God had ever been able to lead me to "know" God like I did in that moment during the Creation story. —*Sharie Bowman*

The power of the arts to convey a felt experience of mystery is profound. In our Awakening the Creative Spirit Program, once we have shared this dance of Creation, we reflect together on its message for us: if God is creator, and we are made in God's image or *Imago Dei*, then we are, in our essence, creators. We are, in our essence, artists. Therefore, when we open ourselves to the expression of creativity, we also open to the movement of the Divine within us.

A good number of those who join us for the journey of this program do not initially feel comfortable claiming the title of "artist." Perhaps this is the case for many in the field of spiritual direction. And yet, as *cantadora* (or storyteller) Clarissa Pinkola Estés describes, we all have within ourselves a *chispa* or ember, a spark of divine creativity. And because of this spark, whether we have never even produced a "work," we are still in our essence artists. Estés suggests that even when that ember is not actively tended, it still remains glowing within us, just waiting for the breath to ignite it and bring it to a leaping, dancing blaze.[11] It is to this awakening that we invite our participants—and hope to invite you as well.

2

An Introduction to the Expressive Arts

Christine Valters Paintner

The soul requires a special crafting of life itself,
with an artist's sensitivity to the way things are done.
—THOMAS MOORE

How do we, as spiritual directors and companions on the sacred path, begin to kindle the ember of creativity within us and within directees? What tools might help us to awaken the creative spirit in ways that are accessible, inviting, and transformative?

In this chapter we turn to the field of the expressive arts, a therapeutic discipline whose inter-modal and process-oriented approach offers special gifts to the ministry of spiritual direction and formation. The expressive arts began as a field within the discipline of psychotherapy, engaging the arts in the service of healing. Over time, their application has expanded, and they are now applied in a variety of contexts including education and spiritual growth. The beauty of this discipline is that the basic philosophy and principles of expressive arts can easily be extended beyond work within a therapeutic context, which we will explore in this chapter.

As Ellen Horovitz writes in her book *Spiritual Art Therapy*, our relationship with God demands more than just passive receptivity and calls for a

willingness to plunge deeply within ourselves. She explains, "authenticity
... is an archaic life force that pervades our inner being and exists solely for
the purpose of being awakened, revitalized, and released."[12] The expressive
arts offer us tools to move into the depth of our experience and be awakened to the vitality of dynamic expression.

Inter-Modality and the Multiple Languages of the Soul

In traditional art therapy, the therapist was trained in a specific art modality such as movement, music, poetry, or visual arts, and used that art form
in the service of the therapeutic process. The expressive arts developed as
a way to integrate the various art modalities and to honor each one as a
unique language of the soul. Working with the arts in an interdisciplinary
and connected way offers deeper insight than when engaged in isolation
from each other.

The expressive arts rise out of an understanding that we each speak a
variety of languages. In our everyday life we may be most conscious of our
verbal, analytic, and linear ways of communicating, rooted in the left brain
experience described in Chapter One. However, we have multiple ways of
knowing within our very being which include the intuitive, visual, poetic,
kinesthetic, and musical.

Educator Howard Gardner has done extensive work in the field of
"multiple intelligences."[13] The premise is that as human beings, we contain
within ourselves, a multitude of ways of understanding the world around
us. He names eight primary intelligences and recognizes there may be more:

- Linguistic intelligence (use of verbal language)
- Musical intelligence (allows people to create, communicate, and understand meanings made out of sound)
- Logical-mathematical intelligence (enables individuals to use and
  appreciate abstract relations)
- Spatial intelligence (makes it possible to perceive visual or spatial
  information, to transform this information, and to recreate visual
  images from memory)

- Bodily-kinesthetic intelligence (allows individuals to use all or part of the body to create products or solve problems)
- Interpersonal intelligence (enables individuals to recognize and make distinctions about others' feelings and intentions)
- Intrapersonal intelligence (helps individuals to distinguish among their own feelings)
- Naturalist intelligence (allows people to distinguish among, classify, and use features of the environment).

Adding a ninth existential intelligence, the capacity to raise philosophical questions about life's meaning, is under consideration. The gift of these insights to our work as spiritual directors is an acknowledgment that we were created to know the world, ourselves, and God through multiple avenues. We are each naturally stronger in some intelligences than in others, more fluent in certain languages we might say. But we can all develop our fluency in each of these languages with some practice. By accessing other languages, we open ourselves to greater depth of insight and wisdom.

The expressive arts enlarge our capacity to see the holy at work in the world. As spiritual directors embracing this way of being with directees, we are reclaiming an ancient tradition of allowing the arts to open us to the multiple ways in which the sacred speaks to us, as suggested in Chapter One. Stephen K. Levine, one of the founding members of the field of expressive arts therapy, writes: "In turning to the arts for healing, we are rediscovering an ancient tradition. In early societies and in indigenous cultures, all healing takes place through ceremonial means. Music, dance, song, story-telling, mask-making, the creation of visual imagery and the ritual re-enactment of myth are all components of a communal process in which suffering is given form."[14]

The integration of different art modalities deepens meaning and knowing in ways one form of expression can't fully access. For example, by moving from poetry to visual art to music to movement, each art modality opens up the experience in new ways. In her book, *Creative Connection*, Natalie Rogers, a pioneer in the expressive arts field, emphasizes the process of allowing one art form to influence another directly. This integration creates insights that do not happen from engaging in just one form.

Using various expressive arts in sequence heightens and intensifies our journey inward. When we start expressing ourselves through movement and sound—moving in response to our feelings—and then go immediately to color or clay, our art work changes. Frequently what we then create comes from the unconscious. We may be surprised by what appears. And if we follow the visual art with journal writing, the writing also comes from a deep place within. By moving from art form to art form, we release layers of inhibition that have covered our originality, discovering our uniqueness and special beauty. Like a spiral, the process plumbs the depths of our body, mind, emotions, and spirit to bring us to our center. This center or core is our essence, our wellspring of creative vitality.[15]

In the expressive arts, our body knowledge, intuitive wisdom, and emotions are expressed through symbol and shape, poetry and color, movement and music, and are honored as valid ways of knowing in and of themselves. Rational analysis is not required to validate the insights gained. Artistic knowing is different from intellectual knowing, engaging us symbolically and in embodied ways, stretching us beyond the limits of the rational, linear thinking upon which we tend to rely. The arts afford us insights into life and the movements of the Spirit within us, presenting alternative possibilities that are not available through cognitive ways of knowing.

The following is a poem written by one of our program participants in response to the creative process Natalie Rogers describes:

> First, wake up your lonesome energy, tell it how you need it.
> Second, slow down, get grounded and hear the stillness
>   inside you.
> Third, find a being or an object or a word that sets your
>   imagination on fire.
> Four, gush gush gush gush gush. . . .
> —Barbara Gibson

Pilgrimage of the Art-Making Process

In working with the expressive arts we are invited to place emphasis on the creative process over the artistic product. We live in a very product-oriented culture. The way we spend our time may only seem valuable if we have something to show for it, if we are productive and "busy." We often measure our own worth by how much we accomplish in a given time and how many goals we reach. In the expressive arts, however, much as in prayer, the focus is on the process of creativity and art-making itself rather than the creation of a beautiful product. Inevitably the art created will be beautiful as an authentic expression of the soul. The heart of the work, however, is to free ourselves from the expectations and goals that can keep us from entering deeply into our own creative longings and expressions.

One of the metaphors we use for the art-making process is *pilgrimage*. A pilgrimage is a journey of spiritual significance, in which an outward physical journey parallels an inner spiritual one. On a pilgrimage, as in art-making, we take a journey to encounter the sacred in a more intimate way in our lives. We prepare for the art-making time with prayer and take only the essential tools. Pilgrims bring an intention for the journey and likewise intention is an essential element for making the time to create art as an act of prayer. In the process we are invited to be fully present to each moment as it unfolds.

On pilgrimage, as in the art-making process, we risk entering the unknown with the hope of being transformed. We leave our familiar world behind. We are also connected to a whole community of people who have taken this journey before us, those who travel alongside of us, and those who will in the future. The journey itself is more important than the destination. We are transformed in the process of the creative act, allowing ourselves to be led through the inner and outer experience by the divine impulse moving within.

Art-making as pilgrimage helps us to understand the arts as a process of discovery about ourselves and about God. The theologian Jeremy Begbie writes that the "urge to make and enjoy art seems to be universal: the impulse to scratch out images on stone walls, revel in the delight of notes strung together, shape and re-shape words into patterns, and so on." He goes on to say that these activities go beyond entertainment and self-expression, that "they can be vehicles of discovery."[16] When we enter the creative process with the intention of listening for the movements of the Spirit in the midst of the work, we discover new insights about ourselves and God.

One spiritual director and artist describes the pilgrim's journey this way:

One of the ways I have found to ease myself onto the pilgrim's road is to surrender to the discipline of sculpting. In the past few years I've begun to learn how to create from the power within me. To create in this manner I must approach the process as a pilgrim. It is a holy journey and, at times, an uncomfortable journey. My heart is stretched as though it were a tent whose stakes are being moved outward to make room for Mystery, a holy and as yet unknown image for God. —*Karen Haddon*

Another spiritual director and chaplain describes the freedom that she discovered from focusing on the process in our expressive arts program:

The instruction to "pay attention to the process, noting what is happening within me as I am doing the project and NOT to be concerned about the finished product" was my saving grace. It freed me in a surprising way! It moved me from being blocked by my awkwardness. My Triptych, Mandala and Mask are displayed in prominent places in my home. They have become symbols of inner movement for me. They remind me to trust the images, thoughts, or experiences that come to my mind during spiritual direction. The theme of being "in the now" as I work with clients has become my modus operandi. I trust it more than my academic learning. —*Cathy Rhoads*

The Arts as Sacred Container or Tabernacle

A complementary metaphor for pilgrimage is that of art-making as a vessel or sacred space. A tabernacle is a dwelling place for the holy. The arts help us to make space for an encounter with God while also creating a safe container in which to experiment and explore new possibilities. Through the arts we externalize our internal processes. When exploring painful experiences such as grief, loss, trauma, or betrayal, the arts can offer directees a safe space in which to experience the range of feelings being stirred within them. Expressive arts therapist Paolo Knill writes: "The practice of the arts, as disciplined rituals of play in painting, sculpting, acting, dancing, making music, writing, story-telling, is and always was a safe container, a secure vessel to meet existential themes, pathos and mystery."[17] The arts allow us to explore and look at new, uncomfortable, or scary feelings by giving them shape and form, revealing new insights to us. The expressive arts create a sacred space to explore our interior process and also give form to what is moving deeply within us.

In working with the arts in spiritual direction or retreat settings, one of our main roles as facilitators of creative expression is to hold the space and make a safe container for directees to explore new territory and encounter the sacred in new ways. The process of art-making invites the participant to be present to the moment and to notice what is stirring within.

The Role of Witness

This being human is a guest house.
Every morning a new arrival.
A joy, a depression, a meanness,
some momentary awareness comes
as an unexpected visitor.
Welcome and entertain them all!
even if they're a crowd of sorrows,
who violently sweep your house
empty of its furniture,
still, treat each guest honorably.
He may be cleaning you out
for some new delight.
The dark thought, the shame, the malice,
meet them at the door laughing,
and invite them in.
Be grateful for whoever comes,
Because each has been sent
As a guide from beyond.
    —*Rumi*[18]

Rumi's eloquent words challenge us to consider the ways in which we are called to bring the whole of ourselves to the creative process. What I call "inner hospitality" is deeply connected to the ideas in Rumi's poem. In the Benedictine monastic tradition, hospitality is a fundamental value. In St. Benedict's Rule he writes: "Let everyone that comes be received as

Christ." The invitation is to see every person who arrives at the door (both literal and metaphorical) as bearing a face of the Divine, even the person who annoys or irritates us, or the person who makes us feel uncomfortable. Welcome them in especially, says Benedict, because they will reveal God in ways we do not expect.

This extension of hospitality is both an external and internal process. We can extend hospitality to ourselves as well. In our interior guest house, which Rumi describes, is our inner life where many dimensions of the self gather. Chelsea Wakefield, LCSW, a therapist and dreamworker in North Carolina, uses the metaphor of the inner round table. She suggests we each contain a multiplicity of selves, different parts and voices, and we might imagine the round table they gather around as the Self, our core which is able to observe the other parts of ourselves in a compassionate way. The Self is the part of ourselves which the mystics describe as dwelling in God.

In any given moment, we have a variety of inner selves or voices that clamor for our attention. The practice of meditation or art-making is, in part, to become present to those voices. Rather than resisting the voices we dislike, our invitation is to welcome them in and open up a hospitable space within ourselves. We often spend so much energy resisting these unwelcome parts of ourselves. When we are in a place of balance, the Self is the center of our focus and each voice has its place around the table in conversation with the others. When our energy becomes channeled toward a particular identity or voice the dynamic shifts away from centering in the true Self.

Thomas Moore offers a similar idea in the chapter "Honoring Symptoms as a Voice of the Soul" from his book *Care of the Soul*. He writes: "care of the soul is a continuous process that concerns itself not so much with 'fixing' a central flaw as with attending to the small details of everyday life, as well as to major decisions and changes."[19] He invites us to focus on observing how the soul itself actually operates, as a means to knowing ourselves more deeply: "Observance of the soul can be deceptively simple. You take back what has been disowned. You work with what is, rather than with what you wish were there."[20] This invitation means looking at the hungers and compulsions of life and listening for what is being revealed there about ourselves and about God. It means welcoming in all parts of ourselves as holding wisdom for our own growth and wholeness.

One of our program participants explores the power of connecting with a part of herself that had been hidden:

We were invited to choose a verse (from a poem) to play with. We memorized it, danced with it, and spoke it. One invitation was to speak our verse in a witch's voice. I'd never even thought of attempting to take on that character before. I discovered a really spooky, dark part of myself, but one with lots of power, that I'm not sure I understand yet. The witch was sinister . . . insisting that no one was beyond her sight and power. She reminded me of Gollum from *Lord of the Rings*. My delivery spooked my partner. She said "the hair stood up on the back of her neck" in listening to me. Since the Awakening Program the witch has shown up with her wisdom in other venues. I'm beginning to make friends with her. She brings an opposing, but unique view to situations, and always tells the truth, no matter how difficult. —*Sharie Bowman*

When we begin to integrate all of our inner characters, even the ones who feel "spooky" or "dark" can offer us new sources of power and insight into who we truly are.

The Self is the calm and non-anxious core we all possess, which is able to witness this internal process. In meditation we cultivate our ability to be completely present to the rise and fall of our emotions, not by becoming detached or disassociated from them, rather by fully experiencing them without feeling carried away by their power. The art-making process offers the same invitation: to be present to what is happening within us, to notice the fears and judgments rising and falling. The witness is the compassionate and curious part of ourselves that is able to look with love and tenderness on this pattern rising up in us and extends a sense of curiosity. We might then ask ourselves: "Why is this coming up right now in this time and place? What does this wave of feeling have to say to me of importance about myself and God? Where else in my life do I experience these voices?" Witnessing is not about fixing something, witnessing is about entering into a relationship with what is and discovering the grace and gifts hidden there.

In spiritual direction, our work is to receive the gift of sacred story from a directee, and to bear witness to all of the story's dimensions—the beauty, the pain, the sorrow, and the joy. This deep seeing and recognition of the self by another person and the experience of having one's story heard, one's art or dance seen, or one's song listened to is profoundly healing and transformative.

The spiritual director, in creating this safe container for directees to be heard and seen, offers a calm and compassionate presence. When the director is able to receive whatever the story, dance, or artwork reveals with compassion, he or she models for directees the capacity for cultivating this internal witness in themselves.

Witnessing may take different forms in a spiritual direction session depending on whether the work is "one-with-one" or in a group. Catherine Moon writes about the sacramental nature of this process: "The sacramental is contained in the coming together of the community whether that be two people or twenty, to make visible the invisible, to bring about recognition of the holy in the every day. At times the art therapist (or spiritual director) may be instrumental in creating the sacramental atmosphere and at other times the art therapist must only 'take a back seat' and support the sacramental process as it unfolds."[21] Being a witness to another person's process is a sacrament and gift offered back to them.

The Arts as a Spiritual Practice

Art and prayer have much in common. They are both rooted in an intense encounter involving a surrender of willfulness, openness to inspiration, and lead to a deep engagement with mystery.

A commitment to spiritual practice engages us actively in a relationship with the sacred dimension of our lives and also cultivates particular qualities and ways of being in the world. Engaging the arts prayerfully helps us to develop ways of deeply listening to what is stirring within us. The arts teach us about mystery, giving us room to live into the paradoxical places of our lives. Through making art we come to know ourselves more deeply and provide space to discover and express our own voices. We take risks so as to become more visible to the world through gesture or color or song. We learn to slow down and to see more deeply with graced vision. The arts help us to give meaningful expression and form to our commitments, values, and ideas, and make beauty present in the world.

Artistic knowing is different from intellectual knowing and, when rooted in prayer, shifts our prayer to other faculties. Art as prayer engages our bodies and imaginations, stretching us beyond the limits of the rational. The arts ask us to suspend our desire for logical information and rely more on intuition. When we engage the arts, we discover the values of improvisation and play as holy acts, as a spiritual director describes in her contemplative practice:

One of the greatest delights and challenge of offering the arts in spiritual direction has been in the area of how I structure activities for directees. In the truest sense of contemplative spiritual direction, one listens moment to moment for the stirrings of the Holy. As a former teacher, I have had to re-learn how to offer an art experience to others. In certain teaching circles, not creating a lesson plan is akin to heresy. Yet through the process of letting go of pre-planning, my directees and I have received graced moments I could never have planned for: healing and insight through spontaneous drawings, improvised prayer drumming and movement, and even a kind of Scripture-based partner *visio divina*. By not being driven by the requirement to create structured arts "lessons," I'm freed to pursue my personal arts making as the Spirit guides me, and I am learning to trust that what may be called for in a session of spiritual direction will emerge, and is often fed, by the work I have done independent of one-to-one sessions.
—*Suzie Massey*

When we create for the joy of the process, rather than for the product, we explore creativity in a deeply intimate way. To be truly creative, we move between states of openness to new associations of ideas and states of focused explorations of these associations. The meditative mind is receptive to flashes of insight because it is open. Similarly, prayer is ideally an act focused more on the process itself rather than the outcome. We engage in a discipline within which we cultivate an attitude of openness to surprise and serendipity, waiting with patience and humility.

Spiritual Direction and the Expressive Arts

As spiritual directors who invite engagement with the expressive arts, we become facilitators of the creative process and witnesses to the work of art-making and its gifts. In this passage, Stephen K. Levine is speaking about psychotherapists, but his vision can be equally applied to spiritual directors and so, in brackets, I have replaced some of his words to illustrate this:

> In fact, in their practice [spiritual directors] function more like artists than like scientists . . . They must, to be effective, let go of theory and be sensitive to the experience in the moment. Their task is to give form to the therapeutic encounter and to thereby facilitate the freeing of the imagination in the [directee]. Good [spiritual directors] are open to metaphor and symbol; they listen with the "third ear" that hears what is not said; they see the potential for development in the person and are animated by these invisible possibilities.
>
> Ultimately [spiritual direction] is itself an art-form. It is an activity in which a person takes the raw materials of his or her life and forms them into a significant whole . . .
>
> The use of expressive arts in [spiritual direction] is thus a restoration of healing to its original source: the imaginal depths of the soul. Only a person skilled in the art of "soul-making" can serve as a guide in these regions.[22]

The process Levine describes is akin to the listening with the "ear of the heart" that St. Benedict of Nursia invites us to in the first line of his Rule[23] and seeing with the "eyes of the heart" that St. Paul describes in his letter to the Ephesians.[24] Levine goes on to say:

> The task of therapy is not to eliminate suffering but to give a voice to it, to find a form in which it can be expressed. Expression is itself transformation; this is the message that art brings. The therapist then would be an artist of the soul, working with sufferers to enable them to find the proper container for their pain, the form in which it would be embodied.[25]

I love this image of the spiritual director as "artist of the soul." I would describe the artist as one who sees and listens deeply to what is happening below the surface, attends to the particular, and then gives outward form and expression. Similarly, the spiritual director's role is to accompany directees on the spiritual journey and help them to a way of deeper listening and seeing, so that they may come to recognize God's presence in all areas of their lives.

3

Guidelines and Principles

Christine Valters Paintner

It takes devotion to create and reverence to enjoy beauty.
—FRITZ EICHENBERG

When integrating the arts and spiritual direction, there are several guidelines and principles we adhere to as facilitators of both individual and group processes. We offer them to you for your own reflection and guidance.

Covenant

When leading art retreats, one of our first objectives is to establish a sense of trust and safety. We begin to create this safe atmosphere through exercises and reflections that connect participants with each other through their hopes for the program and also through their agreement to a covenant for our time together. We recommend using your own adaptation of a covenant when working with individuals and groups to help create a safe container and begin a conversation around what each person needs to balance his or her own self-care and risk-taking for growth.

- Confidentiality: We ask that everything shared be held in strict confidence and no part of any participant's story be shared beyond the group.
- Mindfulness: We invite participants to pay close attention throughout the process to their own inner movements.
- Honoring Limits: We invite participants to recognize their own needs and honor them as well as giving permission for others in the group to honor their own limits.
- Risk-Taking: In balance with honoring one's limits is the invitation to take some risks and move into uncomfortable places. We invite participants to stretch themselves, knowing they are being accompanied and supported along the way.
- Honoring Wisdom: We ask the group members to honor the wisdom each person brings.
- Expressing Needs to the Group: We provide a time for individuals to name any particular needs they have to the whole group.

Initial Guidelines for Using the Arts

1. Become Familiar with the Art Materials You Want to Engage.

Prior to leading a creative exercise, explore it yourself, preferably with a spiritual director or friend, to help you process what it stirs in you. When reading about a new exercise, it may be tempting to dive right in with a directee or group to try it out. In exploring the arts with others, however, it is essential that you have experienced a form yourself so you can become familiar with some of its particular challenges and gifts. As a spiritual director who uses the arts, your commitment to the arts in service of healing and transformation begins with yourself.

2. Frame Art-Making as an Invitation to a Directee.

Suggestions for art-making are best framed as an invitation that can be freely accepted or rejected. Cultivate a sense of safety and trust in the directee's ability to make choices. There is, of course, a great deal to be gained from risking and stretching boundaries, but it is always the directee who chooses when to take a risk and engage in an experience that may feel uncomfortable.

For several exercises in this book, we offer a suggested script to frame an experience. As you implement them, say them slowly, with pauses to allow time for the directee to have the words and images move within. Over time you will develop your own sense of timing and spaciousness in leading interior experiences. Feel free to ask the directee for feedback as well.

3. Build the Freedom of the Experience in Incremental Steps.

When leading others in art-making always begin with experiences that have greater structure to create a sense of safety. A commitment to using incremental steps means that you begin with art-making processes that are simpler and have more structure and then gradually move into experiences which offer more freedom and complexity. The simple, more structured experiences create a strong initial container for the directee. These are especially helpful when the directee is new to creative expression and may feel intimidated. In Part Two, in our chapters on specific art modalities, we will offer simple exercises with which to begin exploration of the arts.

4. Notice What the Art Form Itself has to Teach You.

For example, working with collage is a very different experience than working with paint or clay. The materials you work with can each elicit different kinds of responses. Let the experience dictate what medium is to be used. If a directee is feeling scattered, collage can be a way of bringing wholeness to a life that feels fragmented. Clay or gentle movement can be a good media to get grounded. Singing is powerful for those who are working on claiming their voices. The intrinsic quality of each medium has a powerful effect on the experience. As a spiritual director engaging the arts, explore each of these qualities yourself so you become familiar with the possibilities of a particular medium.

5. Use Breath and Imagination as Ways of Creating Internal Spaciousness.

In Chapter Five we will explore breath and imagination in much greater detail. To begin an experience of creative expression, connect with your breath as a grounding practice. Engage meditation and intention to practice receptivity to images as a way of encountering the holy. Offering a guided imagery experience to begin art-making can assist a directee to cultivate a stance of openness, let go of the desire for control of the outcome, and risk the unfamiliar. Adriana Diaz, in her book, *Freeing the Creative Spirit*, states "creativity is a combination of making something happen and letting something happen. Creative meditation has two stages: one quiet and still, the other spontaneous, active and dynamic."[26] In preparing for creative expression, invite some quiet in which the directee prepares to receive the gifts of the imagination.

6. Engage Intuitive Ways of Knowing.

Encouraging spontaneous expression helps to support directees as they learn not to "think it through," but engage in intuitive responses. Focus directees on the creative process itself, inviting them to notice their places of resistance and flow. Time limits on activities and exercises can be a helpful tool to create structure and safety, and move past blocks by discouraging too much thinking and judging of the process.

7. Recognize Places of Resistance and Blocks.

Part of your role as a spiritual director engaging the arts is to help break down the normal fear and resistance to creating most adults have learned. Creating a safe space and emphasizing the process helps to bypass some of the judgments directees have internalized. Working with resistance takes many forms. Sometimes the time-limited nature of an experience helps to break through the resistance. Sometimes a meditation helps a directee to surrender the mind and become more fully present. There are times when it is most helpful to meet the resistance or block head on and dialogue with it through the creative process. This will be explored further in Chapter Five.

8. Be Present to Experiences of Resonance and Dissonance.

When you invite directees to engage the arts as a time of prayer and discovery, encourage them to listen to what is happening within them for information about themselves and God. Tending to the places of strong emotional response, either resonance or dissonance, can provide extraordinary insights. *Resonance* means richness or significance, especially evoking an association or strong emotion. Similarly, *dissonance* means conflict or lack of harmony and also evokes strong emotion.

When working with the arts we may be engaging externally generated images, such as in collage work or photography, or images that arise internally, such as movement and painting. Both kinds of images can elicit a response of resonance or dissonance that acts as a vehicle of discovery.

9. Be Aware of the Potential for "Image Saturation."

While one of the principles of working with the expressive arts is to move from one art modality to another, this does not mean, however, that more exercises are always better. When working with directees, cultivate a sense of when to deal with the images already evoked, rather than generating further images through another modality. Be aware of the potential for "image saturation" and recognize when it is time to simply be with what has emerged, rather than moving into another art experience.

10. Prepare the Space and Materials.

If engaging in art-making during the session, consider the space, time, and materials. When inviting directees to create art at home, discuss these elements, encouraging them to find ways to make art even in a small space. It is wonderful to have a large studio, but there are many ways to explore the arts in smaller spaces and with limited materials. We will offer some of these possibilities in later chapters.

Ways of Processing the Expressive Arts Experience

Once a piece of art or poem or dance has been created, as spiritual directors we assist directees with unpacking the meaning of their art. There are several possible levels of engagement:

Silence

As an initial invitation following the art experience, create space to simply be with what has stirred in the session. Allow directees to savor and relish the images or experience without having to attach meaning or direction to them too soon. Take time for directees to simply notice the feelings moving in them. One of the most potent responses to art-making is silence, a holy space beyond words. Silence is powerful enough to hold the full presence of director, directee, the art, and the presence of God.

Moving to Another Art Modality

When working from an expressive arts model, consider inviting the directee into another art form as a way to deepen the insight or experience. Most often this includes journaling and written reflection. For example if directees create a collage, they might follow by writing a poem suggested by their images, moving with their images, or singing a line from their poem. Allow the other art forms to help unfold the experience before moving to rational analysis.

We will explore concrete ways of moving from one modality to another as a way to open new layers of meaning in later chapters in Part Three.

Naming the Process

When we work with directees we hold their stories in loving reverence. Their images, words, and movements are to be similarly honored. After resting in silence, or inviting journal-writing or other modalities to expand the experience, spend significant time reflecting on the process of art-making itself and what they noticed moving within them. Invite directees to explore what the process was like and name some of the internal movements of resistance, joy, surprise, and so forth. Ask where they noticed resonance and dissonance. When working with images, invite directees to enter into the figures, colors, or shapes and experience what they are like from the inside, claiming them as parts of their own internal longings to be expressed and explored.

Witnessing

In *Art as Medicine*, expressive arts therapist Shaun McNiff suggests we treat artistic creations as if they were "ensouled" and "approach them as we would a person, who similarly cannot be explained."[27] The art created in prayer contains a depth of mystery, just like the person who created it.

In Chapter Two we discussed the role of the witness in the spiritual direction and expressive arts process. The witness is fully present to the unfolding of the story contained within an artistic expression. There are various ways for us to be present in this way. Sometimes mirroring or reflecting what has been said or naming how we have been moved is a powerful way for directees to see themselves in a new light. This type of reflection can allow the creator to understand the clarity and intention expressed in his or her own work and to take in the information offered at many different levels.

The experience of owning, acknowledging, and revealing the truth of one's experience and having this truth witnessed by another with reverence and care, is an essential element of the journey toward wholeness. Witnessing means listening rather than analyzing or interpreting. Reflect on what you notice in the directee's sharing by repeating phrases to help the person make connections with what is moving within. Your compassionate embrace of the directee's challenging inner voices assists in the process of integration.

In considering a directee's artwork itself, resist imposing your own interpretations. Be present to the images and symbols by allowing the directee to share the story. Ask questions that encourage reflection such as "What are the feelings moving in your body right now?" or "Talk about your artwork in the first person, as if you were the piece of art itself speaking." Take time to be with and inhabit the images, allowing directees to integrate the images with their life story. In *Art as a Way of Knowing*, Pat Allen wisely counsels: "let the images instruct you . . . try to restrain from coming to conclusions; instead, follow your image like a trail of bread crumbs as far as you can. Then let it go."[28] Resist your desire to make meaning too quickly and translate the work into a linear analysis. Allow the images to take the lead in unpacking their wisdom.

Aesthetic Responses and Noticings

As spiritual director and responder to the work, take some time to notice your own feelings and inner symbols that arise when sitting with a directee. Share these with humility and caution, asking yourself whether this sharing serves your own need or whether you can offer your noticing to the directee without attachment. Consider whether this will enhance or get in the way of the process.

Acknowledging how you, as the responder, are touched personally by the work can be helpful and provide a means of acknowledging your shared connections. Get in touch with what resonates with you and which emotions or body sensations arise in response. Avoid making value judgments about the art.

Integrity and the Engagement of Expressive Arts

Engagement in the expressive arts runs the risk of becoming a superficial technique or activity if we do not encourage a prayerful engagement in the process and allow adequate time to reflect on what has stirred within the directee in response to the experience. The arts are in service to the soul. Without taking time to explore the inner dimensions of the experience and the process, the arts can become merely "decorative tricks."[29] We do not include art-making as an "add-on" experience to a session or retreat. To honor the power of the arts, we offer them in service of healing and wholeness as an integral element of the entire experience. We make significant space to listen for what they have to reveal to us.

As spiritual directors who create space for the arts we are called to maintain a commitment to ongoing personal use of creative expression for healing, growth, and connection to the sacred source. We engage in the art experiences ourselves before leading others so we come to know the internal dynamics. As guides for the creative journey, we create a clear frame and transition into the art experience, moving directees more deeply into their embodied and intuitive selves. To be embodied means to experience one's body as an integral dimension of one's whole being. We encourage time and spaciousness in reflecting on the creative process following the experience, and resist offering our own interpretation of the art. These guidelines allow the arts to become a sacred vessel for experiencing God's movements within. What makes inclusion of the arts in spiritual direction or in a retreat setting different from an exercise you might lead in another setting are their transformative power and the invitation to enter a genuine encounter with the sacred dimension of our lives and of the world.

PART II

Explorations of Different Art Modalities

4

Storytelling

Betsey Beckman

Anything and everything are possible in a story.
—JOHN O'DONOHUE

Each chapter in this section focuses on a single art modality. In the individual expressions of storytelling, imagination, movement, visual art, music, and poetry, we explore and celebrate the distinct gifts each art form offers to the context of spiritual direction.

Spiritual Directors International describes its mission as "Helping people tell their sacred stories everyday." Taking this phrase to heart, we might venture to claim that the most natural and essential element of our work in spiritual direction is storytelling. In learning the tools of spiritual companionship many of us may never have considered that storytelling is an art form, and an ancient one at that, springing from our very human beginnings.

If we contemplate the origins of storytelling, our images take us back to the earliest gatherings of humans around the sacred fire. Just as our first ancestors learned to harness the power of fire to warm, transform, and provide, so they learned the power of story to ignite courage, transform despair, and provide spiritual sustenance. We can picture the earliest wisdom circles as hunter-gatherer communities convened around the crackling flames with music and laughter carrying them through the night. As time goes on, we can hear stories rising up out of our collective memory: Greek heroic myths of conquering Cyclops and resisting Sirens, Native American stories of the earth being born on the back of a turtle, Indian epics of the Monkey Gods, and African tales of Ananzi, the spider. We can picture Irish bards singing their love stories, ancient Sumerians recounting Inanna's descent to the underworld, Buddhist mountain monks imparting their koans, and ancient Israelites re-enacting their journey to freedom. Stories such as these inspire, instruct, cajole, remind, and create an archetypal framework of meaning for cultures, religions, and societies. Stories carry us across the threshold into God's imagination.

All of these images hearken back to the time when stories were not written, but told. Stories traveled on the voice, rode the breath, fluctuated with the seasons and the tides, bringing communities together. Through time stories have become more fixed as they have been written down, allowing uniformity, but losing the character of lived expression. For us, the flickering light of the television has replaced the dancing fire-flame, just as Hollywood's hair-raising and spine-tingling multi-media effects have replaced the dynamic immediacy of the storyteller's emotion.

Though we may disparage the paucity of television's many commercial offerings, a good program or movie can stir our souls. It is inspiring that we as humans have engaged the technological advancements from the printing press to the computer to record, express, and share our deepest meanings and truths. And yet, there's nothing quite so intimate and immediate as a story told directly to us, complete with human sighs, tears, and laughter. Many a child has been soothed to sleep through stories ancient or new, some even created in the moment to help imaginatively process the trials of the day.[30] The mystery and power of story's intimacy persists through time. In this ancient tradition, it seems fitting that many of us begin our sessions of spiritual direction and sacred story with the same act our ancestors did: the lighting of a flame.

As spiritual directors, we might conceive of our role as "Storycatcher." Christina Baldwin, storyteller and spiritual teacher, has written a book of this title, where she helps us reflect on how we can attune to and invite the sacred story waiting to be heard. She says:

Storycatchers are people who value story and who find ways in the midst of their everyday lives to honor this activity. Perhaps we're at a party and someone starts to speak about what at first seems an ordinary anecdote but soon grows into something more important. A Storycatcher notices and says, "Come, let's sit down on the sofa. I want to really hear you." The Storycatcher's job is to help us shift into narrative: to make people conscious of the story just beneath the surface of our talk and invite us to speak it.[31]

Many of us discover our calling to spiritual direction through a reflection on our inherent desire to invite and honor sacred stories wherever we find ourselves. We learn that the gifts of being a spiritual director are not studied or learned, but rather, derive from a natural inclination to listen and hear the rhythm of sacred story in those around us. As one artist-spiritual director expresses it:

While spiritual direction has traditionally taken place in office-like settings with two chairs, two people, and a candle, my spiritual companion and musician hats frequently stack atop my head "out in the wild" where I'm equally inclined, if not more so, to bear witness to sacred stories on a park bench, behind the music merchandise table, in lines for women's restrooms during conference breaks, or via email. —*Trish Bruxvoort Colligan*

One of my treasured life rituals is gathering with my entire extended family on the shores of Lake Michigan each summer. There we coax my ninety-three-year-old father to recount the timeless story of meeting my mother seventy years ago and sparking a summer romance, which eventually gave birth to our family legacy. Though my mother has been gone now for almost three decades, continuing to return to the place of the first flicker of their relationship and recounting the stories of our "creation" provides a profound sense of rightness and purpose in our far-flung family lives. Late night gatherings around the beach fire provide opportunities for unspoken stories to find their voice, mixing with the lapping of waves.

How might an awareness of storytelling as an art widen our palette of possibilities in spiritual direction? As we consider exploring artfulness in stories, it is not with the intention of creating a sense of self-consciousness in directees through an over-emphasis on the "craft" of storytelling. But perhaps the tools of storytelling might help set free a sense of participating in the power of myth and mystery that underscores our lives. Calling forth a story might help a directee shift from a place of "figuring something out" to a possibility of co-creation with the Divine. Secondarily, as directors, we might occasionally be coaxed to step into the sacred circle with a gift of story for our directees.

Anthropologist and author Angeles Arrien, in her book *The Fourfold Way*, describes the tools of the healer thus:

> Every culture has ways of maintaining health and well-being. Healers throughout the world recognize the importance of maintaining or retrieving the four universal healing salves: storytelling, singing, dancing, and silence. Shamanic societies believe that when we stop singing, stop dancing, are no longer enchanted by stories, or become uncomfortable with silence, we experience soul loss, which opens the door to discomfort and disease. The gifted Healer restores the soul through use of the healing salves.[32]

As spiritual directors, we can affirm ourselves for generally doing a good job of cultivating the art of silence as a healing and sacred modality. To enhance and expand our openness to other aspects of the Spirit's healing salves, let us look now at ways to deepen our connection to the art of storytelling.

InterPlay®

One of the practices I have found most helpful in my own journey of artistry is that of InterPlay.[33] InterPlay is a philosophy and creative practice developed by Bay Area artists and theologians, Cynthia Winton-Henry and Phil Porter. In the process of developing a system of tools and classes to support creativity, they have engendered a worldwide community of "players" who celebrate the "healing salves" of improvisational song, storytelling, movement, and silence for renewing humanity. As Phil and Cynthia write in their book, *Having it All*, "We dare to stand in front of others without a script or choreography or a score and expect something to emerge."[34] In some ways, this willingness to be in the moment artistically is quite similar to what we as spiritual directors do in each of our sessions: we arrive without an agenda and with no prescriptive set of words or actions. We arrive with a lifetime of experience, a depth of prayer, and a trust in Spirit, and in so doing, we allow the Spirit to guide our sessions with openness to surprise and grace.

Having trained as an InterPlay leader, I have been delighted to integrate these gifts into our program, and many of the forms we describe in this book are inspired by InterPlay's expressive body-wisdom practices. In my personal work, I incorporate InterPlay forms in individual sessions with directees, as well as in retreats, workshops, "SpiritPlay" classes, and meetings. InterPlay emphasizes exploring new possibilities incrementally. That means, we don't have to challenge ourselves to take big leaps in learning new ideas or forms; we can begin with small steps, and enjoy an attitude of discovery. These steps break open new awarenesses, and invite us naturally to new adventures. Along these lines, InterPlay has developed a number of simple storytelling forms that help to loosen our tongues, and invite our natural storyteller to emerge without self-conscious "studying" or "rehearsing." The exercises below begin with a few of these examples. Since one of InterPlay's strengths is building community through creative expression, many of the forms described here were originally developed for use in a group format, but can easily be adapted for use in an individual direction session as well.

Experiential Exercises

Simple Ways to Engage Storytelling in Spiritual Direction: InterPlay Exercises

 Babbling

At a moment when you'd like to invite a directee to an attitude of discovery and play, explore babbling. Begin by standing up and "shaking out." Together, shake out a hand, another hand, a foot, another foot, your head, and "what you've been sitting on." Finally, shake out your voice and your whole body. Then, introduce the possibility that the two of you can open up awareness by exploring words through "babbling." Give the directee a "noun" and invite him to ramble on the subject for about thirty to forty seconds. Following that, to foster an attitude of mutuality and play, you take a turn and "babble" on a random word. At first, it is most effective to choose words that are quite common and seemingly mundane such as:

shoes, pencil, popcorn, rubber band, or clouds. Perhaps the two of you can brainstorm a list, and then take turns "babbling" on the subjects. After a few rounds, take some time to notice what you are discovering. How has the mood or energy shifted? What surprised you? What feelings arose? After several exchanges about seemingly innocuous words, you can take another step to invite the directee to explore words with more emotional and spiritual resonance. These words might arise from personal or seasonal themes from the life-journey of the directee such as: mountain, heartbeat, darkness, adventure, thirst, candle, birth, silence. The light-hearted attitude that you establish at the outset helps to build trust for dipping a bit more deeply into an evocative symbol or theme, inviting discovery.

"Babbling" is a very effective exercise for supporting a group in beginning to feel comfortable sharing experiences from their own lives. InterPlay founder Phil Porter unabashedly claims that in any gathering, three rounds of babbling with different partners begins to form a sense of group body or community. To lead "babbling" in a group setting, have people work in partners, changing partners now and then between rounds. Notice the immediate buzz of electricity that fills the air as folks have the chance to wax eloquent on simple subjects. Amazing insights, anecdotes, amusements, and poignancies are often shared in this simple and non-threatening exercise.

Describing

This next step in storytelling focuses on describing detail. After experimenting with babbling, choose something for a directee or group members to describe. Invite focus on detail: the shapes, the sounds, the texture, the atmosphere, the colors. Examples might be: your kitchen, your car, the view out your living room window, your workplace. After warming up these descriptive capacities, shift to a deeper awareness, suggesting topics with more heart connection such as: a place you go for renewal, a favorite body of water, a church or sanctuary you remember, a friend, a pet.

Describing helps heighten our sensory experience of place, relationship, kinesthetic memory, and right-brain associations. For example, if a directee is floundering or struggling, being invited to kinesthetically describe a positive association springing from her life journey can be a very powerful way to re-center herself.

📖 Storytelling

This exercise naturally builds on the previous two by adding one more dimension: narrative. Simply put, in a story, there's a sequence of events: a beginning, middle, and end. Once folks have been warmed up with simpler forms, you might request a "telling" of certain memories: a time when someone showed you compassion, a time when you experienced death, a time when you overcame an obstacle, a time when you felt alive, a moment of peace, a time you felt affirmed by God. Encourage participants to recount whatever stories happen to "show up" under a given topic. These may be powerful primary stories, or at other times, surprising or forgotten memories that now have the opportunity to be welcomed into the light.

Afterwards, notice what insights have emerged through the experience of telling, and also from the story itself. Focusing on telling can lead directees to discover their innate stories without becoming self-conscious. Before you know it, a storyteller is born.

📖 Three Sentence Stories

In the following InterPlay exercise, invite your "storyteller" to practice telling an experience with only three sentences. Here's an example of how this supported a directee in discovering the heart of her experience.

I've been working with a client who talks nearly nonstop giving infinite details about each experience that she shares. At the conclusion of our last session, she left saying she felt totally empty and worn out from "purging" all of her stories. Today I decided to begin the session by having her say "I could talk about . . ." and then just list the things on her mind. After she came up with a list, I asked her to tell me a Three Sentence Story about one of the things on the list. She told me a story of choosing to take her family to a park instead of church on Sunday morning and how she felt really close to God by following her body's longing. After telling this short story, she explained that it was really hard to limit her words that much! But in doing so, she also found that she emphasized the important part of her story, which was choosing to follow her own inner wisdom—something to celebrate! She was so grateful that by telling the experience this way, the story "went into her own cells" instead of empty-ing out of her body . . . and gave her energy. She reflected on how she might be overwhelming her husband and children with words and perhaps that is why she feels they don't listen to her. Now, she's looking forward to sharing the Three Sentence form with them! —*Sharie Bowman*

Stories of Redemption

If we have particularly painful memories we carry as wounds—such as a family dysfunction, loss or regret, or even a recent frustration—sometimes we can have a sense of being "stuck" in our own life story. A very powerful transformative tool can be a "story of redemption."

To explore this form, invite a directee to tell a life event imagining it as he wishes it could have been, and telling the story as if it had been so. In this way, a directee gives himself the emotional gift of having that which he longs for, and inviting in the healing God would desire for him. For example, around a painful memory of Thanksgiving dinner, a directee might re-tell a story of family harmony instead of arguments. Or around the memory of a mistake, a directee might re-tell a story of being comforted instead of scolded. One of our program participants recounts the grace that flowed from such a re-telling:

My father died in a tragic trucking accident the day after my nineteenth birthday. For years I have carried heavy guilt knowing he tried to call me on my birthday and I was not there to pick up the phone. When I was invited to imaginatively shift a memory, this day rose to the forefront. I resisted for a moment and then allowed myself to imagine answering the phone. I could hear his voice clearly and distinctly. "Happy Birthday, Baby. I love you. How's your day?" Short. Sweet. Simple. I remembered he was a man of few words. With a healing salve, the guilt began to soften and peel away. Through the re-telling, I knew there was no guilt to be had for celebrating my birthday. It was exactly how he would have wanted it. —*Kayce Stevens Hughlett*

Further Steps for Engaging Storytelling in Spiritual Direction

Telling a Mythic Story as Your Own

The previous exercises were focused on methods of evoking story elicited from our personal lives. Another very powerful method of exploring the gift of story is to enter into our inherited texts of sacred story. These can be scripture passages from the Hebrew Scriptures, the Christian Scriptures, the Koran, the Bhagavad-Gita, the Ramayana, and others. They can also come from folk tales, passed down orally such as those from Native American tradition. Some individuals may be drawn to mythology such as the powerful story of Demeter and Persephone. The following exercise might even be done focusing on a beloved childhood story or movie. As we explore the personal significance of transcendent tales, we might consider the wisdom that theologian Megan McKenna teaches: "All stories are true; some of them actually happened."[35] To tap into deep revelatory truth, any story that seems to have a spiritual resonance for the directee can be explored in the following fashion.

This exercise might be called a one-person Bibliodrama, which author Peter A. Pitzele describes as "a form of role-playing in which the roles played are taken from biblical texts."[36] The exercise also has a kinship to a form of prayer taught by St. Ignatius of Loyola, in which one enters a scriptural scene through the imagination. (See Chapter Ten.) The act of praying with the imagination can be further expanded through a combination of storytelling, role-playing, and/or reenactment.

With a directee, choose a scripture passage that has resonance in the moment. In a retreat setting, consider reading and reflecting on a passage with your group. Next invite the directee(s) to choose a character from within the story. This character could even be a non-human witness to the story, such as a tree. For example, I have told the New Testament story of the woman with the alabaster jar from the point of view of "The Jar," and playfully told the story of Christ's resurrection from the point of view of "The Stone that Was Rolled Away." These "characters" became, for me, powerful messengers of the Gospel text.

Once chosen, invite directees to meditate on the character's experience of the story. Feel free to play a short piece of music during which the participants imagine: "How does the character move? What clothing is he or she wearing? What is the scene surrounding the event? What is the character's desire?" Invite participants to allow whatever feelings, images or associations arise, however surprising or "unorthodox" they may seem. Give permission to break open the story rather than just recount it.

Finally, invite the directee to retell the narrative from the character's point of view. If comfortable with the possibility, the directee could include movements as well. Alternately, if speaking a story in the moment seems too big of a step, invite the directee to write the story, either during the session or at home. In either case, once the directee has had the opportunity to share and be witnessed, reflect with him or her on the insights offered from stepping inside the story. Honor the potent gifts revealed in the telling.

One of our program participants entered into the scripture passage of the apostles huddled in fear after Jesus' death. She writes about her experience:

I began telling the story by describing the fear and anguish we disciples were having over the loss of our Lord. I paced and wrung my hands and described how frightened we were: after all, we were His disciples—they killed Him and we were expecting no less for ourselves. My heart began to pound as I described the horrible death Jesus had suffered, how we had loved Him and then deserted Him, fearful for our own lives. We were so distraught. And then from nowhere, I mean nowhere—He appeared! He was with us, in our midst! He was alive; we doubted not; we were thrilled beyond belief! Finally, I whispered in a loud animated cry, complete with real tears, "He is risen, He is with us! I know it is true because I was there!" I was totally blown away with the enactment. It was very real for me and for my partner listening and watching the scene. The experience remains with me in the retelling of it now. —Dianna Woolley

Stories retold in the first person can reveal powerful personal insights into how God is speaking to us as we notice what aspects of the story come into focus. Also, if individuals are inclined, stories told in this way can be refined and shared within the context of a homily, prayer service, children's sermon, or retreat setting. When we coax out the storyteller in our directees, we may find this persona to be bolder than we expected. The liberated storyteller may be called into service as a bearer of "healing salve" for others. A universal story told with breath, bone, and deep personal connection can be a powerful bridge between the human and divine imagination.

Spiritual Director as Storyteller

Since embodying and telling stories is a significant aspect of my own ministry, I'd like to reflect on the possibility of the spiritual director as storyteller. Let us remember that Jesus himself was a storyteller. For seekers from any tradition, Jesus can be a potent model of teaching great mystery through the evocative telling of tales. The primary mode of passing down any faith tradition is through story. As an example of how the Christian tradition has been passed down through the ages, storyteller John Shea comments:

> [T]he beginning of any contemporary retelling of the story of Jesus . . . must start with: "I never saw him. I never heard him. I never touched him. But there were those who did. And they told others, who told others, who told others still, who eventually told me. And now, in my turn, I tell you. And you then, can tell others. And so, you see, there will never be an end to it.[37]

In an informal way, in our role as spiritual directors, we may find ourselves recounting a sacred or scriptural story to our directees. These can be soul-stirring moments. At other times, we may occasionally be moved to tell a personal story. In such an instance, we are intentional about telling the story out of a sense of service to the directee, and not to fulfill our own personal need in doing so. When our own personal stories are evoked in a session, there can often be a palpable sense of vulnerability and honesty that helps to dispel any projection that our directees might have of us being "enlightened beings" and forges a sense of our commonality on the path to God.

Beyond this, the capacity to tell a good story can deepen our effectiveness as presenters, proclaimers, and embracers of mystery. I have been grateful to discover that my own calling to the ministry of dance and storytelling has often provided a catalyst for individuals to delve further into their own spiritual journeys through spiritual direction. Here is an example:

Being a devoutly religious person all of my life I had read and heard the scripture stories over and over. But it wasn't until I saw the stories fully embodied that I began to experience the stories as relevant to my life today, not just historical accounts, or traditions passed down. As a woman it has been particularly difficult for me to relate to scriptures, but when Betsey tells a story, she often focuses on the women characters and brings them to life. What is unique about this kind of storydance is witnessing the embodiment of the intense emotions of the characters as they progress through the stories. When I first saw Betsey tell a story in this way I wasn't comfortable with my own tears or joy or any other strong emotion. Learning that I could move through a whole range of emotion in a twenty-minute period of time was life changing.

I stopped fearing my own emotions and began to accept them as part of the God-given flow of life. —*Sharie Bowman*

Additional Possibilities for Engaging Storytelling in Spiritual Direction

Invite a directee to tell about his or her life in the form of a fairy tale, starting with "Once upon a time . . ." Describing a life experience as a fairy tale can grant a sense of awe, artistry, or even humor, offering directees the grace of seeing themselves through God's eyes. The fairy tale can also be quite effective as a response to artwork or dreams. (See Chapters Thirteen and Fifteen.)

Invite directees to explore various vocal qualities in their babbling, describing, or storytelling. Babble fast or slow, high or low, loud or soft. Tell a story with a character voice, such as a southern belle, an English gentleman, a witch, or a child. Also, play with moving and telling stories at the same time. (See Chapter Eight.)

As mentioned earlier, Bibliodrama can be a potent group technique and "form of interpretive play"[38] for entering and enacting biblical stories. If so inclined, encourage directees to explore this modality. (See the Resource Section for publications.)

To recapture a sense of natural creativity, invite directees to share stories about their favorite ways of spending time as a child. As the Linns ask in their book, *What Is My Song?*, "When in your life have you been so absorbed in something that time flew by without your noticing it?"[39] Or as Bernie Siegel poses the question: "As a child, what were you doing when you were called in for dinner and you came in late?"[40]

For a resource of evocative questions to inspire personal storytelling or writing, explore Christine Baldwin's book *Storycatcher*.[41]

Conclusion

Stories remind us of who we are and call us to become who we hope to be. Stories accompany us in the dark and call us into the light. Through the ancient art of storytelling, we can liberate playful and courageous energy for living God's purpose for our lives.

5

Contemplation and Imagination

Christine Valters Paintner

Our relentless human search for new ways of being and relating,
our dreams of beauty, our longings for mercy and justice,
these are exercises of the imagination.
—WENDY WRIGHT

I have always been drawn to contemplative practices. As a child I remember silence being my natural response to the beauty of nature. I could sit in wonder for hours and not need to speak a word, but simply behold and receive the gift upon which I gazed. As an adult my commitment to contemplative practices has deepened. Practices that ground me in the stunning plains of silence and the vast river of the imagination help me to cultivate a stance of openness and wonder to what the world around might be revealing in a given moment. Moving inward before engaging in creative expression helps to quiet my mind, move my awareness into my heart-center, and allows my art-making time to become prayer. This deep rootedness in the rhythm of my breath, which draws me to the present moment, creates a space in which I can begin to observe my own inner dynamics with a curious and compassionate heart. The art that emerges from this inner space is an authentic expression of the movements of my soul. Creating contemplative space in my daily life and practice supports my ability to hear my directees when they sit and share their stories. I am able to support them in making space for their own process of quieting down and beginning to listen to the wisdom of their hearts.

Spiritual direction is largely about listening. We listen deeply to the story of another through what is spoken and what goes unspoken. We tend to words, body language, intuition, images, gestures, and felt senses. To hear requires that we slow down and make space both in our schedules and within our hearts to create a receiving place. Listening demands we grow quiet, so that we might encounter the essence of things. Because listening involves multiple ways of tending the soul's voice, it becomes a path to intimacy with another person and with God. The practice of listening is a way to go beyond the rational, chattering, divisive mind and feel the language of connection among things and persons.

> **Early December**
> Everything in me
> is quiet like
> a rug spread
> out in the sun to dry.
> —*Barbara Gibson*

Creative Process

In the mystical tradition, there are two main paths to the encounter with the divine. The first is the *kataphatic* tradition or way of images. This is the primary path our work with the arts engages. The way of images is a process of coming to know God through symbols, art, movement, song, sculpture, architecture, and drama. The *kataphatic* path honors the ways in which the sacred is revealed through the sensual dimension of this world.

The second, complementary path, is the *apophatic* tradition or way of unknowing. This is the path of contemplative prayer and moving beyond image to an experience of the sheer presence of God. God is always beyond the words and symbols we use to try and understand the nature of the Divine. The apophatic way honors that the sacred is infinitely more vast than the language and images we use for definition.

These two paths are integral to our spiritual journey. As creatures who know the world through our senses, the physical world points us to an understanding of the multi-dimensionality of God. We discover the sacred in color, shape, form, scent, touch, and taste. However, at some point we must also recognize these experiences do not exhaust the fullness of the sacred and so we are moved to wordless wonder. There is a necessary dialectic between the celebration of the arts as a path to God and the embrace of silence as a way of acknowledging the vastness of the Sacred. The poet Jane Hirshfield expresses it this way: "To speak, and to write, is to assert who we are, what we think. The necessary other side is to surrender to these things—to stand humbled and stunned and silent before the wild and inexplicable beauties and mysteries of being."[42]

In further exploring the connections between spirituality and creativity, we turn to psychologist Graham Wallas who was the first to describe four stages of the creative process.[43] These stages are a general pattern and are not always distinct from each other or even progressive and linear. Creativity is, for the most part, organic and intuitive, but the stages offer some helpful insights into the way creativity unfolds and demonstrates how finding contemplative space and tending the imagination are essential elements of this process.

The first stage is *preparation*. Preparation is a stage of conscious work, readying oneself for the creative endeavor, and involves discipline and training. Artists engage in education of various forms and methods. Persons committed to prayer engage in the discipline of regular practice and formation. Preparation is connected to our intention for ourselves. If we are new to the arts or prayer, we don't wait until we have completed years of study to begin; we commit ourselves to the journey, knowing that there are times when we must practice our craft.

The second stage is *incubation*. This is a period in which the artist does not voluntarily or consciously think about art-making. He or she may be involved in other work, or engaged in some form of leisure activity. In the spiritual life, this stage can also be looked at as a period of letting go, of emptying oneself of expectations and self-directives, and making space for God to enter. This is a stage of simultaneous readiness and surrender to the work of God. Incubation is rooted in the apophatic way or way of unknowing.

The third stage is *illumination*. This is where the flashes of insight occur after the waiting period of incubation. It is a mysterious process likened to the images that appear in our dreams, received as gift from beyond us. In creative moments we talk of being inspired. "Inspire" means to breathe into, drawn from the Latin *spiritus*, and also means to be animated or filled by the spirit. Illumination is rooted in the kataphatic way or way of images.

The fourth stage is *verification*. This is the stage of working to elaborate on those initial insights and developing these intuitions into the creative work itself. It is the stage where we give birth to what has been forming within us. For the artist, this stage is the creation of a painting or song or dance. Scholar Earle J. Coleman, in his book *Creativity and Spirituality*, writes of the variety of ways this stage can come to expression in the spiritual life: "Genuine religion is always fruitful, productive, or constructive, as when religious figures establish hospitals, schools, libraries, and monasteries . . . feed the hungry, teach, preach, inspire, write, translate texts, undertake pilgrimages, and create art."[44] The processes of preparation and surrender lead to inspirations that are meant to be fulfilled by concrete actions and work in the world.

This sequence of stages reflects in a general way what can happen when we work with the arts in spiritual direction or retreat practice. We begin by preparing the space and materials. For example, if we want to paint we gather our brushes, paint bottles, and canvas. If we want to dance, we put on loose clothing, take off our shoes, put on some music, and clear a space in the room for movement to unfold freely. We make clear our intention to encounter the arts as a place of prayer and self-discovery. Then we move into a time of centering, of consciously letting go of our fears and blocks and resistance to creating and surrendering into the unknown. Creativity is always the making of something new, so we prepare ourselves to receive what we have not yet named. Then we begin to create by painting or moving or singing. In the process we become inspired and illuminated. Words, gestures, and images flow through us, some are recognizable and some are strange. Finally we put the paint to paper or move our bodies or open our mouths and allow the expression to come forth. These stages do not usually unfold in a linear way. Moments of inspiration and the actual work of expression often emerge in tandem. Sometimes we need to step back from the work for some more time of incubation, a time to return to our center and become present to ourselves. Silence is also an appropriate way to end a time of creative expression, allowing space within ourselves to receive the fruits of whatever has moved in us.

Working with the imagination in the expressive arts is in part about cultivating receptivity and openness to the space of darkness where it is often uncomfortable to rest. Spiritual direction offers space to rest in the presence of mystery. As companions with others on their journey, our ministry is not to rush directees toward the light, but to honor the dark, fertile spaces of their lives as well. The imagination becomes the bridge between the dark space of incubation, where we are called to surrender control and trust in the wisdom of contemplative space, and the moment of illumination, when the creative act breaks through us calling us to give outward form to our inner movements.

Nourishing a Receptive Stance

When beginning an expressive arts experience it is important to have a way to center your awareness, ground your body, and move into the dark fertile space of your imagination. A time of meditation or clarifying intention can cultivate receptivity to the holy encounter through art. Reading a poem, resting in stillness, getting in touch with the breath, lighting a candle, stating your prayer or intention for the time can all be helpful ways to transition into beginning either a spiritual direction session itself or readying for the journey into creative expression.

Moving inward is a time to cross a threshold in the creative cycle where we trust there will be inspiration and that what is inspired is true and worthy. In the following pages you are invited to explore multiple ways to move into this silent space and begin to open up to the gifts the imagination has to offer. Practice these for yourself and then bring them to your spiritual direction time. Beginning with the imagination helps to move directees into a receiving space, slows them down, releases their inner critic, and helps them to welcome in the gift of symbols at work in their souls. It allows spontaneous expression that helps break through blocks. Consider taking some time before beginning a creative experience to ask the Spirit to guide you in this opportunity for discovery.

Experiential Exercises

Simple Ways to Engage the Imagination in Spiritual Direction

◎ **Begin with the Breath**

Most spiritual traditions have some form of practice which cultivates awareness of the breath. In Chapter One, we described the dance of the Creation story which ends with the image of God breathing life into humanity. *Spiritus* is Latin for both breath and spirit and is the root of the word inspire. Conscious awareness of breath in the creative process helps to access our body's wisdom and frees us to move into spontaneous expression. Attention to the breath brings us into the moment where we have contact with feelings and sensations. In this way we become attuned to the particulars of life.

When working in spiritual direction, consider inviting directees to take a few moments to become conscious of their breath. Here is a sample script you can modify for your context:

> *As you breathe in, imagine the Spirit breathing life into you. As you breathe out, experience the release of your exhale and allow your body to surrender more fully into the present moment. Continue to pay attention to your breath for a few cycles and then allow your breath to carry your awareness from your head down into your heart's center.*

This simple exercise is grounding and helps directees shift out of their thinking and judging mind into a more embodied space of heart-centered, intuitive awareness.

◎ During a session, invite directees to pause for a moment and without judging or changing anything, simply take note and make an inventory of what is going on inside. Notice any images or feelings bubbling up.

◎ At the end of a session ask, "What are you aware of in our last few moments together?" Invite directees to rest in silence and see if there is an image that rises up, perhaps as a symbol for what has happened in the session. Encourage them to name whatever stirs without judgment.

Further Steps to Engage the Imagination in Spiritual Direction
◎ Resistances and Blocks

Resistance and blocks are inevitable dimensions of the creative process. Several of our foundational principles for working with the arts address resistance in a variety of ways: employing incremental steps in the art experiences, using time limits to move past the thinking mind into more intuitive and spontaneous response, and creating a safe space for exploration where the focus is on the process. However, resistance will still come up and may take the form of internal judgmental voices or fear of surrendering to creativity. Directees can expend a lot of energy fighting their resistance or trying to overcome their blocks. Sometimes welcoming the resistance and engaging it directly in conversation as one of the voices present at "inner round table" can be a more fruitful approach.

Through the expressive arts, it is possible to begin forging a relationship with that which we most want to discard. Our fears and resistances have developed for important reasons, most often to protect ourselves from a real or perceived threat. However, once that perceived threat has subsided, we often continue those same patterns unconsciously. Art can help make them conscious.

We can support directees in being present to the messages resistance might have for them as well. While engaged in the creative process, encourage the directee to be present to her inner movements. Invite her to notice places of resistance, as well as places of openness, movement, and flow. When a block comes up—either before, during, or after the art experience—invite her to take a moment to consciously acknowledge this voice, rather than spending energy resisting it, and ask for its support. Invite her to take a few moments to pause and engage her resistance directly through imaginative experience and reflective questions:

> *Take a few moments to allow your breath to move your attention inward. Notice how your body is feeling and breathe into any areas which feel tight or stuck. Follow the rise and fall of your breath and open yourself to any images of your block as they arise. Become aware of colors, shapes, symbols, or simply a sense or energy. When something arises, take time to be present to it. Rest for a while in its*

presence and notice if anything shifts. Begin to have a conversation with the block and ask where it comes from and what it has to say to you. Take some time in your imagination to allow this dialogue to unfold.

When an inner critic shows up—rather than getting caught up in the judgment of that voice—we can support the directee to look on it with curiosity and wonder and discover what it might have to say. The art experience is a microcosm of the directee's life. The blocks and resistance which arise while making art are also present during prayer, work, and relationships and so are valuable to explore.

One of our program participants trains chaplains and here explores working with a client's block:

I was working in supervision with someone who encountered a lifelong pattern within her personality. The supervisory session was going nowhere and she had no agenda for the time, being stuck and frightened to venture forward in her life. I turned my chair away from her toward a window that looked out toward a natural setting. We were now sitting looking out the window together, rather than facing each other.

I sat quietly for some time and asked her, "What color is your stuckness?" Silence. She said, "Grey." More silence. I then asked her, "What is its texture?" She responded, "Like fog." More silence. "What is its sound?" "Silence, it is silence," (said with a kind of fear in her voice). "When did you first notice this grey, silent fog in your life?" It had been there as long as she could remember but it felt like it was closing in on her. I asked, "And what happens to the fog when you are angry?" Silence. Then, "It moves back some."

We continued to sit in silence, looking out over the river. Then the discussion shifted to an article I had sent to her the previous week about how "being nice," as a way of being in the world, stifles love, joy, passion, anger, and a host of other emotions. I asked her how being nice connected with the fog. A portion of her story I had never heard before poured out. We went on to talk and she concluded that this kind of "being nice" that stifled all other emotion was part of what made the fog in her life.

At the end of the session she said, "You know I just couldn't talk about it. I had no words, not even the questions. Your questions on its color, texture, sound . . . I never would have thought to ask myself that. It helped me begin to talk about it, explore it." —*Wes McIntyre*

◎ *Lectio Divina*

Lectio divina means "holy reading" and is a form of contemplative prayer, rooted in Christian tradition, which draws us more deeply into an encounter with the Divine presence in a sacred text such as scripture. This ancient practice is rooted in the assumption that God is fully present in the world around us and can be revealed to us in different places and in a variety of ways. Therefore the "sacred text" might be scripture, but *lectio* can also be engaged to pray with art, poetry, dreams, and life experience.

Lectio divina is a way to invite retreat participants and directees to more deeply engage the "sacred text" of their own life experience. While sitting with someone in direction, there is often a moment of sharing from the directee's experience that feels ripe with meaning and significance. While there are "steps" to help guide a *lectio divina* experience, the movement of this prayer is essentially to listen more and more deeply to the Spirit's movement within. Leading a meditation based on *lectio divina* is a simple and accessible way to invite a directee into a contemplative space. This becomes a time to slow down and listen more deeply to what is moving in them and can also act as a centering experience or doorway into creative expression.

Consider using an adaptation of the following experience with your directee:

(Prepare) Take a few moments to prepare yourself for this experience by becoming still and tending to your breath.

(Listen) Calling to mind the experience you just shared, enter into it with your imagination and be present to it as fully as you can. Become aware of a word, phrase, or image that is calling to you for more attention. Be receptive to whatever this might be, holding it without judgment. Take a few moments of silence to savor it.

(Reflect) Begin to allow this word, phrase, or image to unfold in your imagination. Make space within yourself for memories, images, and feelings to stir in you. Take a few moments of silence to be present to this unfolding.

(Respond) Approach what has been moving through you with a sense of curiosity, wondering what kind of invitation is being extended to you through

these memories, feelings, and images. Attend to the way they connect with the context and situation of your life right now. Is God calling you to anything in your present circumstances? Is there a challenge or invitation being offered? Allow some silence to be present to what is moving in you.

(Rest) Close with a few moments of silence to simply rest and be in God's presence, offering gratitude for what has been revealed.

◎ Body Gratitude Meditation

Practices and meditations to help move a directee's awareness into her body can also be a very helpful way to enter more deeply into a contemplative space and ready the directee for creative expression. A body meditation is also an accessible way for someone who is not comfortable with movement to become conscious of her body's wisdom.

Offer the following guided imagery exercise to a directee as a way of inviting her to become more deeply present to the gifts of embodiment. Begin this time of prayer by inviting her to be where she is, accepting whatever her body offers to her this day and give herself permission to feel the whole spectrum of emotions and memories.

Prepare yourself for moving inward by tending to your breath and to your heart. Put your hands over your heart and give thanks for the wonder of the blood that pumps through your body; give thanks for the breath that infuses you. Take a moment to honor these automatic rhythms that sustain life.

Move your awareness more deeply into your body. Ground yourself in the wisdom of your body, listening as closely as you can. Gently move your awareness into your feet and notice what you feel. Take a few moments to offer thanks for the many ways your feet have served and supported you. Become aware of any memories that rise up and take time to be present to them. Reflect on how you experience yourself being rooted in the earth. Allow any feelings or images that want to arise to have space to move within you. (Allow some time for this.) Breathe in gratitude and exhale release.

Invite the directee to move her awareness to the next area of the body. For each of the following body parts follow the script above—invite a sense of gratitude, an awareness of memories or images that are being stirred, and a time for reflection on the following questions for each area of the body. Allow some silence before moving to the next area and engage the breath as a way to transition.

> *Legs: How do you stand in the world? How do you walk in the world?*
>
> *Pelvis: What are you giving birth to in the world?*
>
> *Belly: What nourishes you?*
>
> *Chest and Heart: Whom do you love?*
>
> *Back: What are you carrying?*
>
> *Arms: What do you embrace?*
>
> *Throat: What wants to be spoken or sung?*
>
> *Face: What is the face you show to the world?*
>
> *Bring your awareness back to the whole of your body. Hold these questions: What is your body trying to teach you? What questions is your body asking? What are your body's invitations? What kind of wisdom does your body offer you today? Where has your body failed you? Is there forgiveness you are invited to offer?*
>
> *Close your time by bringing a sense of gratitude for what has been revealed. Now slowly bring your awareness back to the room.*

This simple meditation can be quite powerful because many of us spend so much time disconnected from the wisdom of our bodies. Here is a description of how one retreat participant experienced the guided body meditation:

We started the day with a body meditation and I found myself feeling quite nervous about our day dedicated to movement. During our meditation we were invited to close our eyes and go to a place of gratitude. As I started to feel gratitude, an image of a wave in the ocean started coming towards me. I then saw myself on a surf board (which I know nothing about!) riding the wave. I looked to the left and there was Jesus grinning and riding the top of a wave, waving with his arms extended to the sky saying,"Woo hoo!" In that moment I knew that I was simply to "trust." —*Delores Montpetit*

Additional Possibilities for Engaging the Imagination in Spiritual Direction

◎ Select a guided imagery exercise to support directees with something they are tending in spiritual direction. See the Resource Section at the end of this book for some suggested publications.

◎ Play a contemplative piece of music for an effective way to center directees and prepare them for creative expression. See the Resource Section on Music for some suggestions of recordings.

◎ The process of *lectio divina* was explored earlier in this chapter as a way to enter into life experience. You can engage the same process to pray with a piece of art a directee has created or a poem he or she wrote. *Lectio divina* can also be introduced as a way to break open a sacred text which a directee has found either meaningful or troubling.

◎ See Chapter Ten for some suggestions on engaging Ignatian Contemplation.

Conclusion

Working with the imagination is a powerful way to invite directees to become more aware of their own internal experience and the symbols stirring within them. When moving into an experience of expressive arts, working with the imagination offers an important space for transition into intuitive and embodied knowing. Contemplative forms of prayer within a direction session cultivate an inner spaciousness and presence to the Sacred.

6

The Dance
of Embodiment

Betsey Beckman

Wherever a dancer stands is holy ground.
—Martha Graham

Whether we like it or not, we all have bodies. Our bodies carry emotions, memories, wounds, joys, and celebrations. Our bodies are uncomfortable, hot, cold, relaxed, energized, stiff, or free. Our bodies accomplish amazing things—building, birthing, healing, walking, typing, climbing. Even when we are still, our hearts are pumping, our breath is cycling, our atoms are vibrating. If we listen, our bodies carry innate wisdom evolved through the ages, teaching us how to assess, respond, intuit, gather, and connect.

Nevertheless, as spiritual directors, we might ask the question, "Why do we dance?" Our ancestors might answer: we dance because the music pulses and our cells respond with rhythm and release. We join with the seasons in their cycles of rebirth. We dance to express our frustrations, ecstatic joys, and deep grief. We dance to connect with community, to embody our stories, and to reveal our inner knowing. When we dance we are lifted up out of the tasks of life into a communion with the rhythms of the eternal, the Sacred, the holy Spirit of life.

For spiritual pilgrims today, perhaps the question becomes, "Why don't we dance?" Truth be told, we don't dance because we're too darn busy. We've forgotten how. It's too revealing. We're too embarrassed. We're too stiff and it hurts! And besides that, some of our religions teach us not to dance. Think about it: dancing releases power and stirs up primordial energy. To dance is to say yes to the sensual nature of life, infused with the movement of the ever-creative Spirit. To dance is to let go of the need to be in control and surrender to the rhythm of the heartbeat of creation. To dance is to open ourselves to a deep wisdom that is beyond us, holding us, binding us together in intricate, energetic beauty.

Despite our culture's distancing from dance, I've been called to it anyway. My life has been flooded with gradual epiphanies inviting me into the ancient dance of life—from a first spontaneous childhood prayer of skipping to the sound of church bells in the yard, to the leotards and tights of classical ballet instruction. From a career as a professional modern dancer in the title role of "The Passion According to Mary," to my twenty-three-year-old funeral dance of farewell to my mother; from improvisations of intense emotion in my Movement Therapy training, to meeting my musician husband while working on choreography. From my "Oh Baby of Mine" duet with our newborn son, to a full repertory of biblical storydances. Over the years, I have danced with bishops, balanced on communion rails, fallen into baptismal fonts, and raced through cemeteries announcing resurrection. Dance has been the vehicle of my deepest grief, my most ecstatic joy, my holiest love.

Along the way, I have had the opportunity to dance at momentous gatherings where contemporary church opens to an experience of the ancient echoes of communal celebration. Each year, I offer workshops at the Los Angeles Religious Education Congress, where thousands of Catholics gather to be inspired in ministry and celebrate the Eucharist in the arena in Anaheim. There I join with other dancers in offering prayers on behalf of the community, and stand in awe when we lift our hands and thousands of others follow, blending into a vast sea of gesture prayer. There, we exchange rhythms with cultural dancers and drummers clad in costumes from numerous nations, and celebrate a sense of diversity in our communion. I share the following poem that I wrote to celebrate the embodied gift of such a prayerful, festival spirit.

So Longs My Soul

The soul wants to sing;
the soul wants to dance;
the soul wants to explode with color
    to sit in silence,
    to reach out in longing
    to leap like a deer
    to dress itself in feathers
    to feel the beat of the drum!

The soul wants a body
so it can kick up its heels.
The soul wants a wide, wide skirt
to wear while it swings and sashays
all the way down the aisles!

The soul wants to know
how mercy feels in the bones,
    in the breath releasing
    in the soft surrender of fear
when love takes over
and all shame, all shadows
are washed away.

The soul wants to feel the awe
of a song rising up
while the dancer
becomes the music,
becomes the meditation.
The soul wants to be the dancer
dancing for us all!

The soul wants to embody
the deep prayers,
rising up from the earth like incense;
the soul wants to become mercy,
to be a balm

for hearts that hurt—
become an embrace
for pain, for poverty, for punishment.

The soul wants a body so it can
be a Bethlehem—
be the place where all that is big
and wide and wonderful,
can put flesh on,
can be born among us into this world,
into this humble humanity.

The soul wants to fly with wild ribbons
rising on the wings of hope.

The soul wants to know you,
God, who soars over time,
who dives deeper than space,
here, now, in our midst,
dancing through us
in this moment, this place
where we are steeped in your mercy,
and so become balm for the world—
souls brimming over with beauty,
moving with your ancient mystery.
Amen!
—*Betsey Beckman*

So, how might we move from these cosmic and grand images of creation and celebration to the quiet intimacy of a spiritual direction session? It is my hope that the stories recounted here remind us that movement is not a foreign language, but a mother tongue for us all. This language may need to be uncovered or recovered, but it remains a primary language nevertheless. Anyone who has a body can be invited in simple ways to allow the holy to break through the gift of our humble humanity.

When I move I feel like my body is talking to me. I feel like God is talking to me.
—*Cheryl Shay*

Dancing Spiritual Direction

I call my own companioning practice with individuals "Dancing Spiritual Direction." Therefore, those who come to me for direction are already seeking an embodied creative expression of their spiritual journeys. They may have varying levels of comfort with movement as we begin, but they invariably come with a desire to learn, experience, embody, and explore. For our sessions, I rent a yoga studio equipped with various "props," and along the way I've seen pillows become a council of elders, straps snapping with anger, blocks forming a sacred path, statues as guardians, and journeys to the balcony as an ascension to heaven.

In working with new directees, whether in a group or individually, there is usually an initial stage of trepidation in opening to dance as a language of experience. The most important element in exploring any of the expressive arts in spiritual direction is first establishing a foundation of trust in the spiritual direction relationship, or in the formation of the group itself. Laughter and lightness seem to be essential tools in my own toolbox for introducing new forms—especially movement.

My individual sessions most often begin with a verbal check-in with the directees to find out what life stories they are bringing for exploration. Then, after twenty to thirty minutes of speaking, there comes a moment of "launching" when words seem to be enough and there is a call to move into a state of prayer and discovery. (These might be the same moments that another director might be inclined to invite silence . . . an open space for Spirit to speak, lead, or inspire.) Directees who are experienced with movement generally need little more than an invitation to take to the floor with their questions, frustration, curiosity, or celebration. I often choose a piece of music that fits the mood of the directees' journey to support them. For newer participants or in a group, the initial invitation to awareness can come through incremental body/movement exercises that help build trust and give permission for all parts of the self and soul to emerge through movement, and to be welcomed by God. Even if the individual has physical limitations, the body can still speak eloquently as an instrument of prayer.

Movement and music are completely energizing to me. As I'm a kinesthetic, rhythmical, and intrapersonal learner, these draw on my innate intelligence and vibrate every cell of my being, which frees energy for my devotion to the Beloved. —*Lisa Sadleir-Hart*

Experiential Exercises

Simple Ways to Engage Movement in Spiritual Direction

In the process of working with a directee, you may encounter moments that are ripe for inviting the insights of bodily awareness. As a directee begins to describe an emotion or concern, the following are some questions and invitations for introducing first steps in movement exploration.

Exploring Sensation

• *Where do you feel that emotion in your body? How about putting your hand on that part of your body and breathing into that body part. What is your experience as you breathe there?*

• *Could you amplify the sensation you feel right there? Could you bring more of your body into that experience? Would it be a contraction, a heaviness, a hunching, a bracing, a softening, a lifting, an opening, a closing, a tensing, a release?*

• *What if I give you a couple minutes of music to explore the subtle movements in and around that body sensation? See what your body and soul might be saying. Remember to breathe.*

• *What if this were your prayer right now? What might you be expressing to God? What is God expressing to you?*

Exploring Gesture

• *How might you express that feeling/experience in a gesture? (Or: Did you notice the movement your hands were making as you were talking? Here is the movement I witnessed.)*

• *Try repeating the movement a few times. What do you notice as you repeat the gesture? Is it satisfying for you? Does the movement want to change or evolve?*

• *Is there a different gesture that might express the longing of your heart? When you find a gesture that feels right, take some time to repeat the movement slowly a few times in a row, like a chant or mantra. Allow your soul to speak through the gesture. I'll join you in that movement.*

• *What is revealed to you as you explore these gestures, bringing your inner sensations to an outward expression?*

Exploring Shapes

• *If you could make a shape with your body to express that, what would it be? How do you feel as you make that shape?*

• *Now how about if I make that shape back to you and see what you notice. What would be the opposite shape? How does it feel to assume that form?*

• *Could you explore moving back and forth between these two shapes a few times to see what you discover?*

• *What might God be inviting you to?*

Postures in Prayer

Contributed by Roy DeLeon

As spiritual director and yoga teacher, I offer this simple prayer of postures.

Bring your body to a posture that suggests or expresses a feeling of sadness, depression, mental anguish, or heavy-heartedness. After a few moments, still in the posture, bring to mind an acquaintance who might be feeling the same, and give your friend company. Be still. Be silent. Pray with them.

Now bring your body into a shape that expresses joy, thankfulness, spaciousness, light. Stay and feel the energy of this posture. Bring to mind one or two loved ones who might be in the opposite pole, and shine on them, dance with them, send them your smile. Close by rubbing your heart center with your palms until satisfied.[45]

First Steps in the Dance—Hand Dance[46]

The following dance forms are all encouraged and supported by recorded music. You will find an endnote listed next to the title for each exercise suggesting specific musical selections you might choose. In addition, please refer to the Resource Section for a list of inspirational musical offerings.

One of the simplest forms of dance that I know comes from the practice of InterPlay, and involves dancing with just one hand. This is a deeply satisfying form of contemplation or meditation, which can be offered for an individual or group, regardless of space or mobility issues. A hand dance can be done while standing, seated, or for deepest relaxation, lying down. You might consider this form to be like opening a window, letting in a bit of fresh air, creating an invitation for body wisdom.

To begin, invite the "mover(s)" to practice a few skills. Allow spaciousness between each of the following invitations:

> *Lift one hand and explore moving it in a smooth fashion . . . then a jerky fashion; explore smooth and fast . . . then jerky and slow. Find a shape with your hand and feel the quality of that shape. Now change the shape, and change it again. Let your hand come to rest on a part of your body and breathe into that place of connection. Find another place of connection and breathe. Finally, see how much space you can cover moving one hand, finding the edges of how far one hand can go. Now, take a deep breath in and let it out with a sigh. I'm going to put on a piece of music and invite you to enter into contemplation. You can draw on all the ways of moving we have just explored. Let your hand be an instrument of play, discovery, and prayer.*

Afterwards, have directees share a bit about what they discovered, noticing insights, feelings, awakenings.

After learning this form, here is what one of our program participants wrote the next morning:

Morning Musings
Before the first light
cozy under the blankets
my arms rise to dance
an expression of love within.
Swaying, circling, diving
graceful, playful, joyful
my heart yawns to the miracle
of life, of breath, of birth.
—*Lois Perron*

Further Ways to Engage Movement in Spiritual Direction

Warm-Up[47]

If directee(s) are ready for exploring full body movement, begin with a warm-up. Put on a reflective or lightly rhythmical piece of music, and lead by starting from one point in your body and gently explore and expand the range of motion of each part one by one. For example, you might begin with the shoulders and shrug them up and release, roll them forward, roll them back, repeating several times. Make sure to include head, face, arms, spine, hips, legs, ankles, and feet, and then add some movements that integrate all parts. Have participants simply follow you, which frees them from having to "come up" with movement, and allows them to begin to tune into what their "bodyspirits" may be revealing to them that day.

Following and Leading[48]

As a next step after a warm-up, consider having participants find a partner to move with. This choice builds group connection and expands permission for a range of expression. In an individual session, you can become a partner for your directee. In either case, the emphasis shifts from being led, to taking turns leading. Within a group, call out when to change leaders so that no one is in the "hot seat" too long. Also, to build energy, shift the music to a more spirited selection. After a while, you can invite shared leadership, letting the dance evolve between partners. It is particularly freeing to invite directees to access their child selves and to explore the space with playful support. Enjoy the opportunity to join otherwise serious directees in crawling under tables and jumping on pillow cushions with radical abandon!

For some this simple act of "moving with" can open powerful doors:

I found it challenging to move in tandem with a partner. That took great vulnerability for me to listen to my soul and move accordingly without self-judgment. My body has been harmed through sexual abuse so I recognize that connection to my reluctance. However, this practice also reaped some of my greatest blessings as I experienced "moving with" as a safe dance in community. —Cheryl Shay

"Exforming"[49]

Exforming is a handy InterPlay term for expressing whatever energy has built up over time in our bodies and spirits. In our fast-paced culture, we take in an enormous amount of "in-formation" on a daily basis. "Ex-for-mation" allows the release of ideas, feelings, frustrations, worries, or even celebrations. There are lots of ways to exform: shaking out, breathing and sighing, walking, jogging, tai chi, swimming, yoga, taking a bath, garden-ing, crying, making love. (You can have directees make a list of their own favorite ways.) When we don't have modalities for releasing pent-up expe-riences, these held energies often become "somaticized," appearing as ten-sion, pain, sinus pressure, and occasionally even more serious crises such as ulcers or heart attacks. One of the most powerful forms of exforming is improvisational movement. Sometimes we may not even know what needs to be expressed until we give permission for the floodgates to open. Here's a story from one of our program participants who discovered by surprise her own capacity for exforming.

While on my individual retreat, I was greatly relieved to leave my gnawing wor-ries from work behind. With the help of my loving retreat director, I moved quite naturally into a welcome holy silence. One day, as I settled into prayer, ready to listen to the lovely, still small voice within, suddenly with no warning and with shattering intrusion, there came a powerful disruption. I felt as though I had been gazing out on the calmest of waters when horrendous "Jaws" lunged out with mouth open and teeth bared!

My body shook so terribly that I realized my pent-up anger had finally reared its ugly head. I could only deduce that "Jaws" was indeed the small still voice getting my attention. Without thinking, I stood up and did something I had never done—I danced my anger! Not knowing that the music I had brought had four movements, I just put it in the player and began to follow its grand invitation to dance.

I still recall the progression of what followed during the next thirty min-utes. First came the notorious release of angry emotion. No gentle ballet, only robust aerobic movements: kicking, punching, shaking, expressing my protest at intense injustice in my work situation. And my thoughts remain unprintable, to say the least. By that time, I was feeling spent. But there was a slight pause in the music and another movement began. My body seemed to begin an eas-ier and smoother swaying. This time my mind shifted away from judgment to contemplating my own part in creating the imbalance at work. I realized I had shown much disgust and a lack of cooperation with the team, with plenty of rash words blurting out. The dance led me in expressions of humility and sor-row—low bows, prostrating, arms lifted for mercy.

Then in the third movement, I found myself coming to a compassionate awareness for my team of co-workers who had limited vision, a whole differ-ent world view, and were easily threatened. I recall a lot of stretching my arms and hands out in front as if to erase the hurts they live with and to receive their forgiveness for my own actions. In the final section, my profound slower move-ments, many bows, and embracing arms told me I had indeed forgiven them—and strangely enough I even felt we had reconciled.

I came from this time of prayer both gentled and exhilarated. But the phe-nomenal part still remained: on arrival back to the workplace, not only did I not have to reengage my anger, but I no longer remembered it! I could move into teamwork with understanding and the willingness to challenge when neces-sary—and do so appropriately. —*Marilyn Peot, CSJ*

This powerful dance of release did not occur within an actual direc-tion session, but in the context of a deep place of spiritual support during retreat. As a growing number of spiritual directors tune into the gift of the body, perhaps more of our retreat experiences will offer support for such embodied expressions of healing. As Alice Walker writes, "No one can end suffering except through dance."[50]

Dancing with a Witness[51]

One of the core elements of dance as spiritual direction is witnessing. This term was originally developed in the movement therapy practice of "authentic movement" and now is widely accepted in many movement modalities.[52] Authentic movement gives prime emphasis to the powerful, shared space of revelation that is created between mover and witness. The witness holds the space and creates a container of safety for the mover to explore her inner territory. The witness also pays attention to his or her own inner responses, noticing whatever associations might be awakened during the witnessing process.

As spiritual directors, we are quite used to entering into a state of deep attentiveness with directees, allowing for intuitions, images, prayers, and affirmations to come through as messages of the holy. Most of us are accustomed to doing this through a state of quiet listening. In Chapters Two and Three we explored the significance of witnessing in spiritual direction in general. With movement, a particularly potent state of sacred awareness can be fostered through the grace of seeing and being seen. How often in our lives are we given the opportunity to be witnessed as we move our soul's deep expressions? How often do we have the honor of gazing on the movement of another with profound acceptance and utmost respect, bearing witness to whatever God might be revealing, coaxing, nurturing, or healing in the moment?

In teaching the art of witnessing, consider inviting witnesses to imagine embodying the compassion of God and seeing with God's eyes. Call the witnesses to a presence of deep breath and openness of being. Likewise, invite movers to imagine that they are moving not before an audience or a judge, but in the presence of God, who is ready to receive whatever expressions arise.

Here are two powerful descriptions of movers being witnessed for the first time.

Stepping Out

We started by dancing together in a large group and eventually we were invited to dance with one person as our witness. I felt so nervous and self-conscious, yet I wanted to be able to do it, so I offered to go first. I started to dance very tentatively, asking God, "How do I get through this?" The words "just step" came to me so I prayed, "just step" and stepped; "just step" and stepped. Gradually, I found the hurt from my childhood experience began to drop away. I hesitated, I tripped, and finally I let go. I became freer and freer, and I found my nervousness replaced with joy and inner abandon. When I was finished, my witness was crying and said, "That was such a profound dance of freedom!" I was deeply touched that God had healed and revealed.

Upon reflection, I realize that when I step out with God, I am empowered. It's the stepping, the trust and the responding that brings joy, wholeness and healing. Now, in the retreats that I facilitate I am including expressive dance and loving every minute of it. An interesting aside to all of this is that the night before our dancing segment, I dreamt that I was dancing in a very small white closet all by myself—I think I am out! Bring it on! —*Delores Montpetit*

A Dancing Relationship with God

During our process together, we were invited to do something called a Solo-witness dance. Our group was divided into pairs and one person was invited to simply witness the other person dance an expression of prayer. I had struggled with speaking prayers for years . . . it always felt like I had to be perfect to approach God and I had never reached that state so it seemed pointless to try to pray. The idea of dancing a prayer filled me with fear. I decided to just pretend no one was watching and dance the longings of my soul. As I walked out on the dance floor, I felt like I was approaching God for the first time and could no longer hide the truth of my pain and sadness; I could no longer be fake with God. As I danced, images came to me that I embodied, emotions rose and fell, movements came forth to express the deep longings of my heart.

When the song was over I was invited to notice with my partner what I had experienced in my "prayer dance." I was totally shocked when my partner related back to me specific images and longings from my prayer. She got it! I decided that if she could understand my danced prayer that had no words, God definitely could too! It freed me to pray from my heart and was the beginning of a whole new dancing relationship with God. —*Sharie Bowman*

We can see that the role of witness is not to interpret or explain the meaning of the mover's dance. As witnesses, we are invited to remain attentive to whatever stirs within our own selves even as we witness another. After the mover shares his or her own experience, the witness can then offer noticings, images, and affirmations that honor whatever grace was revealed.

Additional Possibilities for Engaging Movement in Spiritual Direction

Teaching a Gesture Prayer

A simple introduction to body movement can be for the director to teach a gesture prayer which the directee can then incorporate into personal prayer. For an example of a choreographed gesture prayer, see Chapter Fourteen. Another possibility is to explore creating a gesture prayer together with a directee. Choose a psalm refrain or the chorus of a song. Sing or play the phrase multiple times and experiment together until you find a repeatable series of gestures that flow easily from one to the next and help to enflesh the words of the prayer. No need to be literal; find movements that express the deeper meaning of the text.

Labyrinth[53]

Walking (or dancing) the labyrinth can be a very inviting form of movement prayer, either as "homework" for a directee, or if accessible, during a direction session or retreat. (See Chapters Ten and Eleven.)

Dancing on Behalf Of

Many forms in this chapter, such as hand dances, shape and stillness meditations, dancing with a partner, or moving with a witness can be offered as prayers on behalf of a loved one or world concern. As St. Paul writes, the "Spirit intercedes with sighs too deep for words" (Romans 8:26).[54] Choose a form and invite directees to allow movements to arise spontaneously, expressing their heart's desires on behalf of the concern they carry.

Exploring the Four Movement Patterns

Dancer and movement researcher Betsy Wetzig has identified four basic movement patterns that characterize the range of humanity's different energies and approaches to life. Playing with "hang, thrust, shape, and swing" can provide simple tools for helping directees explore a range of dynamics as well as discover and celebrate the movement qualities with which they naturally identify.[55]

Make a list with directees of ways they already experience embodied prayer (such as gardening, walking, massage, or knitting). For expanding expressive capacities in the journey of embodiment, invite directees to consider such modalities as yoga, tai chi, InterPlay, ecstatic dance, the Dances of Universal Peace, liturgical dance, American Sign Language, hula, modern dance, dance therapy, authentic movement, and so forth. As comfort grows, the language of movement naturally opens up in direction sessions.

Won't You Join the Dance?

As spiritual directors, we might remind ourselves that movement, dance, improvisation and gesture prayer just might not be everyone's calling. At the same time, as we ourselves grow in acceptance, comfort, and respect for the deep voice of wisdom that resides in our bodies, perhaps a growing number of directees might be inspired to join the dance of holy embodiment. And who knows, perhaps some adventurous directees may lead the way!

Visual Art Expression

Christine Valters Paintner

A painting is not about an experience. It is an experience.
—MARK ROTHKO

My parents were not religious people, but they did have a love of art and the beauty of sacred spaces. When I was a child we traveled a great deal and spent many hours wandering through museums and cathedrals, gazing upon the splendor of form emerging from stone, and the color used to express emotional and spiritual landscapes. I remember the cool spaces of those ancient buildings: the upward sweep of the arches drawing my eyes toward the heavens, the luminous glow of stained glass windows on a sunny evening spilling color everywhere, the achingly beautiful sound of a voice rising in song within that "thin place." I began to discover a visual language for the internal longings for which I had no words. My parents often called me the "sensual child" because of my love of color and texture, of taste and fragrance. Somehow I knew that art led me to the heart of something much bigger than anything I could express through everyday language.

Contemplate for a moment the ways religious traditions visually express their relationship to the sacred: the intricate sand mandalas of the Tibetan Buddhist monks, the icons of the Eastern Orthodox tradition depicting the faces of holy men and women, the powerful statues of gods like Ganesh and Shiva in Hinduism rising from their stone forms, the elaborate illuminated manuscripts of Christianity, Judaism, and Islam making sacred texts come alive, or the incredible mosaic tile work found in Islamic mosques.

Through art we can come to an experience of revelation about ourselves and about God. Art helps to support our presence to those places of revelation and creates space for us to receive our inner symbols. Carl Jung said that "symbols act as transformers."[56] Symbols are the language of imagination, revealing the depths of our experience in a non-rational and non-linear way. Both religion and art use the power of symbol to uplift and awaken us to the sacred dimension of our lives. Living symbols are messages from the depths of our being to our conscious selves, messages that reveal things previously unknown about ourselves and our lives. In spiritual direction we are invited to discover the ways symbolic images moving in our directees help to open them to the creative possibilities of the unconscious. We can support their discovery of these images through using guided imagination techniques, attention to dreams, and visual expression.

There are many different media for expression in the visual arts. As a spiritual director you might consider engaging clay, collage, assemblage, paint, mosaic, paper cutting, and fabric, to name just a few. Depending on the medium, your directee may be working with external or found images, as in collage, or internally generated images, as in painting or working with clay. Both approaches are valuable. The materials involved with each medium have their own texture and shape. Allow the experience to dictate the form. For example, notice how the qualities of collage, paint, drawing, and clay differ from each other, and consider what kinds of experiences they seem to support best. Your sense of this will develop over time with your growing experience of engaging the arts for your own growth and transformation.

Experiential Exercises

Simple Ways to Engage Visual Art in Spiritual Direction

Tend to the spiritual direction space visually: What art do you have displayed? What colors do you use? Do you visually mark the change in seasons in any way? Consider the use of colored cloths, various candles, and small sculptures to evoke a sense of the sacred in a visual way.

Collect a set of figurative symbols or small statues and place them on a tray. Invite directees to create an altar space when they arrive to a session with the symbols which are resonating with them that day. Begin by talking about their selections. Or invite directees to bring a symbol of their own to a session to express where they are in their journey. Another approach to this exercise is to use symbols from nature (see below for an example.)

Collect various evocative images from magazines or books and arrange them into a book of your own. When directees are having trouble expressing their feelings in words, invite them to flip through the images and find one that resonates.

Keep a pack of cards with images (such as SoulCards[57]) on hand. Invite the directee to pick one and allow the serendipity of the image to speak to what you are reflecting on together. Another option is to have a variety of prayer cards with different icons printed on them available for directees to choose from.[58] Allow some time for the directee to pray with the image and be present to what its language of images might be revealing.

Offer markers or colored pencils and paper for just a few minutes of quiet visual meditation and expression as a way to center before beginning a session. You might start with a question as a prompt, such as "What is the color and shape of my soul today?" Or "What is my deepest longing this day?"

Further Steps to Engage the Visual Arts in Spiritual Direction

Natural Objects as Art Materials

Contributed by Rachelle Oppenhuizen

Natural objects such as stones and organic materials invite participation without the implications of "performance," a "technique," or "skill" that can be detrimental to spiritual exploration with the more "advanced" (and potentially more threatening) tools of colored markers and intimidating sheets of blank, white paper.

I've found that a basket of smooth stones invites an almost universal appeal to touch. Natural objects such as feathers, leaves, bits of bark, or seed pods that I've gathered over time on my daily walks, offer numerous opportunities for sensory associations, exploration, and reflection.

Presented in a basket or on a simple fabric underlay, directees are intuitively drawn to touch, hold, and attend to objects more closely due to the way they've been gathered and set apart. Allow color, weight, scent, feel, light and shadow, to evoke emotions. Memories, desires, or connections may be stirred from the simple experience of handling, touching, holding, or arranging. "Which object here expresses something about how you're feeling today?" is a simple and elegant way to begin a session with either a group or an individual. Time for examination of the object draws a person into a state of reflective attention which can then become a means of creatively drawing forth connections and finding metaphors for the deeper work of one's heart and soul.

In a liturgical season such as Lent, a basket of stones offers the raw material for quiet reflection after the reading of a scripture text, a meditation or a poem. Direct and indirect work goes on within as the stones are arranged into shapes (circles or cross shapes) or stacked into simple altars or cairns.

Art Journaling

Most spiritual directors are already familiar with journaling as a powerful tool to get in touch with interior movements and as a way to pray with words stirring through us. Art journaling emerges from a similar impulse, but offers access to our visual language. Essentially it is a way of working with both word and image to bypass the inner critic and create a safe space for expression and connecting with our intuitive voice. Spiritual director Jane Comerford, CSJ, describes this intuitive flow of visual expression as "gush art" because it helps us to break through our resistance and work from our feelings and body sense to respond to God and life more freely. As we bypass our internal censors, we come to new awareness of ourselves.

A favorite resource for art journaling is Marianne Hieb's *Inner Journeying Through Art Journaling*. Hieb defines the discipline of Art Journaling® as "the use of simple art materials, the language of design, gazing, written journaling, (and) noticing to help focus, express, respond to, uncover, or clarify inner wisdom."[59]

You can engage art journaling in a spiritual direction session or encourage directees to work in this way at home. During a session, begin by preparing the space, making sure you have the materials and time needed to enter fully into this experience with a directee:

1. Materials Needed: Gather a few sheets of plain white paper and a selection of oil pastels, markers, and colored pencils.

2. Preparation: Light a candle and perhaps play some meditative music, asking the directee if this would be a helpful support. Then invite him to spend a few moments moving inward, connecting with breath and the interior space of the imagination and becoming present to any colors or shapes beginning to take form there. Take time to allow him to move into a space rooted in intuitive wisdom and heart knowing, moving him out of his thinking and judging mind.

3. Framing a Question: Consider beginning the art expression time with a question to stir images. Marianne Hieb suggests beginning with a question such as "What are all the elements that make up my life today?" and allowing later questions to build upon what was revealed in this first experience. Lucia Capacchione's book, *The Creative Journal*,

is also a helpful resource for suggestions of evocative questions to prompt a visual response. The question might also rise up directly out of something the directee is wrestling with in this moment. Encourage him to be receptive to the question that wants to be asked in him.

Art-Making

Once the question has been framed, invite the directee to move into expression with visual art materials. These might include oil pastels, crayons, colored pencils, or markers. You can work with this process using paint as well, but keeping the materials simple helps keep the experience accessible and immediate. A time limit can be a helpful way to move the directee past his blocks and resistance by giving him little time to think things through and encouraging presence to his unfolding experience. Invite the directee to use the materials to express through color and shape his inner movements without worrying about whether it makes logical sense. Allow about ten to fifteen minutes, depending on the time available in a session, to work in this way.

Reflection

Once the time for visual expression is done, allow the directee a few moments of contemplative presence to what has emerged. In the Christian tradition of praying with icons, this practice is called "gazing," which means being present in a non-judgmental and receptive way to the art as a doorway into the sacred. Invite him to receive the image as a gift from the depths of imagination.

At this point in the process it can be helpful to use written expression as a way to invite your directee to explore the insights or questions that have emerged during this time of art-making. Encourage him to take some time to notice what feelings have been stirred and what he noticed as the process of making the art unfolded.

One spiritual director offers this reflection:

I meet with one directee who is VERY verbal, knows herself well and can share with words. But one day she was talking along and she just stopped and looked at me and said, "I'm stuck. I don't know what I mean." I immediately got the pastels out and she easily broke through whatever was resisting her. I almost always encourage people to not worry about drawing a picture or trying to come up with an image, but they almost always do. I try to get them to just pick color and start spreading it around the page. —*Rebecca Johnson*

When the directee has had some time for written reflection, continue to explore the meaning of the art that has emerged through conversation.

Clay Meditation

Clay is another accessible art form to introduce to a directee during a session as a tool for meditation.

Materials Needed: Keep small bags of clay on hand, both self-hardening or non-hardening work well. Sculpey® brand has a convenient package of thirty small blocks that are individually wrapped and come in a variety of colors.

Modify the following meditation as needed for your directee:

> *Take some time to begin working with the clay and become familiar with its feel in your hands. Notice its texture and the way it both resists and yields to your touch.*
>
> *Call to mind the creation story of the Hebrew Scriptures where God shapes the human from clay, gently molding and shaping each fold and indentation. Take a few minutes to experience yourself as coming from the earth and being molded by God.*
>
> *Hold this image in your heart as you continue to mold the clay. Notice how it feels in your hands. Don't worry about making an image, just be present to the materials and to what is stirring inside of you. Notice any images bubbling up. As you handle the clay see if it wants to be formed into a particular shape.*
>
> *Reflect on how you experience God shaping and forming you. Where are the places in your life that feel resistant and where are they malleable? Work with the clay for a while, engaging in the process, tending what comes to you without censoring.*
>
> *As you continue to listen and be present, begin to notice if there are any images bubbling up. Continue to hold the questions in your heart of how God is shaping and forming you. Work with the clay for a while, perhaps five more minutes, engaging in the process, tending what comes to you without censoring.*
>
> *When you have come to a resting place with your clay experience, take some time for gazing on the object that has emerged in this time. Be present to its gifts and notice your own internal movements. How did you feel God moving in you during this time?*

Allow some space for silence following the experience to simply be present to what is moving in the directee. Taking some time for journaling can also be a helpful way to clarify the meaning of the experience.

Clay can be a very grounding experience for a directee who is feeling scattered:

I have used some clay work and poetry with directees. The clay became a way to introduce silence for directees who were buzzing and could not still themselves through any meditation or other focus for quieting. Clay brought in a process of centering that did not need to be named as such and did not result in resistance. Just holding the clay and smoothing it into a ball—which is what they did—brought them through the transition between their daily events and the experience of centering that they were seeking. —*Freya Secrest*

Collage

The most challenging part of the program for me was the visual art. I wrote: "I have no paints. I have no brushes. I fear the empty white page." I just had no background or experience whatsoever with visual art, didn't even take an art class in high school. Luckily we began with collage. Aha! Even I could do this. —*Rebecca Johnson*

Collage is a particularly accessible medium for those beginning to work with visual expression, because it relies on found images rather than accessing images from within and then giving form to them. When working with collage, consider having a stack of images available already cut out from magazines or books. In the space of an individual session, beginning with a small collage can be a simple, non-threatening introduction to engaging the visual arts in service to the soul's longings.

The materials needed are simple: A piece of colored cardstock (approximately 5"x7" for each collage, glue sticks, scissors (although tearing works well too), and a variety of images.

Begin by taking a few moments for the directee to get grounded and move inward to access her interior symbolic language. Then invite her to take a small piece of cardstock and select three images through which she experiences a sense of resonance or dissonance. Then with a limited period of time—about ten or fifteen minutes works well—arrange these images in relationship to each other on the cardstock and adhere them with glue. Because of the small size of the background surface she will have to make decisions about which part of the images to include and which to remove. Encourage the directee to be present to her own interior movements as she works, releasing judgment and thoughts.

After the collage-making allow the directee a time to simply be with what has emerged. Then, using imagination or journal writing, invite her to explore the following (allowing time after each suggestion for written response):

> Notice . . .
> Which images are present?
> Which colors and shapes are present?
> Which images are near to each other and which are far apart?
> What is hidden and what is revealed?
> What is in the foreground and what is in the background?
> Is there any open space or is the surface completely covered?
> Have you extended beyond the edges of the background or stayed within the borders?
> As you notice these elements begin to reflect on how these same elements are present in your own life.
> Take some time to enter into each image and speak from it saying "I am" and explore what it feels like to be that dimension of your collage. Allow yourself to have this experience, noticing feelings, memories, and images. See what you discover about yourself in the process.

Invite the directee to take some extended time for journaling in response to what was stirred by these questions.

Collage Mandala

To offer a more extended collage experience in a retreat setting, invite a directee to create a mandala. The mandala is a sacred form used in many traditions as a tool for centering and prayer. You can purchase round cardboard baking forms approximately twelve inches in diameter from a baking supply store to serve as a sturdy background.

This form works well when a large surface is desired and there is a longer time period available to select and arrange images. Creating a mandala can also be an effective exercise for the directee to do on his own in between spiritual direction sessions as an expression of his soul at a given point in time. When he brings his mandala to the next session, use some of the suggestions and questions from the previous exercise in this book to help him break open the meaning of the images he has used.

The suggestions for the "I am" reflections in the previous collage exercise can be used to explore the mandala as well. These can also form the starting point for writing a poem. Here is an example of an "I am" poem created from a collage mandala:

I am the Sun—glowing, radiating, birth, warming, energizing,
    pulsating with life.
I am the One-with-all—unique yet same, alone yet together, close
    yet distant.
I am the Bride of the Beloved—held in eternal embrace, pure as
    snow, above and beyond.

I am the Moon—waxing and waning, revealing and hidden, full
   and new.
I am the Shell—incredibly created with grace in simplicity, washed
   up on the shores of life.
I am the Balloons—playful, colourful, filled with the Spirit, and
   ready and willing to move to the wind of God's breath.
—*Lois Perron.*

One of our program participants describes the way movement helped
to deepen the meaning of her visual expression and reveal new layers to her
experience:

I created a mandala to express the "Portrait of my Soul." My mandala was filled
with bright colors, glitter, feathers, and jewels, all intertwined and racing
around in manic shapes. It was beautiful. Really. Then I took it home and put
my mandala to movement. That changed everything. Through movement, I discovered that my soul isn't a raucous jumble of colorful art supplies, but is deep,
dark, and still. I flipped the mandala over and colored the entire reverse side
black. —*Karin Ogren*

Labyrinth Collage
Contributed by Debra McMaster
Another shape to use in collage-making is the form of a labyrinth. You can
search online for a pattern to use as the foundation. A simple version is the
Crete labyrinth or a five-circuit round.

Materials Needed: Square paper about 12"x12"; pictures, scissors, pencil, glue stick, bottle of glue, yarn, labyrinth pattern, a variety of images.

This process is similar to the previous collage exercise except that you begin
by having directees create the labyrinth pattern on their paper and then select
images to fit the curves of the labyrinth. If they choose to include an image that
is wider than one single pathway, be sure they redraw the labyrinth curve over
their picture so they don't lose the line. When they've finished cutting and glu-
ing all the collage images, use bottled glue, such as Elmer's, to apply yarn to
highlight the pattern of the labyrinth path. Allow the piece to dry completely
and back the finished labyrinth with foam board to make it sturdier.

When directees have completed their collage labyrinth, invite them to pray
in the following way with it on their lap:

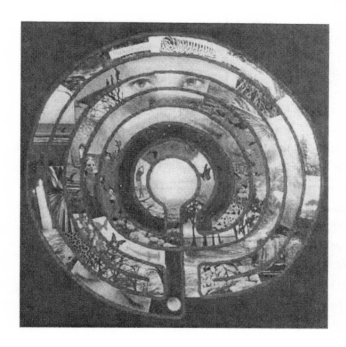

Allow your intention to form in your mind. You may "walk" with a specific request such as intercession for another, for discernment, for inspiration, or simply for gratitude. Let your fingers slowly walk the path. Remember the significance of the pictures you chose. You might want to use your non-dominant hand. You might even want to close your eyes and trust the feel of the path. When you reach the center, take some time to rest in openness to whatever comes. When it seems right, "walk" back to the beginning, taking with you whatever you received on the journey.

As you pray you may want to consider these Three Rs:

Release—setting aside whatever clutters your mind so you can walk with your intention.

Receive—opening to whatever comes on your walk.

Respond—integrating any insights into your life.

Mixed Media Explorations

Contributed by Jennifer Steil

When working with directees, I offer a wide range of media and materials for visual art expression. These include water paint, acrylic paint, chalk pastel, oil pastel, colored pencils, graphite, and ink. I provide various brushes; large and small, course and soft. I also offer collage materials such as magazine images and words, photos, beads, fabric, twine, raffia, threads, shells, seeds, and feathers. I use clay as well. These offer the opportunity for directees to choose the media, texture, and modality which best suits the moment of expression.

I have noticed that directees are drawn toward media, colors, and making marks which are expressive of themselves and give voice to the movements of their soul. In any session, I may offer all of these materials for them to work with. I have found that working in mixed media offers a range of flow. For example, watercolor can be used to express a flowing emotional or spiritual response that is free and allows for spontaneous discovery. The viscosity of acrylic allows for layering and more dramatic and direct expression. Chalk pastel can be used for clear bold marks with a softening and blending potential. Oil pastel calls for a certain direct response in which pressure is applied in moments of intensity. Combined, each of these give expression and awareness to the qualities of interior movements that are a part of our life experience.

I invite directees to enter into any experience of creative expression with a childlike awareness. In this, I encourage them to notice what they are drawn to, whether it be media, modality, or color and then to select it intuitively. This is an invitation to allow the expression of their souls and to trust their intuition as their guide in the Spirit. I encourage them to engage prayerfully with God, to allow for the stilling of the inner voices by noticing conflicting messages that arise but allowing them to pass with a continuing trust in the voice of their souls. If anxiety arises and the inner voices are clanging within, hindering the process of free expression, I invite them into breath prayer, noticing only their breath as they continuously stay in motion with their media.

I find that continuous motion and having several large sheets of paper ready for transitions is very helpful in allowing for the breakthrough of free expression as they are moving towards the still point of their creative selves. I invite them to enjoy pure color, marks, shapes, patterns, movement, and whatever spontaneously appears and to notice how they feel as they arise. I encourage them not to judge or deny the freedom of the moment whether it is joyful or painful, but to stay with it. Through this simple practice with prayerful attention, I have seen tremendous creative, emotional, and spiritual breakthroughs as they flow together. I have discovered that directees, in opening to their creative souls, find themselves open to the voice of God in their inner being.

A directee describes her first experience of entering into a time of visual prayer during a spiritual direction session:

In one of my earliest spiritual direction sessions, my director responded to a long-forgotten movement within me by suggesting that I go to the retreat center's creative expression room and "put some color on paper." Although resistant and awkward at first, I wanted to honor her experience and wisdom by making an effort to follow her guidance. What happened astonished me. While I've always loved the visual arts, my creative talents are limited primarily to the written word. So I was skeptical, to say the least, as I chose a crayon and began moving it across a sheet of paper. But after a time of disengaged critical thinking, I was surprised to see the result of my free-form coloring—a vivid and powerful representation of my current spiritual condition. Since that day some years ago, I have frequently sought out art supplies after sessions with my spiritual director and whenever I've been on retreat. By "putting color on paper," I have clarified Divine guidance for various aspects of my lay ministry, including my calling to become a trained spiritual director. In addition, I've received many blessings of insight, integration, and healing in my writing career and my personal life. —*Constance Bouvier*

A spiritual director describes the way that visual art expression can be a powerful container for strong feelings:

I consider my personal involvement in the creative process and image-making to be what truly qualifies me for the work that I currently do as an artist and spiritual director. My goal is to help others become fully engaged in the present moment and to begin to listen to the voice within. This is done through contemplative prayer, meditation, journaling, and dialogue.

During a particular workshop, one of the participants was extremely agitated and emotional. She was fearful and thwarted by performance anxiety. Tearfully, she expressed that all she could feel was chaos. It was then, that I suggested she try to paint the chaos. She immediately received the grace to begin working. The transformation that occurred was life-changing. Violent marks of red and black paint covered the canvas. As she was painting she seemed to hear another voice instructing her to paint white into the dark paint. She obeyed this voice and began to weep as she realized the "Light" was in her darkness. This was a significant breakthrough and her painting serves as a reminder of this powerful creative encounter. —*Claudia Campbell*

Additional Possibilities for Engaging the Visual Arts in Spiritual Direction

There are many other possibilities for exploration in the visual arts. Here are a few additional suggestions:

- Creating tools for continued prayer and exploration such as an altar or prayer box can be powerful. You can purchase small, plain wooden boxes at craft stores and invite directees to paint and decorate them with meaningful symbols and colors.

- Simple forms of book-making, such as creating an accordion book, can become a place for a directee to place images, poems, and quotes which have become meaningful to them or as a way to honor a particular chapter of their lives.

- Photography is a very accessible and powerful medium. Consider inviting your directee to take a contemplative walk (See Chapters Eleven and Fifteen) and use the camera as a way to be present to and observe the world around them while noticing their internal movements.

- Have a selection of beads and invite your directee or retreat participants to create their own string of prayer beads, choosing colors and shapes that appeal to them. Then invite them to create their own series of prayers to use with them, perhaps a series of significant prayers or poems.

Conclusion

The creation of art is a journey of discovery. We close this chapter with a story told by Karen Haddon, a spiritual director and visual artist. She describes the way in which the unfolding of the art-making journey reveals truths and insights all the way along if we allow ourselves to stay present and pay attention.

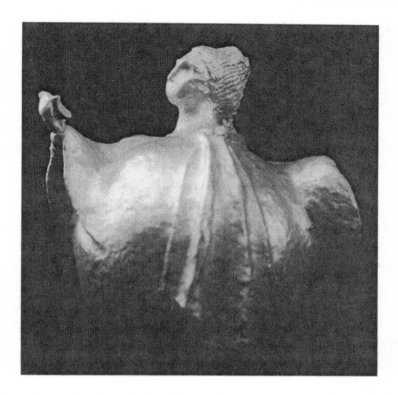

This sculpture is a piece that was born of prayer . . . a time of wonder, awe, and innumerable questions. At the start of a five-day workshop the instructor had given each student a Styrofoam ball and invited us to play—to try something new—become familiar with the materials and use the ball as an armature, to experiment with texture and possibilities. This was meant to be a warm-up exercise.

While that process was true for my fellow students, I surrendered to an interior truth. I found a quiet corner in the studio and slowly began to cover the ball with clay paper. Now and again I would add another layer of paper, building mounds that would become a firm foundation and even the folds of the garment of my creation. I remember my questions and my prayerful confusion as I wondered just what my heart was creating. You see, when I sculpt as a pilgrim I don't know the outcome. It's as though my hands are directly connected to my heart and my mind can only observe. Each night I would go to bed with one of my questions: "What am I creating? What will this become? What is this figure looking at? What is she holding in her hand? What colors will I use?" As I drifted off to sleep I would hear a still, calm voice saying: "Trust me. Watch . . . and see!"

I remember my delight when I began to sculpt wings—She's an angel! I pondered my understanding of angels—beings who bring the light and messages from God. Of course, my next question was: "What will she say?"

When I formed a star in the palm of her hand, I remembered a piece from the creation story—each of us has stardust in our DNA. "Was the star a symbol for me?" To God my process must have felt like a game of fifty questions! Every observation transformed into another question.

I thought I had completed the sculpture when I finished painting it. I had chosen blue for the base because it was my color for prayer, the foundation of my process. As I painted upward, the color had softened and eased into a pearlized white, a color that seemed to reflect light. I mixed up a shade of pink, put a small circle on the angel's chest, and then I took it off. I mixed a shade of rose, put it on, and took it off. All the time I questioned, "Why am I doing this?" Once again I put the rose paint on. As I increased the diameter of the blush—my head caught up to my heart.

The angel's "blush" was her heart's response to gazing at the star—And that star was me!

Instantaneously, the space in my heart that had been created during sculpting was filled with knowing! This messenger was telling me that God felt as she did. When gazing upon me—God's response was LOVE!

Love became a heartfelt experience, no longer just a thought or a teaching of the church. Love was a truth! I am loved . . . and God is my Beloved!
—*Karen Haddon*

8

Music, Voice, and Rhythm

Betsey Beckman

What makes the soul of a poet dance? Music.
—Hazrat Inayat Khan

Music echoes through time as an expression of the sacred. Hear shamans shaking ceremonial rattles and voices in Hebrew soaring with their ancient psalms. Be lulled by Celtic harps reverently releasing the dying. Feel the pulsing drama of the drums: Native American, African, Japanese, Javanese. Be roused by the rhythms of the Indian sitar or the spirited guitar Mass. Rejoice with Beethoven's "Ode to Joy." Dive deep with Gregorian chant or the Hindu "Om." Be stirred by the shofar, the conch shell, or the melodic Islamic muezzin, calling the faithful to prayer. Throughout time, virtually all religious tradition has included music.

What repercussions do the gifts of music have for the art of spiritual direction? As sentient beings, we recognize that music vibrates through the air, enters our bodies, and resonates within our core. Music also originates from our own bodies as we tap our toes, practice our piano scales, find ourselves humming a tune, or lift our voices to join a harmonic chorus. Music has the capacity to inspire us to action, calm us, irritate us, evoke powerful memories, lift us to heights of ecstatic joy, or open the floodgates to the sadness we didn't even know we had.

The process of creating music also has its own unique attributes and benefits. Modern brain researchers have even discovered that when musicians improvise they utilize the same brain circuitry as dreams: inhibition switches off and free expression switches on.[60] Clearly, music gives us access to parts of ourselves not available when we are in ordinary time. These are the ancient attributes and ever-new discoveries that we explore as spiritual directors, inviting doors of awareness and expression to open in the midst of our prayer, our process, and our discovery of the Divine.

How to Begin
Open
Open your mouth
Open your mouth and sing
Let the sounds
rise up
Let the song
be free
Let the lightness
ride
on your soul's
harmony.

What else
do you need
to be free?
—*Betsey Beckman*

The voice is our primary instrument, and so is a wonderful place to begin. Though sometimes soft, shy, or wounded, still, we carry our voice with us wherever we go, and we can access this instrument to call upon Spirit. In fact, the word "invocation" comes from the Latin *vocare* (to call), and is also related to the word *vox* for voice. I offer a story to contemplate this gift:

> The group arrives late afternoon at the log-frame retreat house for their week of Awakening the Creative Spirit. After finding bedrooms, putting

names with faces, and sharing their first meal, the participants gather comfortably before the fireplace in the living room for their first circle. How to begin this weeklong journey of depth and discovery? In the moment, an impulse arises: an invocation. The leader lifts the frame drum and begins a foundational steady rhythm. All gathered take a nourishing breath and sink deep into the grounding of this heartbeat. Then, as if taking wings, the leader's voice opens and springs forth with a spontaneous song-prayer: "Creative Spirit! Creative Spirit! Spirit of the earth, spirit of the air, spirit of the water, moving everywhere. Spirit of the fire—lead us on your way. Spirit of the holy be with us this day . . ."

As the group gathers and forms, the solo voice rises to invoke or call upon the Creative Spirit for presence, support, and inspiration. In the quiet that reverberates afterwards, the group meditates with elements from nature chosen from the altar. Then, after each one shares her insights and intentions, all are invited to join in a sung refrain, adapted from a Rumi poem: "Let the beauty we love be what we do. Let the beauty we love be what we do."[61] The group voices ring out as one—the journey has begun.

Music as Receptive and Expressive

How might we "tune in" to the various possibilities of voice, music, and rhythm in our spiritual direction practice? Music therapist Margaret Warja describes two different ways music is often utilized in therapy. The first is "receptive," where one listens to music—either prerecorded or live—and invites the music to evoke images through guided imagery, artwork, or storytelling. The second music modality is "expressive," where one creates music, either vocally or with instruments.[63] Either of these modalities might be welcomed into our individual and group spiritual direction sessions.

Receptive Music[62]

Receptive music is the simpler of the two modalities in which directees can simply "lean into" the music to receive its gifts. In many places in this book, we suggest playing a piece of recorded music to support meditation or art-making. Another possibility is to engage music as inspiration for movement meditations or improvisations. This engagement of music is "receptive," but we might also call it "responsive," since it encourages active engagement through dance. In my own practice, which focuses on movement, directees occasionally bring in recordings that have meaning for them, which they then respond to through movement. Likewise, in leading retreats and spirituality groups, I use recorded music for warm-ups, energetic or meditative group dances, as well as for solo improvisations or hand dances.

Whether receiving or responding to music, different instrumentations and musical genres evoke different states of being. In some recordings, you may find that the drums stir energy, the cello honors sadness, the harp provides comfort, the flute cries out plaintively, the piano offers a reflective mood. All invite unique responses through movement or in meditation. As you explore your own tastes and inclinations in music, you can begin to build a repertory of musical selections that can support directees in their process. In the exercise section of this chapter, we explore various ways to support you in incorporating receptive music in the practice of spiritual direction.

Expressive Music

"Expressive music," or the creation of music, can also take many forms in a direction setting. We can begin by considering the possibility of accessing our voices as an expressive instrument. If you and/or your directee feel comfortable singing, beginning or ending with a song can be a welcome prayer. Additionally, have you ever found yourself humming a familiar hymn or tune only to realize the song is a perfect reflection of your inner state of being in the moment? These unconscious melodic gifts may arise in direction sessions, and can be invited to become a conscious part of our prayerful exchange.

It has only happened a couple of times, but, during spiritual direction sessions, two different pastors recalled hymns with images that were powerful for them. Both of them smiled as they remembered. The hymns were connected to their feelings and the feelings were not easy to talk about. They could each remember the hymn, sing it and return to the feeling. It was sacred space for them. Both men were able to access through music what they couldn't get to in other ways. I didn't suggest it; the hymns rose from them and their connection with Spirit as expressed in the words and music. —*Billie Mazzei*

We can also support directees in creating songs that express their inner states. Have you explored this capacity in your own life? We need not study the art of music composition in order to invite personal musical melodies to arise in our souls. With a bit of openness, a song can start with lyrics, a phrase, a walk down the street, or an inner rhythm that springs into a melody. We may simply need to sing an improvised phrase enough times so that we can remember it, and allow it to become a part of our own personal repertory. In my own journey, I have found myself spontaneously creating songs while rocking my son to sleep, driving in the car, looking at the moon, praying for a friend, encouraging myself to do household tasks, or amusing a forlorn toddler. Once I have discovered a song, I find it helpful to write down the words, or sing the melody into a recorder to help capture the moment and mood. When encouraged, expressive songs seem to well up in times of frustration, sadness, great joy, or playfulness.

Besides exploring the instrument of our voices, we can also consider other rhythm and melodic instruments as vehicles to express the soul. I have worked with directees who initiated this desire within our practice together. One directee had recently acquired some Tibetan bowls and found their tonal resonance was inviting her into a deep place of prayer. She brought them to our session to receive support for her exploration of meditation and vibration. Another directee had played the piano for years, but never felt comfortable allowing spontaneous music improvisation as an expression of her soul, so we arranged to meet at my home (in my husband's piano studio) for several of our direction sessions, and I had the honor of hearing soul sounds pour through fingers. I have also worked with professional singers who were deeply touched by the invitation to create their own spontaneous songs as prayer, opening them to a new reservoir of direct personal expression.

Both receptive and expressive music modalities can be called upon in the field of spiritual direction to help open the soul to feel and express mystery. Below you will find exercises to support you in exploring both of these modalities.

Experiential Exercises

Receptive Music: Simple Ways to Engage Music in Spiritual Direction

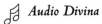 *Audio Divina*

Consider offering recorded music as a form of *Audio Divina*, which means sacred listening. Choose a piece of music to invite a directee into reflective prayer. Play the piece three times, the first to listen, the second to reflect, and the third to respond (through artwork, journaling, or movement).[64]

Music for Contemplation—Make Way for the Image of God

> When walking down the street, imagine a host of angels going before you and before each one you meet, proclaiming, "Make way for the image of God! Make way for the image of God!"
> —*Jewish Midrash story*

Contributed by Trish Bruxvoort Colligan

I wonder: What would the world be like if we approached every person in our path as someone with a piece of God's heart? What would happen if even in a clumsy-but-generous fashion, we could spot Divinity's essence in those around us? As a spiritual director, I am prone to considering such baffling marvels of human life. As a songwriter, such themes wind themselves into the music that I write, perform, and share through recordings.

As a spiritual director, how might I accompany the pilgrim navigating a journey from blame or self-hatred toward compassion, self-love, and forgiveness? When the way seems overbearing or a heart feels rubbed raw, how might I serve? In such moments, I find music to be a gentle, kind-hearted bearer of many gifts. Likewise, I draw upon the *metta*, the Buddhist prayer of loving-kindness. In this practice, we imagine compassion infusing our softening hearts. Then, we widen this loving-kindness, first enveloping a benevolent person, second a neutral person, and third, a person of challenge. Gradually, our circle of loving-kindness expands, including all beings in all times and places.

For a recent CD release, I wrote a song integrating *metta* prayer and the opening Jewish story, in which a variation of the refrain, "Make way for the image of God!" is repeated three times. I have found this to be a helpful meditation in my spiritual direction practice. When using this song in a session, I invite my directee to close her eyes, and while listening for the first time through, to imagine being encircled by beloved companions: *Make way, for here comes an image of God.* The second time through the refrain, she envisions more difficult individuals: *Make way, for you are an image of God.* Finally, I invite the two groups to converge, standing shoulder-to-shoulder as images of God among us: *Make way; make way for we are the image of God!* (See Resource Section for free link to song.)[65]

Artists of life, let us make a world that makes way for each moment and each person saturated with a holy, divine essence!

♫ Music for Contemplation, Guided Imagery, Art-Making, and Prayer

Songs with lyrics can provide powerful imagery for prayer. Another more open-ended possibility for use of "receptive" music within a direction session is to offer instrumental music for meditation or contemplation. Consider beginning your session with a recorded piece of music for centering. If you are comfortable playing a musical instrument, such as flute, you might offer a live piece of meditative music as an opening prayer.

A classic use of music in therapy is to work consciously with shifting moods through the selection of musical genres. If a directee is experiencing a dark night of the soul, for example, beginning with a piece of music that matches that experience of depth brings a sense of resonance and honoring of the place of emptiness. As the session goes on, a gradual introduction of piece(s) that shift energy towards more active rhythms and energy can help the directee experience new possibilities for life and motivation in the spiritual journey. Also, consider supporting a directee in creating a collection of recorded soul songs as a musical support system. Your encouragement for a directee to embrace the life-giving resource of music can be a deep consolation in the time between direction visits.

Finally, "receptive" music can provide a powerful support for guided imagery or prayers. Consider the "Body Gratitude Meditation" in Chapter Five as one that could be supported by gentle contemplative music as a backdrop. There are also many resources for guided imaginations, relaxation meditations, and healing prayers—books as well as recordings—that can be explored as tools for use with receptive music. (See Resource Section.)

Expressive Music: Further Steps to Engage Music in Spiritual Direction

Vocal Coach, April Sotura, has developed a practice she calls "Voicing Self," where she supports individuals in gaining the vocal confidence to express their authenticity and authority. As a backdrop to the exploration of voice as instrument, she writes:

Voice is a mystery. Through the utterance of a cry, a laugh, a word, and a song, we reveal ourselves upon the stage of life. Utterance ushers forth from our responsiveness to the play of life both within us and all around us. The impulse of the natural voice is to respond to life with full resonance and with congruence in body, mind, heart, and soul. Listening to the urgings of natural vocal expression, it is possible to come to know our self more deeply, and to speak true the song of our hearts.

To free one's acoustical voice to inhabit full body expression is both a gift to the world and a life long journey. I find that most voices are tender and vulnerable. We long to announce ourselves to the world only to find our voice locked behind the clamp of tongue and jaw. Conditioned to edit our words before we speak, we find that speaking truth is daunting. The acoustical voice is held in a vice grip and often needs gentle coaxing to move from whispers to willing release, from passionless monotone to melodic, dynamic expression.

♫ InterPlay Vocal Warm-Ups

A first step in encouraging a directee to explore a range of vocal expression can be leading a vocal warm-up. The tools of InterPlay offer a simple and accessible way to free the natural voice by emphasizing playful expression rather than "artistry." To lead an InterPlay-style vocal warm-up, begin by making random sounds (accompanied by whatever small natural body movements arise). Then invite the directee (or group members) to join in. For example, try leading this series of sounds:

> *Ta, ta, ta, ta, ta, ta. Whee! whee! whee! whee! Harrumph . . . harrumph . . . harrumph . . . harrumph . . . Shhh . . . shh . . . shh . . . shh . . . Huh? huh? huh? Binkle-bonkle, binkle-bonkle, binkle-bonkle. Grrr . . . grr . . . grr . . . etc.*

Once you've got the hang of it, you can feel free to explore your own expressive sequence of sounds in the moment. I found myself quite amazed and energized the first time I was led in such a stream-of-consciousness journey of sound. I have since come to relish leading moments of vocal release with other "players." Exaggerating facial expressions can also add another dimension of uninhibited expression to this exercise. As the space of permission opens up, feel free to take turns with a directee, so that each of you has the chance to lead and be led. The result of creating sounds together is a delightful release of playful energy and permission for the full range of our humanity.

If you are comfortable with singing, you can also initiate vocal warm-ups that focus more on tonal and melodic qualities of the voice. (See "Exploring the Melodic Voice" or "Tone Circle" below.) These are especially helpful if you are preparing to lead a directee or group deeper into song. Since many people have wounded perceptions of their own capacity to be "singers," an invitation to create playful expressive sounds can be a liberating first step.

Name Game

I first learned the "Name Game" exercise while visiting a psychiatric-movement therapy group and I have since found it to be simple and effective for many group settings. After extending permission for a range of vocal dynamics through a warm-up, invite participants to go around the circle saying their names in an expressive, altered way (accompanied by a movement). Then have the group echo back the name and movement. Remind participants that they don't have to "plan" what's going to come out of their mouths, but that they can let the expression arise spontaneously. This invitation builds connection between group members and also creates a simple form for taking incremental steps in vocal expression.

After the first time going around the circle, you might do a second round as a check-in, inviting people to give voice to a phrase expressing how they are feeling and have the group echo that back. Members might say and move such expressions as "quiet and still," "exhausted," "walking on eggshells," or "full of life!" A third variation might be naming and moving a quality of Spirit that each participant would like to invite into his or her life, such as "deep peace," "spontaneity," "healing," or "the courage to create."

For individual directees, consider having them "check in" by speaking and embodying phrases that express moments in their journey. Nearing the end of the session, recall key phrases that arose in your work together, and explore a range of vocal expressions to speak and embody these insights.

♫ Exploring the Melodic Voice

Contributed by April Sotura

In my vocal coaching practice, I encourage each client to listen deeply to the sound of her own voice, and to identify what she hears in the quality of tone, the feeling, and the shape of her utterance. This listening includes sensing the voice with somatic awareness. Through this inquiry an individual comes to know her voice as a whole-body instrument of expression. I offer the following exercises as ways to lead clients in a gentle invitation to vocal discovery.

Breathing Softly into Tone

Bring your attention to your breath; feel the beautiful rhythm of your inhale and exhale. Song, tone and resonance ride in the river's current of your breathing. Exhale and sigh gently, releasing the gateway of your jaw, softening your tongue. Sighing is such a wonderful way to release and open the breath and to give utterance to feeling, to release the body. Allow soft "ah" sounds and resonant hums to soothe the sensations within your body and wash you clean.

Inner hum—Soaring "Ah"

Now shift your attention to the ground and deepen your experience with gravity. Exhale and sigh gently, again releasing the gate of your jaw, softening your tongue. Name what you feel in your belly; name what you feel in your heart. Begin an exhale, a hum, a tone deep within your belly and let the tone roam and explore the soft caverns of your body. Sense the resonant tones traveling up your spine to your heart. Open your inner hum to the vowel "ah" and let it soar out into the world. With your soaring "ah," sing to all that is around you and all that is within you. Sing out into the world, your joy, your sorrow, your deep connection with the beauty of life.

One of our program participants describes her experience:

After our evening session of exploring voice, I woke up the next morning singing spontaneously. I had such a profound experience of my body as a temple and my voice resonating through this sacred sanctuary. —*Stacy Nagel*

♫ Tone Circles

Contributed by April Sotura

Acoustical tone is supported by our free-flowing breath cycles and energized by the focus of our intention. To further expand an exploration of toning, soaring and singing together, consider leading a tone circle. This is especially effective in groups, but can also work in an individual session. For groups, form a circle facing the center. Invite participants to find gravity, to soften their jaws, and to open themselves to song.

Choose a vocal tone that is comfortable and in the mid to lower register. Lead the group by launching a hum, and inviting everyone to join in and match your tone. Stay with the hum until the whole group begins to buzz like bees, then open your hum to an "ah" sound. Continue toning together on "ah" for three to five minutes. Listen and sense the connection that emerges in the group, the natural pulsing of sound, and the overtones at the edges of hearing. Feel how the tone shapes you on the inside and in the space around you. As a next step, invite the group to improvise. Launch a new tone, inviting participants to start out by matching your tone, and then move on to choosing different tones, exploring harmony and dissonance, connection, and relationship. Sense and feel how tones weave together. Tone together for three to five minutes.

Consider these playful toning variations:

Listen deeply and blend your voices as one.

Tone with other vowel sounds.

Explore shaping simple melodic patterns.

Tone the expression of different feelings.

When toning is complete sit quietly for a few moments and feel the sound vibrations. Share together about the experience, inviting participants to name their discoveries, edges, and sense of Spirit that may have been generated by this co-creation of song and sound.

The following is a description of the journey of toning:

I am surrounded by a dome of sound; eleven voices bounce off of each other, some matching, some blending, some wildly dissonant, and yet, breathtakingly awesome. My voice moves off the basic pitch up a third, and rests there, while still feeling a rumbling attachment to the center. Suddenly my voice moves

upward in melodic minors soaring over the top and then tumbling back down
into the center. Resting, soaring, resting, it hears another voice and follows,
moves a third, and imitates, moving here and there within that dome of sound.
The world is gone, fears, distresses, plans for the day, are gone. And yet, the
world is imminently there, I am fully connected, I feel the pain, I feel the joy. I
am—we are. This is improvisational "toning." —*Connie Pwll Walck Tyler*

♬ Witnessing the Song

During an individual session, witnessing the vocal discoveries or first songs
of a directee can be a powerful awakening. Likewise, in a retreat setting,
once participants have had the chance to explore melodic improvisations on
their own or in a group, you can then invite sharings, or partner witnessing
of each other's tonal explorations or "ah" songs. This vocal exchange invites
a profound and intimate honoring, especially for those who are allowing
themselves to be heard singing "solo" for the very first time. Partners find
it a sacred privilege to experience with each other such tender shoots of the
soul's expression.

♬ Singing a Blessing

In a retreat setting, as a conclusion to voice explorations, invite participants
to take turns singing a tonal blessing for their partner. There is no need for
words, but if words do arise, welcome them. Singing on behalf of another
person can be a disarming invitation to release self-consciousness and to
offer the prayer as a gift of blessing for another.

   Likewise, consider ending an individual session by singing a blessing for
a directee. Feel free to choose a tune you are already familiar with from your
own spiritual practice, or create a song (with or without words) in the
moment. Offering your voice as a vehicle of Spirit can be a beautiful offering on behalf of your directee. Or feel free to sing together as a means of
sharing your prayer.

♬ Percussion Circles

I live in a house with two musicians—my husband and son. In addition to
piano, my husband plays an array of percussion instruments from around
the world, and my son plays the "traps" drum set with wild abandon. I love

to hear the two of them enter into an altered state together, following their deep, shared currents rising and overflowing. As an honorary musician in our household, I have my own basket of drums, small flutes, and percussion instruments. At our Awakening the Creative Spirit Program, we spend one of our afternoons "jamming" together, exploring an interplay of rhythms and the rising expressive release of an ecstatic drum circle.

To lead a percussion circle, gather a collection of instruments such as drums, rattles, tambourines, bells, chimes, cymbals, and claves. As the leader, choose for yourself one of the stronger drums and set a foundational rhythm, allowing participants to simply explore the sounds made by a variety of instruments. After an initial warm-up period of free play, explore other possibilities:

- Echoes: Go around the circle taking turns with each individual playing a one-phrase rhythm, which the group echoes.
- Name-Rhythm Echoes: Go around the circle having each person play the rhythm of his or her own name. Have the group echo back.
- Add on Songs: Start a rhythm. Go around the circle one by one, having each person add a new rhythm that complements the rhythm you have established. Once all are playing, allow the group orchestra to have a time of fullness, then gradually drop out one by one.
- Drum Jam: (Feel free to have people exchange and try new instruments.) Now move into an improvised group expression. Begin a new rhythm and allow participants to join with you, matching your foundation or creating free coordinating rhythms. Feel free to intensify the sound, to soften the sound, to add voice, and to follow the natural ebb and flow of the improvisation till the song finds its natural completion. Reflect together on the experience of community as experienced through the rhythm.

Clearly, our time with the drums and spontaneous movement was the most energizing part of our week. There was a wonderful sense of community! We knew each other enough by that time to really let go. Drums are like heartbeats and we were all beating together. I have never really made music with others except through singing. It was amazing what came about through the improvisation. —Pam McCauley

♫ Drumming in Spiritual Direction

Contributed by Sally O'Neil, PhD

Yet another way to approach rhythm is to explore its meditative quality. Here is a description of how one of our colleagues incorporates the drum in her practice.

Drumming is heart-work. Heart-work, to me, is the opening of the heart center—dissolving the walls we have developed through our lives that impede our inner growth. Drumming opens the heart center and attunes it to the beat of creation, with compassion for oneself and others, and with gratitude. It carries one's awareness into the sacred very quickly by focusing the mind on the tones of the drum. This allows the mind to rest. It is difficult to "think" when listening to the drum. Drumming fairly rapidly—100 beats a minute—creates overtones that often sound like a chorus of drums or voices.

For those who have been traumatized, as well as for those who are grieving, drumming opens one to the blessings that lie below the heavy emotions (such as hurt, rage, blame, shame, or guilt), allowing these feelings to be more easily released.

Many folks make their own drums, and I often integrate drum-making into my retreat work. Working hands-on with the materials allows participants to put their focus and energy into their own creation. This work provides a "kinship" with the instrument and when complete, we drum together to deepen this connection. I find it helpful to set the intention of the drumming session: sometimes that could be a prayer for themselves or for someone else who is in need, or for the earth herself.

As a spiritual director, I occasionally drum for individuals. If a directee comes to a point where words seem to be failing, or if I'm sensing too much mind-talk, I'll ask, "Would you mind if I drum for you? Let's try this." Afterwards we reflect together on what images emerged. It is most often a deepening process.

I keep a Native American frame drum at hand during direction sessions. When words fail or emotions need to be released, I invite directees to drum, and the drum becomes a readily accessible tool for expressing the depth of their heart. I invite them, as in the Native American tradition, to feel the drum as the heartbeat of Mother Earth, providing a grounding that is always there when needed.
—*Carol Scott Kassner*

Additional Possibilities for Engaging Music in Spiritual Direction

♫ Provide music as a backdrop for art-making by offering a piece of recorded music. Or follow in the footsteps of Deborah Koff-Chapin, the creator of the meditative art form of Touch Drawing®, who often plays and sings live improvisational music to support artists in their meditative explorations.[66]

♫ Invite a directee to sing an emotion, creating vocal expressions that sound like joy, sorrow, disgust, fear, or any other emotion that arises. Offer the suggestion to make up a short sentence such as, "I feel very, very sad." Then improvise a simple melody using those words and rhythms as a guide. This could also be explored on a simple keyboard or rhythm instrument.

♫ Consider a two-person rhythm exchange with a directee. Explore rhythm conversations, where one of you plays a short pattern and the other answers with a brief contrasting pattern. Or experiment with one person initiating a repeating pattern while the other joins in or layers a contrasting rhythm on top. (For further experiences with rhythm circles see Chapter Fifteen.)

Conclusion

Music can motivate us, soothe us, or coax us into the surrender of tears. We listen and our bodies respond, we create and our spirits expand. In spiritual direction, "receptive" music can be a tool for inviting meditation and attuning to the deep places of emotion and surrender. Receptive applications of music can also include the invitation to dance, allowing for playful or soulful release. Finally, "expressive" music, or creating music in the moment, can be a powerful modality for communicating our deepest sighs and prayers. Singing and vocal play invite the possibility of discovering the gifts of voice, claiming and sounding our deepest truths. Musical instruments such as drums and percussion can provide access to rhythms and meanings that are deeper than words, allowing our soulful emotions to find uninhibited expression as an offering to the Divine.

9

Poetry-Writing

Christine Valters Paintner

Poetry is the spontaneous overflow of powerful feelings:
it takes its origin from emotion recollected in tranquility.
—WILLIAM WORDSWORTH

The language of poetry is a gift for spiritual direction and the spiritual journey. This chapter includes a variety of ways to invite directees into writing poetry as a way to tend more deeply to their experiences.

I can remember writing my first poem around the age of eight. I was drawn to the compactness of poetry, to the paradoxical way that fewer words could express more meaning, and to the way I could express myself through the musicality of language. Sometimes I wrote poems combining some of my favorite words as a way to celebrate their sounds. Other times writing a poem was a way to capture a moment in time.

As an adult, collections of poetry form some of my primary sacred texts. My shelves are lined with dozens of poetry books and almost nothing can delight me like finding a previously unknown-to-me poet or discovering a new poem that speaks to my experience in ways I never thought to express before. As I read a good poem, I almost always discover something new about myself. Writing poetry is often a response for me to an interior movement, a moment filled with emotion and tenderness that I want to capture as best as I can. In the process of writing poems I also make new discoveries.

Many of the scriptures from different religious traditions are written in poetic form. Think of the Psalms or the Song of Songs in Hebrew and Christian traditions, the poetry of the Sufi mystics in Islamic tradition, and the haikus of Zen Buddhism. Elizabeth McKim of the Appalachian Expressive Arts Collective says that poetry originates in "primal rhythm and rhyme" and poetic language is a part of our inheritance, the ability to shape experience with words.[67] Poetry and spiritual practice both cultivate the art of paying attention.

Poetry as a Way of Knowing

The medium of poetry is words. However, poems use words differently than everyday language. Poems express ideas in compact images but also invite us to slow down with those images. Poetry attends to "the words under the words," as Naomi Shihab Nye titles one of her poems.[68] We read a poem differently than the way we read a newspaper or a novel. Poetry slows us down and moves us into a different way of knowing. Poetry changes our breath and demands a more attentive presence. Poetry is one way the soul reveals itself beyond the boundaries of reason and logic. The sounds of poetry reach us at a depth that linear thinking cannot. Through its condensation of language, poetry guides us to an understanding of the underlying unity of opposites that permeates our existence. Rather than eliminating life's contradictions, poetry helps us to integrate sorrow and joy, horror and humor, with compassionate awareness. Poetry is a way of being with Mystery. All of these qualities of poetry make it a potent form for spiritual direction. Poems from other writers can be read aloud in a direction session, so the directee receives this gift of language. Poems can also be written in a session as an expressive way of giving form to an experience. Both approaches are explored in this chapter.

Experiential Exercises

Simple Ways to Engage Poetry in Spiritual Direction

As we explored in the chapter on music, there are also two ways to work with poetry in spiritual direction and retreat settings. One is receptive, listening to a poem, and the other is expressive, writing a poem. The receptive mode is a more accessible, less intimidating way to begin working with poetry in spiritual direction. When we read the symbolic and intuitive language of poetry, it helps to signal that the time and space ahead is different, moving us out of our left brain, analytic ways of thinking and into the creative and intuitive sides of ourselves.

Select a poem to read as you begin a spiritual direction session. Poetry can mark the boundaries of sacred space. A moment of transition before the spiritual direction session allows both director and directee to be in touch with breath, stillness, and the movement of Spirit. The use of poetry is meant to cultivate spaciousness and be evocative, not prescriptive, and so there is a gentle caution against using a poem's theme to set a particular agenda for the session. There are several recommendations in the Resource Section for anthologies of poems with sacred themes. You might also consider inviting the directee to bring a significant poem to a session to contemplate together.

I open almost all of my sessions with poetry. Poetry has an openness of words, images, and ideas. I have tried to use excerpts or readings, but it just doesn't seem to work for me. Poetry tends to say much more with fewer words leaving more space for the spirit to listen. While a lot of poetry has an overall theme, it still leaves things wide open for people to ponder. I can read the same poem to five different people with five different situations and experiences and they can all say, "It feels like that poem was written just for me." Frequently a word or a phrase in the poem helps people find a way to begin talking about what is happening. Once in a while, I read a poem at the end of a session and the poem is so clearly and beautifully saying what a directee was just trying to express that she bursts into tears and says, "Yes, yes, that's it," and all that she heard herself say seems to be clarified in the words of the poem and sinks down into her heart. —*Rebecca Johnson*

Poetry often begs us for repetition to live more deeply into its words and rhythm. Read a poem aloud slowly twice, then allow some silence to encourage your directee to be present to the way the images are stirring within them. Suggest he begin to move into his imagination and inhabit the poem's inner landscape, letting its rhythm of words and images guide and shape his prayer. Encourage him to become aware of which words or sounds linger and resonate. Ask: "What images are bubbling up in response? How does being with the poem move you into a different space? What longings are stirred in you?"

Further Steps to Engage Poetry in Spiritual Direction—Writing Poetry

In his books, *Poetic Medicine* and *Finding What You Didn't Lose*, poetry therapist John Fox offers rich resources for engaging poetry as a path for healing and expression:

> Poetry-writing is a pathway to a place within yourself of sensitivity, growth, and transformation. Your writing can encourage a renewed connectedness with nature, with your most essential self, with your daily life, with those you love, with your community, and with God . . . when your poems become the container of your truest feelings, you will begin to experience and integrate those feelings more consciously.[69]

We can offer this gift of poetry-writing to directees and retreatants in a safe, nurturing space where connection to the self is established and an exploration of inner worlds can happen. The writing exercises included below can be used within a direction session as a way of responding to a powerful moment or as a way of breaking open a previous art experience such as visual art expression or movement.

The poet Jane Hirshfield writes that in Japan "it is sometimes thought that no experience is complete until the poem that comes of it is written."[70] Writing a poem is a way of honoring a memory, a new insight, or an important event and giving it form through the beauty of language. It can bring a sense of wholeness to capture an interior movement through an outward expressive form. Poem-writing can also be an act of discovery. By responding to an inner movement and putting it into poetic language, new ways of seeing are revealed. Writing poetry can cultivate practices of awareness, of listening deeply to our experiences, and the world around us.

> Writing poetry—It seems to bring me
> Closer to you—dear Holy One—
>   I trust,
>   I try,
>   I begin

I know the You
    That knows me!
—*Judy Bartels*

When leading a directee or group, engage some of the tools from Chapter Five to support an experience of being grounded and centered before writing. Simply paying attention to the breath can help directees connect to their own primal rhythm of which poetry is one expression. Encourage a setting aside of judgments about what makes "good poetry."

When leading poetry-writing exercises, it is helpful to begin with some free writing in a journal about a particular topic. This writing might be in response to a piece of art that was created, or a movement experience, or simply as a way to begin expressing what the soul is longing for. Free writing is a warm-up for the creative voice when we can begin to practice writing without censoring ourselves. Writing without editing allows images to emerge unfettered. Time limits are also helpful so as to encourage spontaneous expression.

When clients want to talk and talk, using one of the poetry forms has been a wonderful tool to help them slow down and find the right word, to move more deeply into the felt experience of their knowing, and give it shape more slowly, thoughtfully. Writing poetry allows integration of feeling, thought, and focus that they can then carry out into action. —*Freya Secrest*

Writing Haiku

Haiku is a form of Japanese poetry that distills the essence of a particular moment in time and place, usually through strong nature imagery. Most haiku in English consists of three unrhymed lines of 5/7/5 syllables. Because in Japanese this syllable count results in an even shorter poem than in English, feel free to use even fewer than 5/7/5 syllables for your haiku writing.

In writing poetry, the principle of incremental steps we introduced earlier is a helpful one by which to abide. Starting with small, structured forms can provide a safe and strong container, and make writing poetry accessible to even the most fearful of poets.

If a particular word or image has come up in spiritual direction, you can use that as a starting place for inviting a directee to write one haiku or several. Begin with some time for free writing about the word or image. Then invite him to write a haiku using some of the words he wrote down. In the act of condensing language, we are forced to think in a different way and we often have an experience of discovery in the writing process.

Haiku are usually reflective of the particular season in which they are written. A simple way to begin incorporating poetry-writing in spiritual direction is to invite directees to write a haiku about the time of the day or season of the year and the invitation to them in this moment of time:

The Gifts of Morning:
Sun rippling across the sea,
calling me to rise.

As sun scatters dark
She asks me to awaken
to the light in me.

Morning bells ring
Sky unfurling gold ribbon,
Saying Look! Listen!

Bridges beckon me:
cross toward the long dark night.
Go to the Edges.
—*Christine Valters Paintner*

Cinquain

Cinquain comes from the French word for five. It is another simple structured form which encourages the writer to get right to the heart of the experience in few words. Like the haiku, it can be a helpful form to encourage directees to express the heart of an experience.

The modern cinquain is based on a word count of specific types of words. When leading others in writing this form it is helpful to go line by line so that there is no anticipation about what comes next and the element of surprise helps to keep the pen going and bypass judgment.

Have writers choose a word they want deeper insight about and use it as the first line. This might be in response to a dream, a piece of art that has been created, or a song that has been sung.

Line 1—One word (noun) a title or name of the subject

Line 2—Two words (adjectives) describing the title

Line 3—Three action words (verbs) ending in -ing that describe line I. What is it doing?

Line 4—A four-word phrase or sentence that sums up or further describes line I

Line 5—One word referring back to the title of the poem, a metaphoric synonym

Like the haiku form, the cinquain can become a powerful container for capturing the essence of a moment or experience:

Water
Soft Fluid
Running, flowing, swishing
Warm, blessed, alive, new
Baptism

Shadow
Alone, Cold
Cover, Shelter, Embrace
Afraid, Curious, Longing Deep
Freedom

—*Paula McCutcheon*

Using a Poem as a Prompt

Another way to encourage a poem's birth is to use the title from someone else's poem as the starting point. Perhaps the poem you chose to begin a spiritual direction session really speaks to your directee. Invite her to use the title or a single line from the poem as a starting point for her own. For example, invite her to contemplate Mary Oliver's poem title "When Death Comes"[71] or David Whyte's "What to Remember When Waking."[72] Using those as the first lines, what poem wants to then emerge to express your directee's own experience? The following poem was inspired by a poem entitled "I Am Going to Start Living Like a Mystic" by Edward Hirsch[73]:

Promises

I am going to start living like a mystic:

So when I look out the window I will see God in a leaf
pulsing with the rhythm of photosynthesis, and I will catch
the message starlight delivers from the galaxy Andromeda.

I will eat my lunchtime sandwich
as though it were manna offered
straight from the hand of Yahweh.

I will kiss my mate as passionately as Jesus
praying with the disciples that night.

I am going to start living like a prophet:

I will never look away from the least beggar
on the grimy street, even if all I give is my eyes.

I will stop pressing down my tears,
let them leap from my eyes.
Their salt will flavor
what I write, what I do.

I am going to live what I know:

I will shout "Thank you" to the seals
and cormorants in the cold bay
and to the crooked maple tree on the road,
no matter what the newsmen say.

I will never stop welcoming
my fine erotic dreams.

I will learn to die starting now.
I will let the evening come.
                                    —*Barbara Gibson*

Telling the Story of Your Inner Poet

This exercise is inspired by one from poetry therapist John Fox.[74] Begin by warming up a directee's inner poet through free writing or simpler poetic forms. Then you might want to engage poetry as a way to help him claim this voice more deeply and discover where his inner poet resides. Offering questions as prompts for each line of poetry can be a helpful way to lead a poetry exercise as in the following example. In his response, encourage the directee to listen for the initial impulse that stirs in him and to use descriptive language to capture these images.

Read each of these questions to the directee or retreat group, allowing a couple of minutes of silence in between for writing an intuitive response:

> *What does your inner poet look like?*
> *What does your inner poet feel like?*
> *Where was your inner poet born?*
> *What does your inner poet see?*
> *Where is your inner poet recognized?*
> *What does your inner poet know?*
> *What does your inner poet imagine?*
> *Where does your inner poet live?*
> *What must your inner poet speak aloud?*
> *Why does your inner poet exist?*

Take a few minutes at the end to allow the directee to review what has emerged and then invite him to spend a few minutes connecting these images together into a poem.

Inner Poet

My inner poet is French.

Tipped beret and Mona Lisa smile. Her voice rings out with playful
    laughter, her arms wide open, leaping into darkness and light.

She is beautiful and earnest.

Seductive and serious.

She was born on the wings of angels and birthed out of pain
    and suffering.

I recognize her in the first morning light by the gentle shores of the
    sea. She is bathed in God's fragrance and surrounded by belief.

What does this inner poet know for sure?
She is light. She is dark. Complete and unfinished. A creature of
    God. A glorious paradox.
This poet lives hidden from sight. Covered in blue scarves and
    white. Peeking through the window and knocking on the door.
    She lives at home inviting others to come and sit by her fire.

Her imagination is infinite. She dreams of knowing and being
    known, of embracing and being embraced. She desires
    community, fellowship, peace and solitude.
She must speak of everything. The resonant and the dissonant. The
    beauty and the depravity. The joy and the sorrow. The fullness of
    life and the darkness of death.

She sits on the sidewalks of Life, holding a thin cigarette and
    dreaming her dreams.
Her voice speaks in a beautiful accent. Tipped beret and all-
    knowing smile.
My inner poet is a romantic. She is French.
    —*Kayce Stevens Hughlett*

French Pantoum

The French Pantoum is a poetic form that is less tightly structured than a haiku or cinquain. Its structure comes from the ordered repetition of lines and creates its own rhythm and poetry in the process. In spiritual direction this form works well as a way to respond to visual art expression. In Chapter Seven, we offer some ways of working with collage images through responses to reflection questions. Writing a French Pantoum from this free-writing experience can be an engaging next step in the process.

To write a pantoum, invite the directee to take a pen and blank piece of paper and do some free writing for several minutes. This might follow the exercise we suggested earlier where a directee uses "I am" statements to enter into the different images from her collage.

After she has written several responses, invite her to select six phrases from the images she has developed (these do not have to be full sentences) and use the template below for the French Pantoum. For lines 1, 2, 3, 4, 6, and 8 she would write in one of each of the six sentences or phrases from her free-writing, then follow the instructions for repeating the other lines of the poem.

French Pantoum
STANZA 1:
Line 1 (new line): _____
Line 2 (new line): _____
Line 3 (new line): _____
Line 4 (new line): _____

STANZA 2:
Line 5 (repeat of line 2 in stanza 1): _____
Line 6 (new line): _____
Line 7 (repeat of line 4 in stanza 1): _____
Line 8 (new line): _____

STANZA 3:
Line 9 (repeat line 2 of the previous stanza): _____
Line 10 (repeat line 3 of the first stanza): _____
Line 11 (repeat line 4 of the previous stanza): _____
Line 12 (repeat line 1 of the first stanza): _____

When the directee is finished, invite her to read the poem aloud. As director, receive the poem as loving witness. Providing a structure is a helpful way to introduce writing poetry to someone unfamiliar with it. The repeating form of the Pantoum can have a deepening effect. Ask the directee: "What is it like to hear your words and images repeated again and again? How does it draw you deeper into the experience? How might this poem shed light on the art you created, the dance you moved, or the question you reflection upon?"

Here is an example of a poem written in response to creating a collage mandala:

I am a Muslim woman caged in my burka like the birds atop
  my head,
I am a working woman wringing out my sorrow as I would a
  saturated sponge,
I am a woman enveloped in a symphony of jazz and moonlight,
I am a watermelon—sweet & juicy—satisfying your soul and
  annoying you with my seeds

I am a working woman wringing out my sorrow as I would a
  saturated sponge,
I am a hawk ready to consume my prey as I gaze into the night sky,
I am a watermelon—sweet & juicy—satisfying your soul and
  annoying you with my seeds,

I am a mango, avocado and strawberries—toss me together and
 savor my flavors

I am a hawk ready to consume my prey as I gaze into the night sky,
I am a woman enveloped in a symphony of jazz and moonlight,
I am a mango, avocado and strawberries—toss me together and
 savor on my flavors,
I am a Muslim woman caged in my burka like the birds atop
 my head.
—Lisa Sadleir-Hart

Additional Possibilities for Engaging Poetry in Spiritual Direction

If a directee's resistance to writing a poem is high, invite her to write a
poem about the resistance, exploring what it feels like and looks like.
Have her use the poem as a place to dialogue with her block. This could
be a poem which emerges from the exercise in Chapter Five on working with resistance and blocks.

Another wonderful resource for ideas on poetry-writing is Ray McGinnis' book, *Writing the Sacred: A Psalm-Inspired Path to Appreciating and Writing
Sacred Poetry*. The psalms are ancient poem-prayers that offer ways to
approach our relationship to God through praise and lament, thanksgiving and anger. Each particular type of psalm offers a structure or
template for how to write our own poetic prayers. Use this book with
directees to inspire psalm-writing or refer to Chapter Twelve for
instructions on writing a psalm of lament.

Another simple way to inspire the writing of a poem is to use an
image or piece of art. In our program we often have participants engage
their own art as a jumping-off point for a poetry-writing exercise. You
might want to simply have a book available with evocative images you
have collected and use them as starting places for poetic expression.
A small journal called *Sacred Poetry: An Invitation to Write*, contains a series
of poetry prompts, each of which includes a photo and theme to
explore.[75] These prompts could be engaged in either spiritual direction or in a retreat setting.

Invite directees to write poetry as a way to cherish an experience of being present to nature.

As we have explored in this chapter, structured poetic forms and a series of questions can be very helpful ways to loosen up the poetic voice. Free-form writing is an equally valid mode of poetic expression. Often when a directee has enough comfort and experience with writing poetry, poems emerge in their own shape. Here is an example of a free-form poem written in response to an experience of nature:

The Race
Have you seen the clouds
in their race
across the sky?

At sunrise,
the horizon is pulled taut
for a starting line.

They all line up,
elbowing each other
for advantage.

The gull sounds the call
and they are off,
racing towards the mountains.

We all stare from below in amazement
as they dash by us,
sending shadows to mark their advance.

They fly with sails fully open,
tumbling past one another,
even swallowing those in their way.

Who will be the winner today?
The fluffy one that threatens
with its load of rain?

Maybe the thin one that
stretches out like taffy.
What strides it takes.

I'm rooting for the smallest one,
trying to dart and weave
to the finish line.

We won't know who wins.
By the time they get to the mountains
we will see them all deep in slumber.

Draped over the peaks,
not even lifting their eyes
to acknowledge our passing.
—*Pam McCauley*

Conclusion

Poetry offers the gift of language which can lift us to new ways of seeing our experience. As a tool for spiritual direction we can receive the gift of poetry as a way to prepare for a direction session. Writing our own poetry can capture the essence of an experience, allow us to reflect on the creation of a piece of art in a meaningful way, or catch a new glimpse of the Holy.

PART III

Working In Different
Life Contexts

10

Breaking Open Images of God

Betsey Beckman

*Dears, there is nothing in your life that will not
change—especially your ideas of God.*
—TUKARAM

In Part Three, each chapter presents a different life context or theme that may arise in spiritual care. We offer a series of multi-modal approaches to support the exploration of these themes.

How do we imagine God? Many of us grew up steeped in images of an all-powerful masculine God inherited from religious text and tradition. Add to that a collection of traditional Western visual images such as Michelangelo's Creation of Adam from the Sistine Chapel, Doré's Holy Spirit descending as a dove, or countless representations of Christ crucified. While these can be powerful and inspiring works of art, as spiritual directors it is not uncommon for us to work with directees who have been wounded by narrow, judgmental, or punitive images of God, or by churches whose rigid belief structures have closed down budding faith. In our age of cross-cultural global spiritualities, what's a director to do?

As discussed in Chapter Five, the *kataphatic* spiritual tradition helps us to image and celebrate God through our senses. Even so, we understand that in reality, God is beyond all our imaginings. The Divine Mystery can never be fully understood or grasped—only suggested, hinted at, evoked. And yet, as humans, we need images, symbols, names, myth, and ritual to help us feel, taste, touch, smell, and hear the profound ways of the Holy One. Thirteenth-century mystic, Hadewijch of Antwerp, experienced this divine encounter, and she writes about it to a young friend, for whom she acted as spiritual mentor:

> From the depths of his wisdom, he shall teach you what he is and with what wonderful sweetness the one lover loves in the other and so permeates the other that they do not know themselves from each other. But they possess each other in mutual delight, mouth in mouth, heart in heart, body in body, soul in soul, while a single divine nature flows through them both and they both become one through each other, yet remaining always themselves.[76]

As we become conscious of our metaphors for God, we learn which ones are life-giving for us, and which ones might be limiting or constricting. At different points along our journey, our images of God grow and change as we do. In their book, *Good Goats: Healing Our Image of God*, the Linns remind us that we become like the God we worship.[77] So, if we believe in a judgmental God, we will operate with a fair amount of judgment about others and ourselves. Often times, in order for our image to change, certain aspects of our own life history need to be healed so that we can grow more embracing in our relationship with God, ourselves, and the world around us. As spiritual directors, we can look for opportunities to invite directees into deep healing encounters with God, which allow openings for new images to be discovered and revealed. Joan Borysenko reminds us,

> Icons can be dangerous and powerful as projections of the human need for conquest and domination. But they can also have salvific power when they embody the love and compassion of the Nameless One. Our ability to love God in any form or image, as long as we allow others to worship in their own way, opens our heart and ultimately enhances our relationship to our own self and to other people.[78]

In our twenty-first century multi-cultural world, we have burgeoning opportunities to interface with people of numerous religions. When I was growing up, everyone I knew was Catholic. But now I have friends who are

Protestant, Unitarian, Jewish, Quaker, Mormon, Orthodox, Hindu, Sufi, Muslim, Buddhist, Wiccan, Shamanistic, Celtic, and Earth-based. This is amazing. For a long time, because of my embarrassment about the negative associations with Catholicism, I actually felt shy about expressing my tradition in the mix of my circles of friends. As I grew to understand and respect other faith traditions, I also felt called to delve more deeply into my own, uncovering little-known feminine symbols of God, embracing empowering stories of women in scripture, and exploring embodied practices within the liturgy. In the process, I grew to cherish my tradition and share it freely. Now I am happy to proclaim my Catholic identity and to launch into shared prayer, images, and discussion with folks from all walks of life.

Of course, our images of God are shaped not only by religious training and traditions, but also by our own experiences of nature, family, community, health, culture, and even by mystical awareness that breaks in upon us by sheer grace. How might we, as spiritual directors, support our directees in becoming aware of the images of God that are underlying their spiritual journeys? How can we support them in breaking open frozen or rigid images to cracks, letting new light pour through? How can we support the imagination to reveal and nurture potent symbols that invite us into a radical stance of freedom and love?

Emerging

Emerging from the cocoon of Catholicism—is the butterfly of truth
and beauty

Emerging from the cocoon of Christianity—burst forth the voices
of women

Emerging from the cocoon of religion—is the freedom to dance
our prayers

Emerging from the cocoon of patriarchy—are women and men
of equality

Emerging from the cocoon of church—are communities richest
in diversity

Emerging are souls longing to express themselves—
and to be witnessed as one with the Divine.

—*Lois Perron*

Luckily, since we have been exploring a plethora of art forms in the emerging field of the arts and spiritual direction, we have a whole toolbox of possibilities to support us in inviting the wings of the butterfly to emerge from the time-honored sacred cocoons that have formed us in faith.

Experiential Exercises for Breaking Open Images of God

The Senses of God

When invited to engage our senses and imagination directly, we can discover and celebrate our own associations and images of the holy. The following poetry-writing exercise can be led in a retreat setting or individual session. As a storytelling form, this exercise could also be led as a "babbling" exercise, where partners take turns responding verbally. (See Chapter Four.)

Begin by sharing a bit of background on the senses as doorways to the sacred. Then, lead a short meditation of centering, breathing, and grounding. (See Chapter Five.) When they are centered, invite directees to write spontaneous responses to the following series of questions. Allow a minute or so after each one for participants to record whatever images pop into their minds.

1. What does God look like?
2. What does God smell like?
3. What does God taste like?
4. What does God sound like?
5. What does God feel like?
6. What does your sixth sense tell you about God?

Afterwards, give participants a few minutes to craft their words into a poem, and end with an invitation to share their poetry and reflections on celebrating God through the senses.

Sense Poem
God smells like luxurious clean sheets and fresh, rain-filled air
God tastes like the ooze of a hot, flourless chocolate cake, its
     warmth filling my mouth

God sounds like a Native American flute unearthed and played
    after decades of silence
God feels like a baby's skin pressed cheek to cheek with my own
God looks like a beloved grandmother laughing with her
    grandchildren
God is loving, forgiving, nurturing, supporting, ever faithful
—*Dianna Woolley*

Tasting God

You've got to be kidding
Anything but Lay's potato chips
What will others think?
But I can't get enough
I never stop at one
I always want more of you
You are satisfying, comforting!
You bring me joy!
—*Lois Perron*

"God in a Box"

Contributed by Jane Comerford, CSJ

One of the main issues that spiritual directors work with is inviting directees
to name and describe how they image the Sacred. Years ago I read the book,
Your God Is too Small by J.B. Phillips.[79] At the time, I wasn't convinced by the
author's premise, but as I matured I began to see how my God was too small
and that I needed to get "God out of the Box." From my experience, I developed the following expressive arts exercise with two goals in mind: to help
directees recognize how their image(s) of the Sacred have evolved in their own
journeys and to give expression to their current Sacred images through visual
art. This experience is designed for a small group setting but can also be done
by an individual.

    Steps in the process:

1. As facilitator, share your own evolutionary journey and illustrate how your
   images of the Sacred have shifted. (Since I have traveled extensively to
   sacred sites, I often do this by showing slides of many sacred images

drawn from various world faith traditions. Or I tell my own evolutionary God-image story by using a variety of boxes in different sizes and designs that symbolize various God images.)

2. Lead participants in a quiet meditation with soft background music where they review their own God-image history. (See Chapter Five.)

3. Distribute cardboard shoeboxes that can be easily turned into sacred shrines—or Triptychs—by opening the ends and tapering the sides. Invite the participants to give expression to their current image of the Divine by creating a sacred shrine with paint, collage materials, and magazine images. Allow about two hours to complete the project.

4. When the shrines are complete, invite the participants to place their Triptychs at various places in the room. Next the group goes on a "pilgrimage" to visit the various sacred shrines. The creator of the Triptych can speak about his or her image or remain silent and let the image speak for itself.

5. After the "pilgrimage journey," gather as a group and discuss how the process has affected participants.

6. End with a communal blessing prayer invoking and praising the Divine for the multitude of sacred expressions that exist.

A program participant from the Jewish tradition shares a helpful insight on the "God in a Box" Exercise:

Working with images of God and using a Triptych are both challenges from a Jewish perspective. Judaism neither uses nor allows use of images of God especially in a religious context. Further, the Triptych is typically a form used in Christian art work. Although there is no Jewish mandate against using a Triptych, I was not comfortable working in a historically Christian format. I overcame the cultural hurdle by knowing the facilitators' intention was not meant to be exclusive and feeling the experience I brought was welcomed with open, loving arms.

For the exercise, I brought an image of the Hebrew letters "yod, hay, vov, hay," the unmentionable name of God, which is spoken in prayers as *Adonai*. In Judaism, there are at least 100 different names of God, each with a slightly different quality. Rather than making a Triptych, I kept my shoebox as a box, covering it with paper inside and out, and put the "yod, hay, vov, hay" image on the top. I lined the inside with four colors of tissue paper to represent the Four Worlds of Creation as defined in Kabbalah. Using clay, I made a representation of a personal prayer and placed it inside the sacred container. Another group member named my piece, "Kabbalah in a Box." —*Cynthia Gayle*

Another participant describes her adaptation of the Triptych exercise for a retreat:

For years I have saved magazine pages with beautiful or interesting pictures; recently, I learned why. As co-leader of a group of clergywomen, at one Lenten gathering I had each person create a collage. Using a cut-up shoebox as a Triptych, the women expressed with images their needs for resurrection in their lives. —*Marilyn Marston*

Finally, the following is a description of a Triptych process offered to a directee as "homework."

After working with a directee for about eight months, I began, little by little, to introduce the arts. After the powerful experience of making a mask (See Chapter Fourteen), he noted that the expressive arts were not something he would have considered doing four to five years ago, but they were working for him, helping him give expression to his inner dimension. I then suggested he might want to continue this work and create a Triptych. He liked the idea and left with a written set of instructions and a level of enthusiasm I had not experienced with him before.

He came back with a relatively small, but immensely expressive piece of work. His left panel had a central image of his ongoing depression surrounded by icons of fear: the fears that he battles in his mind that rob him of hope. The middle panel pictured a large spring-fed pond overarched with a blue sky; and he was gradually able to articulate that the water represents a deep source or well of spiritual sustenance, hope, and peace. The right panel also had an image of water overlaid with pictures of important guides: Jesus, Thich Nhat Hanh, St Francis, Thomas Merton, and an African American woman who has appeared in his dreams. As we concluded the session, he volunteered that he keeps his Triptych in a place in his office where he can see it often; it is sacred to him. —*Wes McIntryre*

Embodying Images of the Sacred

Grounding our work in the inter-modal emphasis of the expressive arts, it is often helpful to follow one form of art with another in order to enrich the process. After making a visual image of any kind—clay, drawing, painting, or collage—invite directees to embody their artwork. This can be a very effective exploration of parts of the self, and can also be a powerful exploration of images of God following an exercise such as the God-in-a-Box/Triptych exercise above. God's qualities are beyond our human capacities, and yet, they also infuse us, calling us to our most vital selves.

Have participants place their collages around the room, (preferably propped up on chairs) so they can be viewed from a standing position. With a piece of meditative music as support, invite participants to choose one of the images of the Holy as represented in their collage and physically take on the posture or shape. Give them time to notice their felt experience. Then, encourage continued movement with the qualities presented by the image. For some, this might include sounding or vocalizing as well. After a few minutes, invite them to return to their collage and bow to the face of the Sacred that has been revealed to them through this exploration.

To continue, have participants embody a succession of three or four images of the Divine. Another possibility is for them to choose an image from another person's collage to explore. Finally, invite sharing of movements and verbal reflections with a partner to further embrace the wisdom of the body as revelation of the Sacred.

As another example of embodying images, Christine and I led a day retreat exploring the story of Mary Magdalene. We cut paintings of Mary Magdalene from second-hand books and offered these images for participants to draw from to create collage mandalas exploring her qualities as a spiritual guide and foremother in faith. Here is the voice of a participant describing her experience:

As the retreat unfolds, Betsey asks us to pose in front of our mandala in a way that embodies what we are attracted to from our images. I am drawn to the rich brown-skinned image of Mary Magdalene; she is kneeling beside the tomb as Christ stands before her telling her not to touch him. I bend my right knee and begin lowering myself to the floor. I find I can't lower myself down. I straighten, examine my leg, swing it, bend it. All the parts work. I again bend my right knee and attempt to lower myself to the floor. I remain half down, half upright. I straighten and shake my head sure everyone else is already in a position. A third time I begin to lower myself to the floor. I cannot.

Then I remember: this is what happens to me when I am not listening to a deep part of myself. Wondering if I'm breaking some rule, I slip to the tables where the pictures lie scattered about. I've got to find another "right" image. Immediately I am drawn to a distant, formal Magdalene. I must need this image, though her solemnity puts me off. I return with the new picture. Quickly I prop it up in front of the kneeling picture and assume the tall stance of the new Magdalene.

Lo and behold, I feel ten feet tall. I feel an authority inside like I am my own trusted counselor. I don't look for permission to some outside force; I am aware I have wisdom to share. I hold up my right hand as if holding the alabaster jar and feel I have something of value the world around me needs. Instinctively I feel glad to finally be standing on my own. My newfound sense of clarity feels wonderful, yet scary too. I give thanks, and decide I can keep both images. —*Patricia Doheny Tyllia*

Hand Dance with a Healing God

As mentioned in Chapter Two, Howard Gardner describes a variety of intelligences or different ways of knowing. If a directee happens to be oriented to the kinesthetic and/or interpersonal intelligence, moving with a partner may be the most powerful modality for encountering an image of the Divine. The following exercise invites participants to an experience of God through touch. It was created by InterPlay leader Sharie Bowman, based on the InterPlay form, "Hand to Hand Contact."

Originally designed for a retreat or class setting, this exercise could also be shared within an individual session, depending on a directee's familiarity with the language of movement. Within my own practice, which focuses on movement as the primary modality, it is not uncommon for me to dance with a directee as part of the session, and our co-creation in movement is a powerful form of shared prayer. Because the exercise below focuses on "hand to hand contact" the particular parameters provide a healthy sense of boundaries for physical contact. However, there are many situations where inviting physical contact with a directee could be awkward or inappropriate, in which case, you could keep this form in your tool-box for leading a group.

One of the most powerful aspects of Christian theology is its emphasis on incarnation. In Jesus we have a model of the human and the Divine becoming one. Christ invites all people to this calling, to embody the holy. Many accounts of Jesus depict his healing capacities and his desire for humanity to experience physical wholeness. In the Gospel of Mark, we find the story of Jesus curing the man with the withered hand (Mark 3:1-5).

In preparation for the following exercise, read the Gospel text from Mark and invite participant(s) to reflect on whatever aspects of their lives may need healing. This could be done through writing, poetry, a hand dance, an art meditation, or simply by naming aspects to a partner.

When you are ready to shift into movement, have participants practice the following InterPlay skills with a partner. (You can choose a simpler version of this "duet" where participants remain seated, or a fuller version where partners are free to move through space.)

Find a partner. Now raise a hand and put your hand palm-to-palm with your partner's hand. Together, move your hands through space, exploring your range of motion up, down and around, fast and slow. Now come back to stillness and push your palms together exploring your shared strength. Now clasp your hands at the wrist—and lean back a bit, pulling away from each other and sharing weight. Put your palms together again, then change the shape of your contact. Make a shape and a new shape and a new one. Now move your hands again—and allow your inner "trickster" to be involved—and feel free to move off your "spot" through space together. After a few moments, separate your palms and move apart a bit, a bit more, a bit more, maintaining energetic contact. Now, for a moment, drop your contact . . . then have it again. Come back to your partner.

Once participants have become comfortable with these movements, invite them into a shared hand dance meditation, where one takes the part of Jesus and the other becomes the person with the withered hand. Find a meditative piece of music, and as a beginning, have the person with the "withered hand" take on the affliction as a symbol of his or her own need for healing. After this partner moves alone for a minute or so, then invite "Jesus" to enter the dance and figuratively offer the invitation to "stretch forth your hand." Allow the shared hand dance to take its own time, with no need to move quickly to the finish, allowing the invitation for healing to find expression, and to evolve into a dance of co-creation.

When the music comes to a close, have the participants change roles and repeat the form, so that each has the chance to dance the "healer" and the "healed." End with shared noticings about how images of God may have shifted or expanded through the embodied experience of meeting the Holy One face-to-face, hand-to-hand.

Conversation with God
Dance-Talk-Dance-Talk-Dance-Talk

There's an engaging InterPlay form called "DT3," which stands for Dance, Talk, Dance, Talk, Dance, Talk. After directees have basic experiences in storytelling and movement, this is a "next step" form that provides an intermingling of words and movement in a non-threatening way. Once directees or retreatants are warmed up, you can demonstrate the form of a DT3 by doing one yourself. Begin by moving in silence for thirty seconds to one minute. Then stop in a posture, and speak spontaneously for about thirty seconds to one minute. Allow your body to speak its own questions, reflections or wisdoms, which may come out quite philosophically or playfully. Then move again, repeating the Dance-Talk sequence three times. Beginning with movement brings access to quite different verbal reflections than just "talking," providing a wonderful connection between right and left brain.

The DT3 can be led as a form to explore particular themes such as "I Believe" or "My Creative Journey." One of our program participants decided to use this form as a conversation with God. Here is what happened:

Our invitation was to take turns doing short spiritual direction sessions with a partner. My partner and I decided we'd like to explore our sessions on the labyrinth, and I volunteered to go first. We both entered the labyrinth and I began dancing, then periodically stopping and talking for a while. I shouted my questions and frustrations to God. I was surprised when God (my partner) began answering in ways I never would have thought of. Gradually I was able to ask God more about my mission in life and playfully begin to dance the vision of my calling. The words came out my mouth "I am the priestess of play! Hurray!" It made us both smile. Later, my partner made the priestess a colorful scepter that stands in my living room as a reminder of my call when I lose focus.
—*Sharie Bowman*

Her partner also writes:

During the serious play of the DT3, my partner began with an initially agonized wrestling with the word "mission." Gradually, we entered the discovery of "permission!" There on the labyrinth, we ended up skipping, dancing, shouting, and laughing in the rain beneath the expansive benediction of a fragrant northwest cedar. —*Rachelle Oppenhuizen*

The New Story of the Universe and the Expressive Arts

Contributed by Jane Comerford, CSJ

For the past ten years a large part of my ministry has been spent introducing people to the "new story" of the universe through workshops and retreats. I am passionate about telling this story and helping people shape-shift their images of God, themselves, and the universe by coming to know this powerful mythic drama of our origins.[80] As part of an introductory workshop entitled, "From Stardust To Us," I use many images taken from space and incredible views of the universe seen through the Hubble telescope to begin to expand participants' worldview and illustrate our place in the evolution of the universe.

To invite participants into the evolving mystery, I place a great focus on "unitive experience" and include time spent consciously in nature, being in communion with all that is. One of my favorite activities is to invite the participants to go out in nature and greet six subjects (people, rocks, trees, flowers, sky, etc.) with this mantra, "I am. You are. We Are." This helps them realize that all is One! Another meditation includes dancing to the song, "One" by Jan Phillips and then going out in nature to contemplate one natural element to invite an experience of this unity.[81] Afterwards, I invite participants to give expression to what is moving inside them through art and writing, or movement and sound. These art forms are wonderful methods for helping the universe story become embedded in people and for helping expand their images of the Sacred.

Other expressive art projects that can be used in conjunction with the new story include:

- creating evolutionary necklaces and bracelets with beads that tell our nearly 14-billion-year-old story
- creating a timeline ribbon with art work illustrating the universe story
- writing short plays that tell one part of the story and performing them

- writing songs that tell the new story of the universe
- creating "gush art" after meditating with images from the universe
- listening to the symphony of *The Planets* by Gustav Holst.

◎ Ignatian Prayer

Contributed by Mary Lou Weaver Houser

St. Ignatius of Loyola, the founder of the Society of Jesus, believed that it is through the senses and emotions that we experience God. He developed a series of Spiritual Exercises that encourage us to pray with scripture by putting ourselves into the story by way of the imagination. As we enter the scene fully, we heighten our awareness of our senses, having conversations with various figures and characters, listening closely to the feelings and invitations that present themselves. Specific images that arise are then received as God's way of getting one's attention. As a director for those exploring the Spiritual Exercises, I invite retreatants to respond to their images from scripture with any of the arts: music, drawing, painting, collage, clay, poetry, or body prayer. These art forms serve to deepen the prayer experience and one's investment in the given scripture. The artworks often become personal icons that serve as a shorthand for recollection long after the experience.

The story below is a beautiful example of a personal icon created through Ignatian prayer.

For more than twenty years I have integrated the arts and spirituality in my life as a Jesuit, spiritual director, artist, and art therapist. I share the following creative process as a personal adaptation of the Spiritual Exercises of St. Ignatius Loyola.

One prayer method Ignatius suggests is to imagine a scripture scene using our senses so the story becomes more vivid. I was praying with the story of Bartimaeus (Mark 10:46–52). Jesus asked me, the blind man, "What do you want?" I told Jesus I wanted to know and love him more and I was afraid to accept a new mission. Afterwards, I painted a double portrait that included St. Ignatius in the upper section and Pedro Arrupe, SJ, (Jesuit Superior General, 1965–1983), in the lower section. I was looking to their stories for inspiration. That night, I dreamed that the face of Ignatius was covered in red.

The next day, I painted over Ignatius' face. I wondered: what does the painting need? I recalled Arrupe's prayer after suffering a stroke: "Now, more than ever I find myself in the hands of God who has taken hold of me." I felt moved by the thought that Arrupe could not be other than he was in his weakness. Then I imagined Jesus bending close to my ear and whispering, "I trust you." I began to paint again, not knowing what would emerge. I found myself making abstract designs with the palette knife where Ignatius' face had been covered over, and then I began to see the torso of Jesus on the cross.

For me, the final image captured both the spirit of Ignatius and the prayer of Arrupe, two mentors who surrendered themselves to God with eyes fixed on Jesus Christ. —*Robert Gilroy, SJ*

♬ Chanting the Divine Name

Contributed by April Sotura

My spiritual and musical path led me to India, where I spent years in daily practice of meditation and *namasankirtana* (chanting). From dawn to dusk we immersed ourselves in the profound reverberations of chanting the name of the Beloved. From this sacred practice, I offer the following exercise to support the creation of your own chant.

> *In supplication, devotion, and love, we bend the ear of God to our hearts by repeating the name of the Beloved over and again. Sacred chant is prayer comprised of the name of God, melody, rhythms, and repetition. To start, hold the name of God on your tongue and taste it. Repeat this name out loud; feel how it rolls off your tongue, how it resonates within your belly. Sing this name on one vocal tone that satisfies you; feel the rhythm of that one tone supported by your breath. Play with variations: singing the name of God on one note loudly, softly, with different rhythmic pulses. Find yourself curious about the feeling qualities. What is it stirring within you? Explore these feelings. Saturate the name and your one tone with your rising feeling.*
>
> *Melody expresses our subtle feelings; finding melody within encourages us toward deep listening and trust. Allow yourself to shift through a series of vocal tones until you feel the tug of three or four notes that hold a melodic pattern that satisfies you. Keep it simple. Explore how this melodic pattern feels as you repeat it over and again. Open yourself to song and prayer. Let the name of God and your melodic pattern merge. Launch your chant repeating your melodic pattern and prayer. Explore your prayer rhythmically with sustained breath support. Play with the weight and balance, the texture and duration of each cycle.*

Build up in rhythmic speed and intensity and then allow your chant to slow down. When complete, sit quietly for a few moments; feel how chanting the name of the Beloved reverberates within you.

Additional Possibilities for Exploring Images of God

The Muslim tradition offers a hundred names of God, and the Hindu tradition includes devotional chanting of the thousand names of God. As a preparation for creating a personal chant (as in the exercise above) consider having directees write a poem exploring their own names for God. (See Chapter Seven.)

Invite a directee to sculpt, paint, or draw an emerging image of the Divine.

If time does not allow for the creation of a Triptych, consider inviting a directee to create a mandala collage exploring images of God. (See Chapter Seven.)

As another alternative to a Triptych, invite directees or retreatants to create a timeline of personal God images as described below:

At the start of the Spiritual Exercises, I encourage retreatants to recall and pray with their own life stories. They create a visual, three-dimensional timeline of their early God-images, favorite childhood getaways, significant events, persons and places. Photos and personal symbols, sacred writing, and snatches of musical lyrics, all form a kind of altar for a more intimate way of praying.
—*Mary Lou Weaver Houser*

Conclusion

The Divine is ever present, and yet always new. As we work with directees exploring images of the Divine, we can support them in accessing the arts and imagination to dive deeply into sacred traditions to touch the depth of mystery in these living streams of faith. We can also engage the arts to support them in discovering new, personal, astounding and healing encounters with God. May the Holy One continue to surprise us with sounds, sights, sensations, stories, and images that draw us ever more deeply into lived relationship with mystery.

11

Engaging the Arts for Transitions and Discernment

Christine Valters Paintner

Traveler, there is no path. Paths are made by walking.
—Antonio Machado

The arts help expand our ways of knowing God beyond the cognitive level. They open up paths for listening to new possibilities. They especially help us tend to times of discernment, when images are being birthed within us before we have the language for them.

During my own times of discernment I often experience a high degree of synchronicity between my dreams, my art, and the rest of my waking life. Images appear in one domain and then repeat in the others as a way of calling my attention to them.

I remember a time when I kept having dreams about cellos—my favorite instrument. As a way of honoring this repeated image I often played a recording of Bach's "Solo Suites for Cello" either for meditation or as a soundscape for my art journaling. After my third dream about cellos I went on an extended morning walk to allow the dream images to move through my body.

As I passed by the art school in my neighborhood, I discovered a woman playing the cello on the lawn. It was a brisk October morning and

I had never seen anyone play music out there before. The serendipity was a call to pay close attention. A few days after this experience, I received a contribution for a book I was writing on *lectio divina*. The writer likened spiritual practice to learning how to play an instrument and used the cello as an example. He wrote about the way we start out being highly conscious of the details of our practice, the steps and stages, and gradually as we learn "by heart," our playing and praying become more fluid, and we become immersed in its rhythm, rather than trying to impose our own. These layers of images—from my dreams, to listening to music, to my walk, to the woman playing on the lawn, to this piece of writing gifted to me—each contributed to my discernment process because I was paying attention to the resonance and repetition of images.

Discernment is a growing sensitivity to and awareness of the action of God in one's daily life. Discernment is a practice that helps us to encounter God in the center of our being and listens for God's desires for our own growing wholeness. Many times, directees first come to us for spiritual direction in the midst of transition. They want help in listening to the still, small voices within them, guiding them towards life-giving choices. In discernment we listen to the truth of our authentic voices as distinct from all of the other voices both within and without that demand our attention and energy.

When we enter into a process of discernment, we are entering a threshold space in our lives. What has come before is different than what comes after. Even if we ultimately choose to make no outward changes, we have approached our lives with intention and deep listening, and thus make new choices about how to live in a meaningful way.

Liminal is derived from the Latin *limen* meaning threshold. Anthropologist Victor Turner describes the liminal as "creative darkness," the time and space of transition integral to all rites of passage.[82] Entering this condition, a person leaves behind his or her old identity and dwells in a threshold state of ambiguity and openness. Discernment often thrusts us into a place of unknowing, waiting, and listening.

Structure is the order of our lives, when we can articulate who we are and where we are going. Anti-structure is a time of chaos. Liminal experiences are those transition experiences when we move from one to the other.

Image or symbol is vital in the anti-structure experience because image is the only language left. Carl Jung said that meaning comes to us in images first and only as conceptual thought after.

Experiences calling us to discernment often subvert our everyday worlds and carry us out into the experience of wilderness and disorientation. Our words cannot yet carry the weight of the new meanings being born in the darkness of anti-structure. In these times, image can be a vehicle for carrying the feelings and the meanings we cannot yet articulate. Images help us to hold onto the experience, stay with it, and communicate it.

> Waiting—lines, long, patience required,
>> Unknown, not knowing
>> Frantic with desire
> Desire to know when the waiting will end.
> —*Paula McCutcheon*

Gradually we develop words to go with the images. The symbol gives rise to thought and reflection. The image has helped to capture the intuitive-feeling side of the experience and give it some manageable form. The concepts begin to capture the understandings resulting from the experience and help to define our world and what we now need to do and become. We are back in the structure again.

The arts hold this liminal space in the threshold and transition times, when we dwell in life's cracks and edges. This creative act of transforming our lives, of allowing something new to break forth and be birthed within, is the fundamental human capacity for the creation of new meaning. One of the most valuable things we can offer our directees is our willingness to be fully present to them in this space and time of waiting and offer them tools that honor the vulnerable in-breaking of new possibility.

Engaging the arts helps us to connect to the voice of our authentic selves. The arts also honor possibility, imagination, questions, and mystery that are integral to discernment. Because the arts are rooted in the existential capacity of the imagination to transcend literal reality, they can serve to present alternative possibilities of being and afford us insights not available through cognitive means.

Experiential Exercises

Exploring Soul Questions through Collage

The poet Rainer Maria Rilke wrote, "have patience with everything unresolved in your heart and try to love the questions themselves . . . Live the questions now."[83] Discernment is about living and loving the questions of our lives, the unresolved places. The arts help us to dwell in that space of the question by allowing us to honor the images and feelings without having to move to linear and logical thinking, the thinking that wants to find answers. Soul questions are those which speak to the deepest desires of our heart. They ask in different ways "How I am seeking to create a meaningful life?"

The following exercise exploring soul questions was inspired by a process led by expressive arts therapist Jane Goldberg. The materials needed are simple:

Three medium-sized rectangle-shaped pieces of watercolor paper (about 4x6 or 5x7), watercolors, brush, jar of water, collage images, glue, drafting tape, and scissors.

Gather the materials and invite the directee into a time of reflection using the following script as a suggested format. Creating some limits for an art experience is helpful. Suggest choosing only one magazine from which to choose images and limit time to between a half hour and an hour.

Take some time in silence to reflect on what your soul questions are right now. Write down three of these soul questions, one on the back of each piece of paper. Then shuffle the papers so you don't know which paper holds which question. As you move into the visual expression experience, let the questions go for the time being.

Take a roll of drafting tape to create a frame around the edges of each piece of paper and secure them to the table. Begin by using watercolor paint for the background, choosing colors you feel drawn to . . . After painting for awhile, shift your attention to images. Gather images through which you experience resonance or dissonance and create collages for each of the three cards. Keep returning to your breath as a way to stay grounded in the present moment, allowing your intuition to guide the process of placing the images in relationship to one another.

When the three pieces are done, take some time to reflect on the process of creating each collage. What did you notice in yourself? What were the voices and judg-

ments that arose? Which of the collages felt the most liberating to create? Which one felt the most challenging?

After exploring the process for a time, turn each image over to see which question corresponds with which image. Notice your own internal response as you discover what the synchronicity of images reveals about your question. See what wisdom they have to offer to you. Take some time to journal about your discoveries. If no immediate connections occur for you, take some time to meditate with the images over a period of several days and notice if any new meanings emerge.

See Chapter Seven for questions you can use to help the directee further break open the collages created.

Reflecting on the Path Ahead
Contributed by Pam McCauley

At two different retreats, I have used images to help facilitate spiritual reflection and sharing. Prior to these retreats, I collected various images of paths from the Internet. They ranged from peaceful paths in the woods to quite arduous climbs up a mountain. Some were winding, others quite straight, some with stairs or doors to open. I had the retreatants choose a picture without giving them much instruction, mainly saying that they should not take much time in the selection. When they came back and sat down, I went through a number of questions for them to reflect on. These included things like:

- Is your path winding or straight?
- Is it difficult or easy?
- What do you feel looking at the path?
- Where are you in the picture?
- Where is God?
- Where is it leading?
- How might it express your spiritual path?

Then, I had them write for about five minutes about other things that they might discover in the image. Next, I had them share with one other person what they had found. I encouraged them also to exchange pictures, so that the other person could share what they saw in the new image. There was an immediate and enthusiastic outpouring when they had the chance to speak as if they had discovered a treasure.

Clay Meditation for Discernment

Contributed by Marianne Hieb

As spiritual directors, we often encounter people struggling to make graced decisions. With an individual or a group engaged in discernment, I will frequently suggest adding the ancient material of earthenware clay to help focus that prayer.

After a meditation during which participants write down their discernment choices, they receive a lump of clay and are invited to divide the clay into pieces that will represent the decisions under consideration. Some will just break the clay in half. Others will break the lump into many more pieces.

In prayer, participants are invited to create an image for each choice, and gaze at the results. Then they engage in written journaling to describe the qualities of each piece, and record any feelings each may have unleashed.

A woman discerning community leadership shared that her first clay representation was lumpy and unformed. She was assailed by a feeling of lack of freedom. Her second representation, strong and well-defined, confirmed remaining in her current healthcare ministry. An older gentleman noticed the wide-open strength of one of his vessels, contrasted with a second one, whose walls were too thin, and kept collapsing. He sensed that this weakness was a parable for the misdirected energy he would need to expend were he to choose the alternate task. A young woman wanted to image her relationship with God. She divided the clay into two halves, one representing her, the other representing God. She came back, humbled and in awe: she only had to utilize one of the pieces. Her clay piece revealed that she was within God, part of the same structure, not separated from and at a distance as she had imagined.

Including clay in a discernment process can enhance the insights that emerge as individuals consider all their graced alternatives.

Awareness Examen

The Examen prayer was developed by St. Ignatius of Loyola and is a simple but profound way of tending to interior movements over time. It can be done on a daily basis for personal prayer, but is also easily adapted for a monthly spiritual direction session. Essentially the invitation in this prayer is to have directees quiet themselves, take some time to reflect on the previous month, and ask: What in this past month has been life-giving? What in this past month has been life-draining? Recording these patterns of what Ignatius called consolation and desolation over time in a journal, can be extremely helpful in a time of discernment.

The following is an adapted and expanded version of the Examen prayer, using gentle arm movements to access the wisdom of the body and felt sensations. You can invite a directee into this gentle way of being present to the body's knowing in a time of uncertainty:

Preparation:

You may do this prayer sitting, standing, or entirely in your imagination.
Begin by moving your attention inward.
Center yourself by getting in touch with your body and breath.
Become aware of the presence of God within the earth of your heart.
Listen deeply to your body and its messages.

Reaching both arms down:

Become aware of your connection to the earth and its support beneath you.
What do you need to ground you and bring your awareness to the present
   moment?
What concerns keep you from being fully here?
Can you allow God to hold them for this time?
What is awakening in the ground of your being?

Reaching back behind you with right arm:

Looking back on this last month, what was most life-giving for you?
Where did you feel most filled with love? Hope?
Take a few moments to experience this in your body.
How does revisiting this moment feel for you?
Where do you experience a quickening?
Is there anyone you want to thank for this memory?
Spend a few moments dwelling in gratitude.

Bring your right arm back along your side.
Reaching back behind you with left arm:

What in this last month was most life-draining for you?

Where did you feel most restless? The least hopeful?
How does revisiting this moment feel for you in your body?
Take a few moments to experience this.
Is there anyone to whom you want to offer forgiveness for this experience?
Spend a few moments seeing if you are moved to extend forgiveness.

Bring your left arm back along your side.

Reaching both arms forward:

Holding a heart of gratitude and forgiveness, how do you want to
   move forward?
What are your hopes? How are you being invited to follow the Spirit now?
How do you nurture the new seeds of life stirring within you?

Reaching both arms upward:

What guidance do you need to support you?
What do you want to ask for to help you move more fully into your hopes
   for the day?
How might you call on God for this guidance?

Reaching inward:

Bringing your hands to prayer position or leaving them open in a receiving
   posture, what new things do you notice now stirring within you?
What is awakening within you?
What desires and insights invite further reflection?
What new questions do you bring to your discernment process?

Following this experience, spend some time in conversation with your
directee about what unfolded, or invite her into a time of journal reflection.

Finger Labyrinth

Contributed By Eunice Schroeder, D. Min.

One day I offered my finger labyrinth to a client before our spiritual direction
session as a way of centering and grounding her. "Oh, no," she replied smiling,
"I don't want to go that deep!" She was well aware of the depth to which a
labyrinth can take one. And that is precisely why labyrinths are so powerful as
a resource for spiritual direction.

When clients are wrestling with a decision or unresolved situation or feeling, invite them to walk a labyrinth. One need not have a full-sized labyrinth nearby. Finger labyrinths can be just as helpful. If using the latter, invite your clients to "walk it" with a finger, their eyes closed, and using their non-dominant hand. This engages the opposite side of the brain and allows for deeper more integrated discernment. (See Chapter Seven for how to create a finger labyrinth.)

Directees may find it helpful to write down their question beforehand. Encourage them to make it open-ended, not a yes or no question. For example, instead of "Should I take that job offer?" make it "Who might this job offer be calling me to be?" or "How does my spirit feel when I envision myself taking this job?" As directees walk the labyrinth, invite them to let go of their question—not to think about it—just letting it float.

Afterwards, clients may want to journal, draw, make a collage, or write a poem based on the images, thoughts, feelings, and insights they gained on their walk.

Labyrinth Walk

Contributed by Debra McMaster

The church where I meet with a number of directees has a beautiful outdoor labyrinth. Two large oaks and a pair of benches frame its entrance. When the weather permits, we prefer to meet there rather than inside. I often prepare myself for meetings by walking the labyrinth to release my busyness and make room for the One to come. When a directee arrives rushed and late, I suggest that she stand in the center to breathe and collect herself. I might suggest when a moment of insight occurs that the directee may wish to walk with whatever has come, taking it in, open to however it is unfolding.

Two experiences are etched in my memory. I once walked the labyrinth with a visually impaired person. Fiercely independent, she hadn't thought the labyrinth was for her. When I asked if she would like to walk it together, her face lit up. We walked slowly, her hands on my shoulders. At one point, her grip loosened dramatically, and I stopped, thinking, "Oh no! She's going to pass out!" But she nudged me to keep going, so I did. Afterward, she told me that was the moment when she began to let go and trust both the path and the guide.

On another occasion, I walked behind a woman who struggles daily with depression and mental illness. In the center, in silence, facing one another, our eyes met in a long gaze. Her expression was full of suffering, her eyes brimming with tears. Mine filled too with tears of compassion—for her, for myself, for all sufferers. Our gaze was Godde's*, looking with us in infinite love and compassion. We walked out in silence; no more needed to be said.

Storytelling: Consulting with Guides

Contributed by Maggie Yowell

I had the honor of leading ten women in a four-day SoulCollage® Retreat. SoulCollage® is a process of collaging cards reflecting different aspects of one's soul. These sacred parts of ourselves have much wisdom to impart to us, and can speak to us powerfully through images. The following exercise was inspired by SoulCollage®, but could also be led using other forms of collaged or painted cards.

On one evening during our retreat, I invited each woman to go on a "journey." To prepare, I led a meditation inviting the women to consider three Guides they would like to consult on their journey and to form a question they would like to carry with them. When we were ready, we entered the sacred space of the chapel and took turns focusing on each woman. The person making the journey named the three Guides she had chosen and assigned these parts to three other women in the group. For instance, some desired to consult the Priest, Shaman, Wise Woman, Mother, Joyful Child, or Moon. The Guides then chose a Wisdom Card that symbolically represented the particular character they were to portray, and stationed themselves around the chapel.

When the Journeyer arrived, she asked her Guide, "Who are you?" The Guide revealed her chosen card and answered in an intuitive way, such as, "I am the Moon. I hold ancient wisdom, and mirror the light. I light the path even when you are in darkness." The Journeyer then asked her questions, such as, "What are my next steps in nurturing my soul?" "How can I best heal my heart?" or "What advice do you have to give me about embracing life fully?" The Guide replied in the voice of the image, looking into the eyes of the Journeyer.

---

* A note about the use of the term "Godde" from Debra McMaster: I've become increasingly dissatisfied with the pervasive presentation of "God" as masculine. This spelling both includes and enlarges upon that limited image. I first encountered this more inclusive alternative in Women's Uncommon Prayers. The footnote there simply says, "Godde is a feminine spelling of God." This seems more complete to me.

The Journeyer continued on, and each of her guides answered the same question, true to the role she was portraying and the images within the cards. Perhaps most striking was the Journeyer who had recently lost her Mother, and so she asked each of her Guides to be her Mother. This dialogue offered her a chance to find closure to a significant life question. The wisdom, tenderness and healing that emerged and was shared by these women was tremendous.

Contemplative Walk for Discernment

Consider inviting directees or retreatants on a contemplative walk. Being out in nature can be a powerful experience of prayer and the seasons of the year have rich questions to pose to us, especially in times of discernment. The contemplative walk could either happen during a session or suggest it between sessions before your next meeting. Going out into the woods or along a shoreline can help, but even a park or tree-lined street helps us to connect to nature again.

Here is a suggested format for a discernment walk:

Begin by simply being present to the world around you; notice how your body is feeling. Listen to where you are being led; try not to think about it. Allow your body's own intelligence to guide you. Encourage a deep listening to your body's messages and intuitions. Let this time be a pilgrimage of the heart noticing where you are being invited to go and where to linger. Try to let go of any goals you have for this time. Even if you walk only a few steps and simply notice, that is enough. After spending time slowing down and being present to what is around you, begin tending to the questions stirring within you in response to nature's presence.

Each season has its own profound questions to ask: In autumn you might consider what you need to let go of, or what is dying within you? In winter you might ask where the bare places are in your life, or where are the seeds lying dormant? Spring evokes questions about what is burgeoning and blossoming, or where do you discover the new life within? Summer might elicit reflections on the fullness of life and time for play.

As you walk through the world, what questions does nature ask of you at this particular time of your life? Finally, once you have become present to the questions of nature, ask yourself how do you walk in this world? Embody your response in the actual movement of your legs and feet across the ground. Then ask, how do you

want to walk in the world? Notice how your body feels and wants to respond.
What does this have to say to your discernment process? How does what stirs within
you and your body's response give you new information?

Other Expressive Arts Possibilities

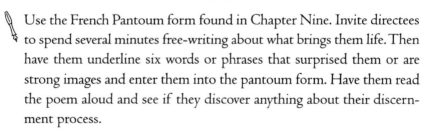 Explore the exercises in Chapter Thirteen on dreamwork. Tending the
images in dreams can be extraordinarily helpful in the discernment
process.

The hand dance which is explored further in Chapter Six can be very
effective as a way of allowing the body to reveal wisdom about questions of discernment. After directees have verbally explored a question
they are addressing, have them practice a playful InterPlay® gesture of
release. Invite them to physically touch their brow, gathering whatever
worries might be lodged there, and throw them up in the air saying
"Whee!" Following this, choose a piece of music and invite them into
a solo hand dance without the intention of "finding" an answer, but
simply exploring sensations. Invite them to pay attention to the ways
their hand wants to move without judgment, simply allowing the experience to unfold. Afterwards, take time to notice together what the
body reveals about the soul's longing.

Use the French Pantoum form found in Chapter Nine. Invite directees
to spend several minutes free-writing about what brings them life. Then
have them underline six words or phrases that surprised them or are
strong images and enter them into the pantoum form. Have them read
the poem aloud and see if they discover anything about their discernment process.

Conclusion

Discernment can be an unsettling time of waiting and not knowing what
the future holds. The arts respect the mystery of the person while also
offering windows into the newness being birthed within. Engaging the arts
in times of transition can help directees to cultivate the inner wisdom and
trust needed to support their discernment process.

Butterflies Know

Can a butterfly see when its wings are complete?

Do they have a mirror inside their cocoons?

I think not!

They have an inner wisdom that says . . . NOW.

Butterflies know when it is time to fly,

   So do you.

Trust your wings.

—*Delores Montpetit*

12

Embracing the Arts During Grief and Loss

Betsey Beckman

Bereavement is the deepest initiation into the mysteries of human life, an initiation more searching and profound than even happy love.

—DEAN WILLIAM RALPH INGE

If asked, "When did you learn the depth of your own capacity for grief?" you would have a story to tell. Here's one from the Buddhist tradition:

> There was once a lovely young mother named Kisagotami, whose joy was made complete by her beautiful baby boy. Passersby smiled just seeing the delight in Kisagotami's eyes as she gazed upon her child. But one day, Kisagotami arrived with her beloved child in her arms—lifeless. He had died in the night. The bereft mother was beside herself, yet on fire with determination. She sought out the Buddha and pleaded with him, "Please, please help me to find the herbs I need to bring my son back to life!" This time her eyes were filled with blazing intensity.
>
> The Buddha gazed upon her kindly, saying, "Of course I will help you. But first you must bring me a mustard seed from a home that has never seen death." Kisagotami went from house to house, searching the long day through, but each house she visited shared with her their story of grief. In the evening she returned to the Buddha with a tender new wisdom, knowing now that she was not alone. Together, they buried her son, and from that moment on, Kisagotami became a seeker of truth.[84]

Grief is universal; it is part of the fabric of our humanity. Buddhist teacher Pema Chödrön writes, "When we don't close off and we let our hearts break, we discover our kinship with all beings."[85] At the same time, grief is rarely a welcome guest in our homes. As spiritual directors, we know that with a foundation of love and support, we can come to honor the deep well of wisdom and compassion that is carved out in us through grief.

What gifts might the arts offer to us in navigating the watery depths of grief? Through the dance of embodiment, we learn to surrender to the powerful waves of emotion that grief unleashes in us. As storytellers, artists, singers, and writers, we begin to give expression to all the phases of our protest, suffering, emptiness, and eventual re-creation. In fact, the arts can lift us out of desolation into recognition of the beauty and holiness inherent in our grief. The psalmists captured this poignancy in their poetic descriptions: "Deep is calling to deep. Your waves, your breakers, have rolled over me."[86]

Expressive arts therapist Stephen K. Levine speaks about the emptiness of grief as the precise moment that calls forth *poiesis*, or creation, which is in itself an act of affirmation. He writes,

> It is essential to human beings to fall apart, to fragment, disintegrate, and to experience the despair that comes with a lack of wholeness. To what can we turn, then, in this moment of crisis? I believe that it is at this critical moment that the possibility of creative living arises. If we can let go of our previous identities and move into the experience of the void, then the possibility arises for new forms of existence to emerge. *Poiesis*, the creative act, occurs as the death and re-birth of the soul. The integration and affirmation of the psyche are one and the same. But this new identity only lives in the actuality of the creative process. We are called upon to constantly re-form ourselves, to engage in what James Hillman calls "soul-making" . . . The soul finds its form in art.[87]

One of my first encounters with the soul-making aspect of grief happened through the arts of story and dance, which, in turn, opened to show me my life path. While in high school, I auditioned for a play based on the Gospels. I was cast in the role of Mary the Mother of Jesus, and was asked to dance the death of my son. At the tender age of sixteen, I had no idea how to dance from a deep place of emotion. My instructors never taught me that in ballet class! And yet, I prayed, "Mary, mother of the broken-hearted, teach me how to love with your passion, to feel with your heart, to dance with your depth." In this awakening I discovered the purpose for my dance was not to have the highest arabesque or smoothest pirouette, but to express the depth of my soul.

Not long after, I learned even more about grief; this time, for real. Here, the arts walked me through the land of desolation. When I was twenty-two, my mother was diagnosed with lung cancer. After a year of rallying valiantly, we all surrendered to the realization that her time was drawing near. On Mother's Day I awoke with an image: Mother Lake. The following are excerpts from what I wrote that morning.

> She is the lake. Mom is always there, just like Lake Michigan. She's always there, though sometimes we forget to drink in her beauty and watch the sunset. Then other times we remember, and catch a glimpse of the sun descending over vibrant rolling-breaking waves. We know the night is coming, and that only serves to draw our gaze upon this lovely Mother-Lake. And when the night of our days descends, it is almost as if she is gone, disappeared from sight, buried herself somewhere. Ahh, until we learn to listen. As always, she laps her love to us, or crashes it out like a symphony of timbrels telling of her love. . . .

I was profoundly stirred by this image that arose as metaphor for my mother's ongoing presence—even as I anticipated her departure. When I completed my writing and went into her bedroom, she was watching TV. I asked her what she was watching. "Oh, a program about Lake Michigan," she replied. I was astounded. This launched us into a teary-eyed sharing, and through the course of the next two months, the reading and re-reading of "Mother Lake" offered a tender source of solace for the two of us, and for all who gathered at the funeral as well.

Meanwhile, I thought death would come in the dark of night. Instead, it arrived as we gathered by my mother's bedside at the first light of dawn. A few hours later, I sat somewhat stunned, and slowly, carefully penned this poem:

> new morning
>   silence
>   borne away on the breath of dawn
>   born

Though I witnessed my father's immediacy of tears as he released his beloved life-mate, there was a deep quiet within me. Later that day, however, my brow began to throb with pain. My sister-in-law tended to me, laying a cool cloth on my forehead. With that act of motherly compassion, my heart broke open. I had never experienced the intensity of emotion that had been awakened, moving through me with powerful force. I am grateful I knew enough to trust the deep expressions of my body.

First, I found myself kneeling on the floor, clutching my pillow and rocking back and forth, crying, "I want you back, Momma! I want you back!" Next, a deep protest emerged as I struck the pillow with clenched fists over and again—shouting "no!" Tears streamed down my face as my voice opened in sobs of despair. Then, I had a deep urge to rip something, to somehow physicalize what had been ripped from my heart. I ripped at the pillow and as I did, I heard words echoing in my head ". . . and they rent their garments." This ancient voice somehow reassured me I was participating in a timeless and holy act of mourning, an ageless expression coming through my own body and soul.

When I was done, my headache receded, replaced by deep breaths connecting me to the life-force in my core. Sadness remained, but my unchoreographed outpouring of grief had washed me clean, teaching me to trust the presence of the Sacred even in the tender land of loss.

A Time for Mourning

Grief arises with shattering intensity when we encounter the loss of a close loved one. As spiritual directors, we may be called to support others through these times of raw re-invention. However, there are many other kinds of losses in life that also nudge us into varying states of sadness. These might be loss of a hope or dream, loss of health, loss of friendship, loss of a job, a home, or an opportunity. Often our culture does not make room for the time-out-of-time disorientation of our grieving. In attempting to "stuff" our feelings, we may not even be aware of the level of sadness that is wavering just beneath our conscious attention. However, in the sacred space of spiritual direction, when one experience of grief opens, it can also be an invitation to heal other ungrieved losses from many different times in our lives.

As spiritual directors, we may invite the arts to support directees at any stage of grieving: to break through a shell of distance or denial, to touch into a forgotten sadness, to provide an emotional release, to honor emptiness and disorientation, or to offer images of consolation or connection. The arts are a potent vehicle for release and a sacred tabernacle honoring emptiness and rebirth.

Experiential Exercises for Exploring Grief and Loss

Psalms of Lament

The Hebrew Psalter offers a dynamic collection of poetic songs expressing the whole range of human emotion in relationship to God. Most intriguing is the fact that the psalms of lament outnumber any other kind of song, including the songs of praise. These ancient prayers of protest and pain offer us a powerful template for our own poetics in our outpouring of suffering and grief. At whatever stage of grief we find ourselves, writing our own psalms of lament can help to give structure and form to the deep tides of emotion that pull inside of us.

Following is a general outline of the format for a Psalm of Lament. Feel free to slowly guide directee(s) through this writing and prayer exercise.

I. Address your prayer to God with an invocation as your initial cry.
2. Express a complaint to God, describing your source of suffering. (This is the body of your lament; allow time for your outcry to find voice. Describe how your grief feels, tastes, smells, looks, and sounds. Employ as many details as you can to portray your experience.)
3. Now consciously write an affirmation of your trust in God's ways.
4. Write a petition or plea for God's help.
5. Express your assurance that God hears you.
6. Write a vow of praise—what you offer in response to God's grace.
7. Close with a hymn of thanksgiving for God's action in your life.

Depending on the intensity and immediacy of the grief, it may be enough to simply invite directee(s) to express the first stages of lament (stages 1 and 2) during your time together. In the midst of raw grief, moving through to an expression of completion can be premature. Scholars conjecture that the original psalms were written over a period of time in order to allow for the cycle of grief to find its own gradual movement toward thanksgiving. If needed, invite your directee to continue to pray with writing over time, and return to the evolving psalm together as desired.

Psalm of Lament
O Christ/Sophia
I'm drowning in an ocean of grief
my lungs ache for air
my legs weaken and my arms
have lost their strength

My tongue stings with the bitter taste
of hatred and despair. I'm drowning.

The world is a giant killing field,
poisoned with cynicism and greed.

Sophia, I know your heart is breaking.
I'm hoping that your rage is ready to explode.
Tell me this won't go on forever.
Tell me the time of justice is near
like a herd of strong horses pounding
just beyond the next hill, bringing mercy
to the poor, justice to the nations
and relief to the long-forgotten.

Come soon. I know you hear me, Sophia,
I know you're listening to the whole world.
Tell me what you want from me.
Tell us, your people how to find hope.
—*Barbara Gibson*

My Psalm of Lament

Kind God, you know and see all.

I ache deep in my soul and belly;

I feel unable to stop pain!

No one cares or hears me.

I must stay happy and not feel.

My pain is sensual yet shameful.

I hate what I feel and resolve not to remember.

I am numb but no one knows . . . or cares.

Children's vulnerabilities are stripped of innocence and safety.

Betrayal is everywhere from those who say they love.

My mind reels with feelings that confuse me.

My child, I saw and I cried tears

when you couldn't.

I gave you courage beyond measure.

I ushered you into unseeing

for a season and a reason.

I stood by you and I know all.

God, rise up to break my chains.

Vindicate me.

Bring redemption.

Free all the children and cleanse

this family.

Let truth be known so freedom will reign.

Let peace come to all.

Kind and gracious God,

you are my refuge.

Your healing will come.

Heaven draws near to all

and you are near to me.

—*Cheryl Shay*

Embodying the Psalms

As Celeste Snowber points out in her inspired resource, *Embodied Prayer,* the Hebrew Scriptures offer us a rich pattern of embodied lament that can encourage our own somatic prayer.[88] The psalmists used powerful bodily images to express their grief such as shaking, weeping, bowing, prostrating, groaning, thirsting, being crushed, sinking, and being cut off or cast off.

Embodying the psalms can bring a deep sense of visceral expression and help us release or "exform" the physicality of our grief. If a directee is working through grief, you might have him choose one of the Lament Psalms (such as Psalms 5, 6, 38, 40, 42, 51, 69, 88, or 142) or work with his own Psalm written from the exercise above. Invite the directee to begin by memorizing a few lines from the complaint section and simply explore embodying the images. This could be done during a session with you, or as "homework." Playing a contemplative piece of music can help provide an energetic container of support for the expression.

In a group setting, this exercise of embodiment can be explored first by individuals or in small groupings and then shared with the community as witness. Some might like to speak or sing their own psalms as they move or have the text read slowly by another while the mover(s) share their bodily response to the images.

During the retreat, the life experience I chose for healing was my sense of deep abandonment when my mother attempted suicide while I was a child. I chose Psalm 22 as my biblical prayer. After I told and embodied my story of my mom's suicide attempts, I danced and sang over and over, "My God, my God, why have you forsaken me?" Through my movements, I poured out my utter sense of despair. Eventually, Betsey sent another participant to dance with me and play the part of God. I continued singing and sobbing even though this person was saying, "I'm here; I'll never leave you." She was even attempting to hold me, and I kept pulling away. Finally, I felt as if I had sung all the forsakenness out of my soul and I collapsed in exhaustion into the other dancer's arms. The fight was gone, and I could feel God's love pouring in on me. My tears of bitterness changed to tears of love, washing away my deep loneliness. I surrendered into the arms of God. *—Sharie Bowman*

♫ Telling a Story in Movement

After a directee has shared a story of loss, if she seems to be having a hard time accessing the emotions to accompany words, you might have her experiment with telling the story again—this time through movement. Assure her that it is not important to mime each of the actions, but to enter into the felt experience of the underlying feeling tone of the story. Encourage her to exaggerate or repeat motions rhythmically so that her body can begin to speak the story instead of her head.

I was in the early stages of a dark night of the soul, though I hadn't realized it yet; I just knew I was feeling sad about some career disappointments. That day, we were asked to move out an expression of a story we were struggling with. I didn't really know what I would do at the beginning, but I found myself acting out a huge sense of disappointment. I found myself circling round and round to show I was getting nowhere. Amidst this action and this realization, I broke down and sobbed and felt that I could keep weeping for hours. Expressing the story with my body brought deep emotions to the surface that I hadn't been able to get in touch with. I knew I had opened a deep reservoir of pain that would take months to deal with. It was the beginning of healing my deep vocational disappointment that I needed to express and let go. —*Kathy Bence*

♫ Giving Voice to Grief

Contributed by April Sotura

When the heart is too heavy to hold the torrential emotions of grief and loss, the voice is a gift of healing. The river of voice functions as a channel allowing deep-rooted emotions to flow. Its gift of healing comes from the expression of acoustical resonant tone with depth of emotion.

> *Release the breath and allow the belly to soften. Invite the jaw and tongue, the gatekeepers, to unhinge. Step into the river and sigh. Breath flows in, and flows out; into this river of breath allow sigh, hum, and tone to awaken and release the depth of feeling within you. Let your body shake and tremble; let your voice explore the tender tones that assuage your heart.*
>
> *Allow your voice to ride on the current of your heart's lament, from tender tones to depth of song. Explore the range and scale of your expression, the high tones of the head voice, the resonant tones of the heart cavity, the deep tones*

of your belly. Add a word, a name, and a phrase. Sustain, sing them loudly and softly; repeat them; find the wild rhythm of your heart song. Sing of your loss, sing of your love, sing your goodbyes, and sing your blessings. When your soaring is complete, rest in a true tone that hums in your belly, grounding yourself to the earth. Know that you are washed clean.

Moving Anger

Well-known psychiatrist Elisabeth Kübler-Ross suggests there are five stages of the grief cycle including denial, bargaining, anger, depression, and acceptance.[89] In my years as movement therapist, I found a great deal of empowerment in becoming familiar with the tools for healthy expressions of anger in movement. For the following exercise, have access to a pillow and arrange to meet in a place where it is acceptable to make noise. As an introduction, you might explore with the directee her own sense of permission for allowing expressions of anger. You may choose to reflect with her on the account of Jesus' expression of anger in the temple (John 2:13–17). You can also lead a gentle warm-up to begin to prepare the body for opening channels of expression. (See Chapter Six.) When you are ready, lead the following exercise and support the directee to move and sound with you.

To support large expressions in the body, begin by establishing your grounding. Stand with your feet parallel and inhale a deep breath, allowing your breath to fill your belly. As you exhale, let your knees bend, and your weight drop down toward the earth. Continue with a slow pulse of your legs, bending and gently straightening your knees (without locking them), inhaling deeply and exhaling fully. After you have established a grounded rhythm, soften your jaw, your face, your shoulders. Allow your spine to move and undulate, creating a flow through your torso while maintaining your connection to the earth. Continue to deepen your breath.

Once your grounding has been established, you can move into specific movements and vocalizations designed to help release or "exform" anger. Take the pillow into your hands. Begin to growl and exaggerate your facial expressions. Allow the lion in you to emerge! You can claw, bite, and grasp at the pillow as you pace and feel the energy building. When you are ready, practice lifting the pillow above your head with your back slightly arched so you can release the pillow forward and downward, rather like the release of a slingshot. As you do this, allow a vocal release with breath and "Hah!" (If you are in a smaller space, you can release the pillow onto a couch or bed.) After repeating this gesture a number of times, you can experiment with other releases such as punching the pillow or stomping on the pillow. Feel free to experiment with sounds such as "No!" allowing the expression to find release through your face, hands and feet.

When your discharge of emotion feels complete, return to a place of safety through grounding. Bend your knees and take full deep breaths. Feel the flow of energy in your body traveling down your legs and connecting you to the earth. Give thanks for the holy power of anger as an energy designed to protect all that you hold dear.

Since anger is often an emotion covering over a deeper sadness, it is not uncommon for the release of anger to be followed by release of tears. You may want to follow the anger exercise with the exercise below on "rocking." Or you may find that a sense of empowerment and exhilaration has been accessed through opening the channels of anger. In either case, reflect with the directee on what emerged through the expression. Acknowledge her for claiming permission to feel her anger, and for choosing safe and healthy ways to express this powerful emotion.

Since working on anger expressions in our program, I have shifted interiorly knowing that anger is energy needing to be released. A number of my pillows have been thrown to the floor with much gusto in my house and I have survived! I have even gotten to the point that I am laughing after my outpouring of anger. —Delores Montpetit

Rocking

One of my most healing memories from childhood is being held, soothed, and rocked by my father as he sang his own little lullaby for me. Holding and rocking my own baby son just as my father had soothed me, brought a deep sense of connection and contentment. Can we image ourselves being rocked in the arms of God?

Invite directees to explore the quiet intimacy of rocking. While seated on the ground, kneeling, or even standing and swaying, have them explore this simple action, discovering what seems most comfortable. Singing a lullaby to themselves, or listening to a psalm of comfort, or a reflective song can bring a deep sense of consolation from the Divine for those in the tender stages of grieving. If they have recently lost a loved one, holding and rocking with a pillow, and imagining rocking the one they have lost can be a powerful sensorial experience of deep communion. (For further exploration of rocking as a healing movement, see Celeste Snowber's *Embodied Prayer*.[90])

Additional Exercises for Exploring Grief and Loss

Collage-making creates a contemplative space for images that can honor the wounds of grief as well as the journey to wholeness. (See Chapter Seven.)

As we began our collage process, the deep loneliness of my childhood engulfed me. The first pictures I chose were children with tears dripping down their face to match my own. Gradually, I found an image of a beautiful mother holding her baby. I longed to be that baby held so lovingly. As my tears began to dry the image of a strong bear called me. Then an elephant mother and baby, and sea anemones, all in a group. Then a final image of women healing another woman, embraced by the hands of God. Finding a home for each of these images on my board allowed some of the grief to move through . . . and I could find my truth as woman and healer. I could feel gratitude while embracing my wounded child. *—Sharie Bowman*

When words fail, consider offering the tools of visual art. Drawing in the midst of despair can open a channel of deep expression. (See Chapter Seven.)

I was working with a directee who was in a dark night of the soul. Every level of her life was dark and seemed void of the Beloved's presence. She was so angry she couldn't even talk to God. During one session, I invited her to draw a depiction of her life and soul. She drew a closed, darkened window. (In a previous workshop, she had drawn a series of windows reflecting the seven stages of pilgrimage, which were all were open and colorful.) While words were too much effort, her window image spoke volumes and gave her another way to express and process this dark passage in her spiritual journey. *—Lisa Sadleir-Hart*

The art of creating mosaics out of disparate pieces offers a powerful metaphor for reintegration after loss.[91]

I recently had a group of women at a retreat create mosaics out of tiles and pottery they had broken in response to Stephanie Kallos' book, *Broken for You*.[92] The process of breaking the pottery and reassembling the shards, a key image from the book, was very powerful for the women there. It became a metaphor for the broken places in their lives and their ability to create something beautiful out of those places. —*Carol Scott-Kassner*

As a powerfully supportive process for the bereaved, consider inviting a directee to integrate a variety of art media, stories, and photos to honor his or her loved one.

Recently, an intern in the Clinical Pastoral Education training program suffered the death of her mother. As grief flooded over her life, we shifted her assignments away from her more academic project, adapting her focus to be processing her grief through the expressive arts. She had already created an altar in her home, and so we invited her to add items from nature and from her mother's life to create a visual honoring of her mother. Other expressions included a Triptych, (See Chapter Ten), journaling, remembering and writing stories of her mother, and creating at least one collage for each story. —*Wes McIntyre*

Conclusion

Grief upends us, disorients us, and opens deep spaces within us. At these times, when chaos seems unmanageable, we as spiritual directors can offer simple tools of expression. The act of bringing creation out of chaos can be an affirmation of life even in the midst of death, an invitation to compassion even in the midst of desolation.

> **Christine Tells Us**
> Don't be ashamed.
> Your suffering is worthy.
> Your suffering links you
> with the whole wide world.
> —*Barbara Gibson*

13

Bringing the Arts to Dreamwork

Christine Valters Paintner

God is the dream maker revealed through the dream.
—MARION WOODMAN

Sleep is the Prayer of the Body
Sleep is the prayer of the body
shrouding itself in holy surrender.
It is an act of supplication,
with its secret longing for the things
embodied in luminous darkness.

What happens in that moment of
great release into the total eclipse
of night when the body descends
into the cradle of dreaming?
Does the breath suddenly become slow?
Does the heart become still,
barely perceptible, in its faithful work?

Or do they labor more heavily
to make space in the body for the rhythmic eruptions
of story and symbol
that beg me to awaken to a bigger life?

This is a lawless land. No
gravity or perpetual motion,
relativity or Murphy to guide me.
No map or compass either.
Where East is North and
South is nowhere to be found.

Is there ever a moment when the body
is so reluctant to return
to this waking world of prayer
bathed in the harsh
blinding light of morning?

Or does it hesitate, longing to stay in the place
where the bigger life
is not so
frightening?
—*Christine Valters Paintner*

About four years ago I had the following dream in the midst of a period
of serious discernment:

> I am driving around Vienna looking for the home of an old friend. I keep
> stopping the car to look at the map closely and find my way and then
> search again. At one of the stops two koala bears jump through my open
> window into the car and begin playing. They try to get my focus away
> from the map I am holding so I can give them some attention.

I had been spending a lot of time listening deeply to where I was being
called to devote my time and energy and for what brought me greatest joy.
Soon after that dream, I was at our Awakening the Creative Spirit Program
when we were focused on the arts and dreamwork. Betsey invited us into a

movement exercise. We were to take time to embody the different dream figures for ourselves and enter into the experience of being the different elements of the dream. I began with myself driving the car, looking at the
map. I felt very determined and serious, set on my goal of finding my
friend's home, and was uncomfortable with being lost. Then I moved into
experiencing the koala bears of my dream, leaping joyfully, playing, and
eager to get some attention.

The next step was to partner with someone and teach her to embody
one of the characters or symbols from my dream so that we could interact
with each other while taking on specific roles. I showed my partner how I
was driving the car, how I would stop and look at the map in a very focused
way, and then let her take that role. Then I became the koala bear, following her around the room, being playfully annoying, trying to grab the map
out of her hands, and wanting her attention.

This is where my "Aha!" moment occurred—that moment in dreamwork where something shifts and a part of the meaning of the dream is
unlocked. For me, it feels just like the tumblers of a lock falling into place
and the door opening onto a room within me, a room I did not know before.
My discernment process up until that point was much like driving the car
and carefully following the map, trying to get to my destination. The koala
bears symbolized God, inviting me to be more playful, to give up my maps
for a while, and stop taking my discernment process quite so seriously.

Dreamwork is one of my primary spiritual practices. It is one of the
paths that helps me to listen for new images of God and new invitations.
I deeply believe that our dreams are gifts from a sacred source, originating
in a wisdom that is far greater than our waking consciousness, and they
encourage us in the movement toward healing and wholeness.

One of my favorite resources for working with the arts in dreamwork
is *The Art of Dreaming: Tools for Creative Dreamwork* by Jill Mellick. She encourages her readers to receive dreams as messengers from another realm and to
remember that in sleep, our state of deepest surrender, we are deeply creative and expressive in shaping stories and images that invite us to live a
bigger life: "Dreams prove that in our inner world we are effortless and tal-
ented creative artists—superb wordsmiths, mythmakers, fine artists, and

craftspeople capable of simile, metaphor, symbol, and imagery unbounded by the cognitive restrictions of waking life. By using simple multimedia arts practices, we can let our dreams express their artistry in our waking world as well as our dreaming world."[93]

Dreams let us know how we really feel and think, not the way we pretend to think and feel. Dreams reveal what our conscious mind doesn't know. They move us toward an awareness of deeper truths not always apparent in our conscious, waking state. "Dreams use the narrative structure of the soul, a logic that dispenses with cause and effect, that exists in a timeless, spatially unbound universe where we are allowed to do the impossible."[94] Dreams are always inviting us to a bigger reality than the one in which we live.

As a spiritual director, you may have had the experience of a directee bringing a dream to a session that he wanted help in breaking open. Perhaps you already have some level of comfort in dreamwork and so you were able to bring your skills and tools to this sharing that opened wisdom from the dream and moved the directee into a new relationship with himself or with God. Working with another person is an essential piece of dreamwork, largely because dreams are inviting us to see things we have been resisting. Dreams often reveal our blind spots. Other people can notice things we do not.

Directees often bring dreams they want to unpack to spiritual direction sessions, and when someone is in deep discernment, I encourage this even more. Talking about the dream can be very valuable. Having a place where dreams are honored as gifts is often enough to encourage the dream to release some of its wisdom. The role of the spiritual director is to open up possibilities for exploration. However, dreams speak in a symbolic language and the arts offer especially helpful tools to help break open their meaning even further. Dreams have multiple meanings and layers of significance. We have never fully exhausted the meaning of a dream.

Echoing our initial guidelines in Chapter Three for working with the arts, we recommend working with the dreams of others in spiritual direction only if you are already working with your own in some way. Recognize that any insights you may have into the dreams of another person are always from your own projections, and consider the ways in which you articulate these insights. Dream worker Jeremy Taylor suggests using the words "if it were my dream . . ." to preface your comments and to keep your thoughts in the first person as much as possible. Only the dreamer can say with any certainty what meanings his or her dream may have. Insight usually comes in the form of a wordless "Aha!" moment of recognition.

After a year of monthly meetings with one directee he brought up a powerful dream he'd had, wondering how it might assist him in discerning a possible change of direction with his career. Using some art and movement we explored this dream. Over the next three to four months, he referred again and again to this dream and his understanding of it as a very potent source of guidance for him. At one point it helped him redefine how he was relating to his spouse and shift a pattern of interaction that was draining for her and hindering him in his discernment. The dream became a touchstone for him, for us, in this work together. —Wes McIntyre

Bringing the Arts to Dreamwork

Our dreams are not bound by the cognitive restrictions of our waking life—they speak in the language of poetry, image, and symbol—a different language from our usual linear and rational thinking. Draw or color your dream, move your dream, embody a dream character. Notice what it feels like and create a collage with images from your dream. Any or all of these experiences help to give honor to the dream wisdom and gently crack open the content waiting for us. The insights that came out of the movement exercise were powerful for me. Often by engaging in the right-brain language of the dream itself, more doors open onto the messages of the dream.

A growing component for me is to incorporate the creative arts in dreamwork—of my own dreams, the dreams of my directees and participants in a dream group in my church. As a spiritual companion, I listen carefully for movements in others that suggest new material surfacing. When it seems appropriate, I encourage drawing, painting, sculpting, or otherwise creating images to represent the feelings, thoughts, or experiences that so often elude verbal definition. —Constance Bouvier

Experiential Exercises

Write Your Dream in Color and Symbol

When we write our dreams down we tend to take a pen to paper and write in our usual linear fashion across the page. Invite directees into the following experience as a simple way to begin accessing their intuitive wisdom in listening to the dream's language:

> *Take a blank sheet of paper and a box of markers or pastels. Pause for a few moments before you begin, to ground yourself in your body, and notice which colors you feel drawn to. If a dominant color appeared in your dream, you may want to begin there. Write out the story of your dream again using colored pens. This time rather than write line-by-line, write the dream in a different direction or shape such as in a spiral. As you write, consider creating your own hieroglyphics or symbol system. When you come to a noun, for instance a dog, draw a small simple sketch of a dog rather than the word. When you come to an action or verb, use squiggly lines to indicate the quality of that motion. For example, if the action is fluid draw some waves, if it is sudden or jerky, draw some sharp peaks.*

Invite directees to notice what this process reveals about the dream's meaning. When I write my dreams down in the morning, I sometimes take a colored pen and then turn my journal ninety degrees and write my dream out that way to indicate that the dream speaks in a different direction than I would in my waking life.

Wisdom Cards and Dream Journals

Contributed by Carol L. Flake, Ph.D.

Images, poetry, and myth are the language of the soul. Collage allows us to work with images from our dreams and intuition. This process becomes a tool for "SoulCraft."[95] Heidi Darr-Hope, a faculty member at The Haden Institute's Spiritual Direction Program, gave me the idea of creating my own "Wisdom Cards." Wisdom Cards are made from 4x6 collages, using both sides of the paper, and then enclosing them in self-laminating plastic. (Laminating pouches are available to order from office supply stores.) After transcribing my dreams for many months, I distilled them to their essence and then created my own deck of Wisdom Cards. Words and images convey the themes emerging from my dreams and the cards can be used for contemplation in a more personalized way than Tarot or other types of Wisdom Cards.

Collage is also very effective for dream journals, an idea that came from Jeremy Taylor. An artist's sketch book provides a sturdy canvas to create collages on the front and back. Images can come from magazines, greeting cards, or photos. Clear contact paper can be used to laminate the front and back covers of the dream journal. A computer program can also be used to create collages from photos. From this rich experience I encourage directees to develop their own Wisdom Cards and Dream Journals that speak to their own unique soulprint.

In my own life, I have found collage to be a very powerful medium for working with images from my dreams. I offer this story to illustrate the possibilities of allowing our dreams to continue to speak to us through art. Several years ago I had this dream:

> I am at a party and a woman walks in, she is older and African-American. When she sees me, her face lights up and she approaches. "Do you know who I am?" she asks me enthusiastically.
>
> "No" I reply.
>
> She says: "I am your birth mother; your parents adopted you from me when you were born. Didn't they ever tell you that?"
>
> "No" I reply again a bit stunned this time.
>
> She replies: "Well I thought it was about time that you knew" and she wraps her arms around me. My overwhelming feeling is one of gratitude for having a mother again.

In my prayer the morning following this dream I knew instinctively this dream was about God. I am very comfortable with mother imagery for God, but this dream brought the image to a deeper level for me, one that was much more intimate and made me realize how in the absence of the physical presence of my own mother I am mothered by God.

I later brought this dream to my dream group and in our prayer time I began to experience a connection between this dream and two others I had in the previous few months, but I couldn't articulate the connections clearly. As we shared our insights with each other, one of the other group members suggested that maybe the other two dreams were images of God as well: God as child and God as lover. I had an "Aha!" moment that confirmed that there was some deep truth for me in this. The timing was blessed too as I was leaving for a week's retreat the next day. I spent the first three days of my retreat creating a collage Triptych, making three icons of these new images of God presented to me in my dreams. When I was done I kept them in a prominent place and prayed with them each day listening for what God as Mother, Lover, and Child might have to teach me at that point of my life. On returning home they hung above my altar for many months while I allowed their wisdom to continue to unfold in me.

Sand Dreams or Sand Mandalas

Contributed by Carol L. Flake, Ph.D. and the Rev. Diana McKendree, M.Ed.

We developed our sand-dream techniques throughout a year of intensive work. We purchased a child's sandbox in the form of a green turtle along with twenty-five pounds of sand. We gathered items from throughout our houses, including small figures we had collected in our travels or that we made in pottery, as well as from several local toy stores to use for the creation of a sand scene. When working with a directee, we light a candle representing the Presence of Spirit and spend some time in silence to begin. Directees are invited to manipulate the sand and then to choose items to place in the sandbox. Because the turtle's belly is round, each sand dream is a mandala. Images or scenes from dreams along with waking images or myths are combined in the creation of a guiding myth or image for the current soul work of the directee. We work with the sand dreams as if they were conscious dreams using the projective technique of dreamwork developed by Montague Ullman and popularized through the Haden Institute and Jeremy Taylor dreamwork programs. The directee is asked to describe the sand scene and then we, as facilitators, ask any questions we might have for clarification. Finally, we project into the sand dream using the phrase, "If this were my sand dream, I would think (or consider, or ask myself). . . ."

Others who use a similar approach talk about creating "sand prayers." Some people ask that five or six sand scenes be created before any commentary is provided. I find that working in the sand helps to concretize the images or guiding myths that represent the current state of the directee's soul-crafting process. As time goes on, the waking and dreaming realities start to interplay with the creation of the sand scenes.

Turn your Dream into a Fairy Tale

Invite a directee to either re-write or re-tell her dream as a fairy tale, beginning with the words "Once upon a time . . ." and tell it in past tense. Invite her to give each important dream symbol a name and capitalize it, making each a character in the story. She might exaggerate or embellish the background and setting of the dream, emphasize the colors and the surroundings. Add the words "always" and "never" wherever she can and use as many descriptive words as possible. Read the fairy tale out loud. See what insights or new connections appear from this form.

Embodying a Dream Symbol and Moving the Images

Consider inviting your directee into the discovery that comes with dream embodiment. See Chapter Six to find some ideas for warming up your body and getting grounded. The following exercise is an outline of the movement experience I shared in my introductory story and can be done on its own with a dream, or in response to the collage experience. Invite the directee to choose one of the symbols of the dream or one of the collage images and have him explore how it feels to be this dream element. Encourage him to enter into the experience with some of the following prompts:

> *What does it feel like in your body to be this symbol or element? What shape does your body want to take? Which movements do you want to make? What kinds of sounds? Give yourself some time to explore the different possibilities until you have a felt sense of the inner experience of being this symbol. Allow yourself to fully become this character and explore the qualities of the inner experience.*

Have the directee take some time to embody another symbol in the dream or collage and repeat the process of exploration above.

After embodying the second symbol, ask him to teach you how to be one of these characters or symbols. Have him explain how it moves, sounds, and feels. You embody this symbol for him while he embodies another one and interact with each other for a few minutes. Invite your directee to become aware of what happens internally as he brings the dream figures into external space. Feel free to let the dream characters evolve in their interaction beyond the dream's actual scenario. What does the directee notice or discover about the relationship between the dream symbols? What new discoveries does this experience reveal?

Other Expressive Arts Possibilities

Have directees make a mask of one of their significant dream figures. (See Chapter Fourteen.) As a spiritual director you can help directees to create a mask of their face as a way to honor a significant dream.

Once the mask has dried, employ paint to illuminate the dream symbols and colors on the mask.

Offer directees some clay to create figures from their dream, molding and crafting them while meditating on their dream's wisdom. When they are done, have them engage the figures in dialogue with each other.

A concise form such as haiku (5/7/5 syllables) or a cinquain can be a helpful way to capture the essence of a dream. (See Chapter Nine.) Invite directees to write a poem exploring the meaning of a dream.

Engage the *lectio divina* process (See Chapter Five) to invite the directee to pray with his or her dream as a sacred text.

Begin by inviting your directee to simply explore what kinds of sounds or voices each dream character or symbol might have. Then invite her or him to make up a song about each of the figures or symbols in a dream. Let it be playful or serious, creating space for the sounds that want to emerge in response.

Conclusion

Dreams speak in the language of symbol, so engaging the arts can be especially helpful to break open their meanings. Many of the other experiences outlined in this book can be adapted to dreamwork with a little ingenuity. Begin by working with your own dreams in this way and then offer the arts as a fresh approach to accessing the wisdom of directees' dreams.

14

Celebrating the Seasons of Our Lives

Betsey Beckman

Ceremony makes the ordinary extraordinary.
—GERTRUDE MUELLER NELSON

As described in our introductory chapters, our earliest ancestors celebrated the cycles of days, seasons, and lifetimes. They danced, sang, and costumed themselves, created altars and artworks to honor birth, puberty, marriage, sacred vows, and the passage of death. They honored the turning of the seasons, the planting, the flourishing, the harvest, and the inner work of winter. From as early as 40,000 years ago, our ancestors even offered flowers to the dead, as evidenced by the great amount of fossil pollen found in Neanderthal graves.[96] Anthropologist and philosopher Ellen Dissanayake suggests that the purpose of art is "to make special."[97] When we create art, ceremony, or ritual, it is not for the practical purpose of accomplishing a task, but to reflect our deepest meaning and our core values. In the act of creating, we invest ourselves in a process of making special; we dedicate our life-force to beauty; we honor the moment, the medium, and the message as sacred.

In my own life, even beyond the formal sacramental ceremonies of my religious tradition, I have discovered countless life transitions as occasions for ritual, dance, poetry, song, and art. As a child of ten moving to a new house, I went from room to room saying goodbye to my beloved childhood home. As a girl of twelve, alone on the beach, I found a plastic shovel, and decided that it was time to bury a childhood toy to make way for my emerging puberty. When a friend graduated early from high school, I wrote her my first friendship poem, honoring her life shift and mine. In college, I choreographed "Life-Dance," the depiction of an elderly woman reliving all the stages of her life, and then releasing her soul to die.

When I was preparing to be married, my dream group drummed me into my new life partnership. While I was pregnant, my closest women friends held a weekend ritual, where we all ended up sharing stories of our grandmothers—the ancestor women who had given birth before us. When my niece reached her menarche, all of the sisters-in-law gathered on the beach with our teen-age daughters and nieces, telling stories of our own "blood mysteries" and anointing the emerging women in our midst. At my fortieth birthday, my friends created a ritual where I recapitulated crawling through the birth canal and was "re-born" into my wisdom years. When my dad turned ninety, I spearheaded a book celebrating his life with poems, photos, artwork, letters, songs, and celebrations of his amazing gifts to us.

In exploring the origin of the arts, Ellen Dissanayake remarks, "What was chosen to be made special was what was considered important: objects and activities that were parts of ceremonies having to do with important transitions: such as birth, puberty, marriage, and death; finding food, securing abundance . . . and so forth." She goes on to comment about our contemporary society, "Caring deeply about vital things is out of fashion, and, in any case, who has the time (or allows the time) to care and to mark one's caring?"[98] Herein lies the heart of our focus in spiritual direction: offering time and space for individuals to feel, reflect, care, create, honor, and celebrate.

As spiritual directors, we are first called to commit ourselves to a process of honoring and making special our own life seasons. From this commitment, we can support directees in honoring the significant moments in their lives—births and deaths, liturgical cycles, daily rhythms, professional shifts or retirement, home and family cycles, aging, menarche and menopause, global changes, and seasons of the earth. We can also support directees in honoring and making special the cycles of our work together, which include the beginnings and endings of our sessions as well as the rhythms of our continued work and completion.

Let us explore a few examples of the seasons of life as creative thresholds where the arts invite us to deepen our intimacy with Great Mystery.

Experiential Exercises for Celebrating the Seasons of Our Lives

Celebrating through Gesture

Marking the beginning and ending of the day is an ancient practice of devotion. Praying with gesture is a simple invitation to embodiment, and can also be a meaningful communal form of movement prayer when one is leading groups or retreats. As we support directees in finding a rhythm for their own daily prayer, here is an example of an embodied morning psalm. These gestures were choreographed to Michael Joncas' musical setting of Psalm 63, "As Morning Breaks,"[99] but the gestures can also accompany the spoken text.

Morning Prayer—Psalm 63[100]

I. As morning breaks . . .

In preparation, with palms up, lift your hands to eye level. As you speak or sing the first line of the psalm text, turn your palms away from you. In one smooth motion; overlap your hands at the wrists, then move them apart from each other. As you spread your hands, envision clearing the clouds from the sky, or dispersing the fog from your morning mind.

2. I look to you . . .

   Turn your palms upwards again, and draw your hands together into
   a cup, still at eye level, lifting your gaze to the Spirit beyond.
3. I look to you, O Lord, / to be my strength / this day . . .

   If you are sharing this movement with a group, on the first part of
   the phrase, "I look to you, O Lord," take a partner's hand on one side.
   On the second part of the phrase, "to be my strength," take a partner's
   hand on the other side. (If you are alone, do the same action as if you
   were taking your imaginary partners' hands, calling to mind the people
   you'd like to stand with that day.) On the final part of the phrase, "this
   day," raise your hands in solidarity before God.

4. As morning breaks . . .

   Now repeat the second movement of the form, releasing your partners' hands, and drawing your palms together into a cup at eye level.
5. As morning breaks.

   Finally, repeat the first movement, turning your palms away, overlap-
   ping and then uncrossing your wrists—clearing the clouds. Then let your
   hands turn palms up and float down to receive the gifts of the new day.

   After teaching this refrain, pray it together with a directee or group.
   Feel free to read the verses of the psalm interspersed with the gestured
   response. Or play a recording of the song, singing and gesturing the
   refrain.

Celebrating Through Ritual

Whether a directee is moving through an ending or beginning at work, a marriage or separation, a significant anniversary or birthday, consider creating a ritual to mark the occasion together. (Or support directees in designing a ritual that they can share with a group of friends.) Rituals can be planned or impromptu. One directee who was in the process of selling her house requested we meet at her home to create a ritual of honoring the memories of her life there. We went from room to room singing, dancing, reading poems, and praying. Another directee who was honoring the end of her discernment process used props within our yoga studio to create the end of a path, with statues to represent the spiritual support she had received along the way.

To create a ritual, consider marking the beginning and ending by ringing a small chime. Include ideas from the pages that follow. Incorporate poems, dances, songs, gestures, and artwork. End with a blessing. Allow the Creative Spirit to guide you in the moment! As an example, one spiritual director describes a nudge from the Spirit that brought forth a ritual moment of completion for one of her sessions.

Recently, I was centering myself in preparation for a directee. I had a piece of music playing and was blessing the room, creating sacred space. I turned and swirled, imagining I was dancing with Jesus. The thought occurred to me, "I wonder if my client dances?" Toward the end of our session, I asked and she responded "not normally, but this morning I danced in preparation for coming to spiritual direction." We decided that a fitting way to close our session would be dancing to a piece of music called "Prayer of Good Courage."[101] —*Cathy Rhoads*

Celebrating through Poetry

Writing poetry is a meaningful way to reflect and honor significant moments and seasons in our lives. In completing a cycle of work with directees, consider inviting them to write a poem reflecting on the moments of growth and Spirit they have experienced. (See Chapter Nine for additional exercises.) In my personal practice, I have grown into a yearly rhythm of meeting with directees from September through June and then taking a summer break. In our June session, we reflect on our journey through the year, acknowledging the revelations in our work together. I have chosen a practice of composing a poem for each of my directees at year's end. Here is an example of such a poem honoring the spiritual direction journey.

Teach Me Your Ways
In the beginning—
What shall I do?
How shall I move?
Show me the way!

Slow small listening
beginning to remember the body
here, now, alive, sentient
leading the way
Spirit enfleshed.

Birth, remembered,
felt in the bones
pain, possibility,
now giving birth to self.

Song, quiet, voice arising.
Drums, setting free
rhythms of earth
heartbeat of deeper longings,
trustings.

Piano, claiming the keys,
letting the music come through
heart and hands,
not just head.

Death,
opening the floodgates
teaching the way of grieving,
the ancient way.
Body prayer—
each direction blessed
finding movements
earth, air, fire and water
alive, around, within.

Judgment and regret slowly softening.
It all comes through the body.
Sometimes simple,
sometimes deep tears,
sometimes the joy of gratitude
overflowing.
Now the dance is not so studied.
Now you can venture into the silence
and open space
to let your body lead,
let the Spirit speak,
let the mysteries unfold
in hand and foot
muscle and music and movement.
Imagine that—
it's not controlled,

it's not decided,
it's discovered!

Woman of faith,
dancing deeper
into the arms of God.
—*Betsey Beckman*

♫ Launching Poetry into Song

Contributed by April Sotura

Poetry is the pure utterance of the heart. Song invites the soul to fly free. As vocal coach and lover of Spirit and music, I offer some ways to play with launching poetry into song. The following exercise can be done with a directee or in a group setting where participants are paired together.

> *Choose one section of your poem to explore. Read this section aloud and allow your witness to listen to the sounds of your soul. Savor the feelings that arise in you as you deepen into the meaning of your poem.*
>
> *Bring your words before you again. In language, our words contain both vowels and consonants. The consonants create shape and form, while vowels fill that shape with meaning and beauty. Choose a new or familiar section of your poem. On one note, focus on singing only the vowels in each of the words without the consonants. With breath support, maintain a steady tone as you open from one vowel to another. Repeat this three or four times. The vowel is the courier of all your feelings, and contains all the beauty and resonance of the voice.*
>
> *Now shift your focus to singing the consonants on one vocal tone. Use your lips and tongue to shape your words while minimizing the vowels. Let your poem become a rhythmic dance! Move quickly or slowly; bite and chew the words; clap your hands; stomp your feet. Repeat this three or four times. Feel the rhythmic power in forming consonants.*
>
> *What difference did you find between vocalizing vowels and consonants? Continue playing and launch your poem into song. On one, two, or three notes, sing your way through your stanza. Explore the delicate and delicious rhythmical dance between vowels and consonants. When you find a melody that satisfies*

you, deepen into it; expand it. Bring your poem to life. If you like, teach your
song to your witness, and sing it together, celebrating the song of your soul.

Celebrating through Dance

Dance provides a wonderful release of celebratory energy. At the culmination of events in the life of a directee, consider inviting him or her to celebrate the journey in dance. A basket full of scarves can be an excellent inspiration and an apt symbol for the fullness of life experience. The use of props can be a meaningful extension of our creative expression through color, costume, and dynamics.[102]

In the dance pictured below, each colored scarf came to symbolize a different part of the year, and culminated in a life-size mandala with the directee in the center, enveloped by the Spirit.

Art Journal for the Seasons

Once the possibility for creative practice has been awakened, individuals and groups often have a desire for support in continuing to explore art as a spiritual expression. As we neared the conclusion of one of our Awakening the Creative Spirit Programs, participant Lisa Sadleir-Hart suggested that we join in creating a Round Robin Art Journal, a form she adapted from a Round Robin Quilt exchange. This is the process she designed:

1. Each participant chooses a theme that she would like to explore and submits this theme to the organizer. The organizer then assigns each of the themes to a month of the year, and creates a list of participants and their addresses.
2. Each participant purchases or makes a blank art journal. Then she creates art for its cover and opening page as a means of consecrating the journal and preparing it for its journey.
3. The journals are then sent to the next person on the list of participants. All create one art expression, centering on the group's shared theme. At the end of the month, (with a reminder from the organizer) all the journals are sent to the next person on the list, and the process is repeated each month. (With twelve participants, this creates a monthly rhythm for a year, but can be adapted to any size group.)
4. After all the months are complete—the journal ends up back with the original owner—with an entry from each of the participants throughout the year.

I was astounded at the variety of prayers and artwork that came through my hands each month. One of the participants began composing songs on her computer, and submitting them in the form of a CD on a page in the journal. Others created journal entries with their photography, poetry, collage, painting, or slide meditations on DVD. At the end of the year, each of us had a hand-crafted treasure imbued with the spirit of each of the other participants. One of our group members reflects on the process:

Our group kept up with each other monthly by means of a shared art journal. This was a wonderful reminder to keep creativity flowing on a regular basis. I was going through treatment for breast cancer the whole time—surgery, chemo, and radiation. The art journal was something simple that I could do that did not take a lot of time or energy, and it became very healing in keeping the connection with my "sisters" of similar artistic and spiritual inclinations. —*Pam McCauley*

Integration through Mask-Making

The art of mask-making is one of the earliest art forms practiced by our ancestors, masks often played an essential part in ceremony. In our Awakening the Creative Spirit Program, we save mask-making for our concluding session. This is in part because the art experience is fairly complex. The process begins with shaping plaster strips to the face of participants, which requires a high degree of vulnerability and trust. The second step consists of painting and decorating the masks after they have dried. Third, the completed masks then inspire an integration of visual and dramatic arts. The "persona" discovered and explored creates a wonderful opportunity for integration on many levels. The following exercise is designed for a group format, but could also be done with an individual directee over a series of a few sessions.

Materials Needed:
- Fast-Drying Plaster bandage. This can be bought in a roll from a medical supply company or in pre-cut strips from craft stores. You will need about 50 strips for each mask in varying sizes (1" x 2" to 1" x 4").
- Small bowl of water for each mask-maker
- Shower cap to protect hair
- Plastic wrap for protecting the face
- Large pieces of plastic to protect the work surface
- Paper towels
- For decoration: acrylic or tempera paints, brushes, glue, feathers, beads, etc.

Preparation: Lead a meditation on the soul, as below:

> *We all wear "masks" expressing different roles in our lives. Often these masks project a certain image or protect us from harm, but they can also hide our true selves from the world. Today you will have the opportunity to create a mask of your*

soul, of your true self, the self you are called to be. What face of your soul is long-
ing to emerge? Who are you becoming? What in your soul has been awakened that
desires expression this day?

Give space for reflection. Following the meditation, invite participants to choose a partner and decide which one will begin as mask-maker. Have the receivers discuss whatever variations they may need for the process: half mask, mold of a hand instead of face, remaining seated rather than lying down, etc. The mask-maker then creates a "station" equipped with the necessary supplies from the list above. Choose an extended piece of meditative music to support the mask-making process.

Process: Have the receiver lie down on a prepared plastic sheet, or assume some other position. The mask-maker then places two sheets of plastic wrap over the face of the recipient. One covers the upper half of the face, the other the lower half of the face, leaving a small opening for the nostrils.

The mask-maker dips the bandage strips into water, gently removes excess water, then begins to cover the recipient's face. Begin with the bridge of the nose, and work out from there, taking care to have enough support under the chin. Leave an opening at the nostrils. Smooth each strip after placement, covering the entire face with two to three layers of bandage. During this process have the mask-makers communicate gently whatever is needed to create a safe and trusting encounter for the recipients.

Once the face is covered, let the mask dry for about ten minutes. When the mask begins to harden, the maker will feel a bit of release from the face when pulling lightly upward on the edges. Carefully lift the plaster off and allow the recipient to see the first impression of his or her own face. Then, place the mask on a smooth surface and allow it to dry for at least four hours. If necessary, build up any weak edges before allowing it to set. Another possibility is to poke holes about an inch from each edge, in line with the eyes, for later additions of ribbon or string. In a group setting, place labels next to each mask with the name of the person to whom the mask belongs.

Decoration: Once the mask has dried completely, invite directees to discover what "face" wants to emerge through the addition of color, feathers, objects from nature, etc. There's no need for them to plan their design; allow the process to be intuitive.

Exploration: After the painted masks have dried, invite participants to gaze on their creations, allowing the face of the masks to speak to them silently. Engage questions from Chapter Seven to help participants explore the meaning of their masks. Consider these other possibilities for exploring the mask:

- Vocal Exercises in Chapter Eight for exploring the voice or song of the mask
- Poetry-writing Exercises in Chapter Nine for reflecting on who the mask represents
- Movement Exercises in Chapter Ten for dancing with and embodying qualities of the soul-character expressed in the mask

Finally, invite participants to share their discoveries with one another. Below you'll find a series of responses to the mask-making exercise, a tribute to the power of the process and its invitation to healing and integration.

Healing Hands

At the beginning of the mask-making exercise, I knew quickly that I wanted a cast of my hands, instead of my face. I placed my hands together in a receiving type of gesture, almost like receiving communion. At first the wrapping felt very binding. So, when it came time to pull them out, it was almost like a new birth of my hands, setting them free. Because my work has always been more head-oriented, the "new birth" of my hands has been a kind of awakening to explore new artistic expression. —*Pam McCauley*

Face of the Soul

One man who came to me for spiritual direction was experiencing clinical depression. He was under appropriate medical care, but wanted to address how the depression and his faith were related and interacting. After about eight months of work together, I suggested he make a mask and use it to create an expression of the face of his soul. In one session I assisted him in the first stage of creating the mask. During this time, as he lay vulnerable on the floor, he could not see me while I formed the mask to his face and over his eyes. With music as a backdrop, we worked on trust-building: trust that I would take care of him and keep him safe in the process. He later noted specific things I had said to him during that time and had held on to them as if they were vital resources in his life.

He took with him that day the material he needed to paint the face of his soul on the mask and the following month returned with a remarkable piece with color, design, and expression exuding from his mask. Each had symbolic meaning for the state of his soul and its emerging qualities. —*Wes McIntyre*

Discovering the Self

The experience of making the mask was life transforming. I felt the healing Spirit of God upon me as my partner placed each layer: cool, comforting, peaceful. I felt I was connected to my innermost being and whole self. When I decorated my mask I felt very strong with wisdom filling me, guiding me to what God desires for me. Whenever I am down or lacking in confidence I look at my mask and remember my experience of wisdom. —*Paula McCutcheon*

Mask-Making with Chaplain Interns

I use mask-making with chaplain interns. Interns make masks together and paint their masks with whatever is the focus of their life at that time: the face of their souls, the face of their grief, the face of their joy, anger, etc. During the first stage of mask-making, I encourage the active partner to practice building trust by communicating about all their actions and the receiving partners to attend to what this experience of vulnerability is like for them.

After making the masks, we reflect on the experience as parallel to visiting patients in the ICU who are vulnerable to whomever enters their room. This experience becomes a model for the interns when they do a chaplain visit to a person in ICU. The interns understand the significance of remembering to announce who they are as they arrive, what their intentions are, where they are in relation to the person in the bed, telegraphing their movements ahead of their actions, and asking permission.

When the masks are complete, the interns talk with their peer group about what the masks represent for them and receive responses from their peers. The masks are then hung on the wall of the meeting room and I find

myself "consulting" with them in the midst of our group work. I find that looking at a mask in the midst of group work can "suggest" intuitions about the
person who is presenting casework that day. The intern who struggled to
name his feelings had a mask with a white face and a large blue question mark
from forehead to chin. The mask with shades of light and dark merging across
it was from the intern who was wrestling with the light and darkness in her soul
and integrating the two in her work. The mask with the huge scar spoke of a
core wound and on and on. Through the making of the masks, the interns
often experience a deepening of their experience of knowing and being known
by each other. —*Wes McIntyre*

♫ Blessing

In the closing circle of our Awakening the Creative Spirit Program, participants are invited to share their masks and reflect on what has awakened in
their own souls in our time together. Then, we invite participants to name

a quality of Spirit that they would like to have accompany them on their return home. We sing the following refrain, asking Spirit to bless the participants with the quality they have named. Feel free to adapt as necessary.*

Creative Spirit
Copyright © 2009 Betsey Beckman

Repeat and add verses as desired   Betsey Beckman

Cre a__ tive Spi i rit,__   Bless us with your play ful ness.__
                                                      com pas - sion.__
                                                      your pa__ tience.

Additional Possibilities for Celebrating the Seasons of Our Lives

Support directees in exploring the wisdom of the seasons during a contemplative walk. Refer to Chapter Eleven for seasonal questions.

Since the subject of creating ritual is a field large enough to warrant its own book, please explore the Resource Section for publications that offer ritual designs, outlines, and prayers for honoring the seasons of the year and significant life passages.

Support directees in creating a personal art journal where they can reflect on significant moments in their lives and visually meditate on the journey over time. Include gush art, collage, photographs, poems, significant dreams, etc. (See Chapter Seven.)

Conclusion

Our lives hold countless moments of meaning that call forth artistry from our hands and hearts, voices and souls. Simple ceremonies help to honor, dignify, and make special the shifts and seasons we move through. When we invite a space for creativity, we give our directees a chance to be immersed in the beauty and grace of their lives. As a conclusion, and to celebrate the holy circles of endings and beginnings, we end with a poem.

---

*The English translation of the Antiphon (adapted) from *The Liturgy of the Hours* © 1974, International Committee on English Liturgy, Inc. All rights reserved.

As The Class Ends I Write This
beyond this circle of people and chairs
a ragged flock of pigeons
beyond the pigeons a snowy mountain
beyond the mountain
my daughter awake in Boston
beyond my daughter an ocean, a continent
beyond that, a war
beyond the war the Dalai Lama
beyond him mountains and another ocean
beyond the Pacific ocean
our circle again, where we sit, on the edge, with pigeons
—*Barbara Gibson*

15

Arts-Centered Supervision

Kayce Stevens Hughlett and
Christine Valters Paintner

Supervision is engagement in Holy Mystery.
—MARY ROSE BUMPUS AND
REBECCA BRADBURN LANGER

This chapter explores the gifts and possibilities the expressive arts offer to spiritual direction supervision. As we grow more comfortable with the arts, we can begin to access the arts for our creative and professional support in this ministry.

What Is Supervision?

Maureen Conroy, RSM, is the author of one of the first books to explore supervision of spiritual directors in depth. She describes supervision as both art and science: "It is an art in that it requires constant attentiveness to the spiritual director's interior space and to God's lively presence . . . It is a science because it involves disciplined focus, a clear process, and specific skills." She goes on to describe good supervision as bringing together this art and science in a "congruent approach."[103]

Supervision is an integral part of both personal and professional development. It offers a space for us as directors to name places where our free-

197

dom has become limited within a particular ministry relationship and to celebrate those places where the Spirit is moving freely. The arts offer a container for attention to our interior space and God's movement in the context of our compassionate listening to others.

Supervision is invaluable in helping us grow in the self-awareness and interior freedom that enables us to become more fully present to directees and to God's invitations in the context of our ministries. Supervision creates an intentional place to practice good self-care and to explore what has been stirred in our own interior lives while extending presence to another person. As spiritual directors, counselors, or other compassionate listeners, we sometimes forget how critical self-care is to our own health and the vigor of our ministry. If our personal issues overtake the space inside us, there is little room left to receive what others will bring.

Background on Arts-Based Supervision

After leading the Awakening the Creative Spirit Program for several years, I (Christine) realized there was a lack of strong supervision resources for spiritual directors, and nothing available that engaged the arts. Kayce, a licensed therapist and spiritual director, had participated in our Program twice, and was working in a graduate school setting, providing supervision to students who were preparing for ministry as counselors. Our collaboration on the process of creating arts and supervision groups was a natural fit. We began by forming a group of six ministers (including spiritual directors, chaplains, counselors, and a pastor). We discovered that including people involved in a variety of ministries of compassionate listening offered the participants a lovely sense of how their work fits into the larger field of soul care.

Because our focus was on the supervision of spiritual directors, we chose themes carefully to reflect some of the pertinent issues to professional development we had each encountered in our personal work and with others. These themes include exploring our roles and identities, finding our rhythm, and our relationship to shadow and light.

In our supervision group, we act as co-facilitators and receive our own supervision from another source. However, the sample sessions which follow can be easily applied to a peer group process, where each member takes a turn to facilitate and create the art experience. Establishing the facilitator's role as the one who maintains the supervisory focus of the sessions and exercises is important for the effectiveness of this work as a source of professional development. Supervision can also be offered in a one-with-one format where the supervisor offers a creative experience to help the spiritual director unpack the meaning and personal impact of a particular encounter with a directee. We offer the exercises in this chapter as a guide to help you move into whichever supervision format works best for your context.

Overview and Structure of Sessions

In a group setting, we recommend having four to six members, with two people having a formal supervision experience each time. Over a period of two to three sessions, each person has the opportunity for a formal supervision session. The purpose of this experience is to offer some focused time to each of the group members to help break open issues emerging from their spiritual direction work so that they can move to a place of greater internal freedom. As facilitator, request those being formally supervised send you responses to supervision reflection questions[104] a few days in advance of the supervision session.

We suggest designing a fairly consistent format. The schedule below is how we structure each monthly three-hour session:

10 minutes—Opening prayer and theme for session

45 minutes—Checking in (what has moved in you in response to our last session)

60 minutes—Expressive arts experience (see below for three outlined sample sessions)

10 minutes—Time for those who are not being formally supervised to share what they noticed in themselves from the art experience

25–30 minutes for each formal supervision process (two people presenting)

5 minutes—Closing prayer or blessing

Choosing Themes

The gift of working with the arts in a group setting is that even those who are not receiving formal supervision in a given session also engage the creative process and experience personal and professional growth as a result.

When you create your own sessions, allow the theme to emerge from your sense of what would be helpful to the participants' growth as spiritual directors. Build the theme on insights that emerged in prior sessions. In choosing a series of art experiences, keep in mind the principle of allowing the theme to guide selection of the particular art process. As you contemplate a session focus, which art experiences seem to have a natural resonance? Keep in mind the whole spectrum of modalities we have explored in this book. After selecting a core art exercise, choose imaginative experiences to help participants move into the creative process, as well as experiences (such as journaling, poetry-writing, or movement) that follow the art exercise to support participants in reflecting on the meaning of what has emerged. Select an opening and closing prayer for the session to further strengthen your theme.

In choosing themes and designing particular supervision sessions, we usually did so well in advance of receiving the responses to the supervision reflection questions from our supervisees. We discovered that the art process always opened a space for the participants to move more deeply into their reflections, no matter what the experience they bring for focus. However, it would also be possible to design sessions in response to particular issues being raised by the participants on their written supervision forms.

Similarly, in a one-with-one supervision context, the choice of the art experiences could be much more spontaneous, because you might choose a particular medium in response to something a supervisee has shared in the moment.

The following art experiences are designed for both personal awakening and insight into the role of spiritual director. These sessions offer space for participants to become more deeply aware of the personal challenges or patterns of behavior that may limit them as spiritual directors. They also invite insight into how God is active in their experience of themselves as ministers. Begin each session with a gentle reminder to participants to keep a focus on their role as spiritual directors throughout the experience.

◎ ⟍ 📖 **Exploring Our Identities and Roles**

Theme and Background: In an initial group meeting, it can be helpful to explore how different roles may be assumed in the position of compassionate listener. As individuals, we each bring our own perspective or lens into the relationship, no matter how well trained we are to stay impartial. This is a natural behavior and, while it cannot be avoided, it is critical we are aware of our own biases and how our identities influence our interactions with others.

This exercise is designed to heighten awareness for spiritual directors of the roles with which they naturally identify. They are then able to consider how this tendency may potentially affect their presence with directees. The expressive arts process opens with the reading of a haiku, followed by a meditation on the poem. Then participants are invited to draw with crayons using their non-dominant hand, and complete the experience by writing a short fairytale.

In contemplating the haiku (see next page), there are three roles or perspectives the participants will be asked to imagine: the child, the mother, or the cherry blossoms. This process allows the supervisee to become aware of the possibilities for different roles and to experience where their inner guide leads during the exercise.

When writing or drawing with our dominant hand we work out of a place of strength. Non-dominant hand work[105] invites us into an experience where we have less control of the outcome and therefore write or draw more intuitively. The practice also helps eliminate the pressure of creating a perfect product, focusing on the process and alleviating anxiety over end results.

Fairy tales, like other story traditions, are typically composed of three parts: beginning/middle/end. In the beginning there is a person with a problem, need, or desire. The middle contains a struggle, wrestling, or contemplation. The conclusion offers transformation and realization. Thus, a fairytale can be made up of as few as three sentences. When beginning with "Once upon a time," these stories have a natural tendency to fall into place and eliminate worries about story structure.

Materials Needed: Meditative music, crayons, drawing paper, pens, and journals.

Exercise: Begin with a brief overview of the structure and theme, an opening prayer, and a brief check-in from each participant. Then move into the art experience. Read the following haiku aloud to the group.

> A blind child
> Guided by his mother,
> Admires the cherry blossoms.
> —*Kikakou*

After introducing the haiku, continue the exercise using the following meditation.

> *Sitting comfortably, close your eyes and take a few deep, cleansing breaths. Settle into your body. By following your breath, begin to clear the clutter from your mind. Breathe.*
>
> *Now listen as I read Kikakou's haiku again. (Read the haiku again.)*
>
> *As you breathe slowly, I invite you to identify with and become the blind child admiring the blossoms he can't see. Continue breathing slowly and see the child in your mind's eye. What does the child look like? What is the expression on the child's face? What do you think he is feeling? (Pause. Allow some silence.)*
>
> *Slowly and gently, with your eyes still closed, listen to the poem again. This time as you listen, I invite you to identify with the mother—the loving other, guiding her blind child to a beauty they can share, but never experience the same way. (Read the haiku again.)*
>
> *Continue to connect with your breath and explore what it feels like to be the mother/guide, showing another the beauty of the cherry blossoms. How does she do it? With words? With gestures? How does she describe the colors? What does she look like? Anxious? Relaxed? Worried? Loving? (Pause. Allow some silence.)*
>
> *(Read the haiku one last time.) This time, become the cherry blossom. What is it like to be the blossom? Listen carefully to your inner voice and see what this evokes in you? Be still. Breathe. Be the cherry blossom. (Pause. Allow some silence.)*
>
> *Slowly and gently, when you are ready, let the imaginative experience fade and come back to the room. Softly open your eyes, but continue to stay in a meditative space.*
>
> *We are now going to move into another art form. While continuing to rest in silence, with your non-dominant hand, I invite you to use the crayons and draw-*

ing paper to create the essence of what you just experienced. Try not to focus on a "literal" depiction. Perhaps it was all color. Maybe a particular image came to mind. This is not expected to be a work of art. Remember this is about process, not product. As you begin, I will read the haiku one more time. (Recommended drawing time: ten minutes. Consider playing some meditative music softly.)

Upon completing your drawing, use this opportunity to write a response to your imaginative experience and drawing in the form of a fairy tale. Please write from the perspective of one of the roles: child, mother, or blossom.

Once upon a time, there was a cherry blossom . . .
Once upon a time, there was a blind child . . .
Once upon a time, there was a mother/guide . . .

Don't hold too tightly to structure. Fairy tales naturally fall into order. The only guideline is to begin with "Once upon a time" and follow your intuition in writing the story. (Recommended time: twenty minutes.)

After this exercise, offer a brief time of sharing for participants. Invite each member to reflect on his or her own experience with the group. You might open the discussion with questions: "What happened for you during the meditation, the drawing, and the writing of the fairy tale? What was the experience like? What was stirred? Did any one part have significantly more impact than another? What insights did you gain into your role as spiritual director?" Have participants consider if there was a quality, word or image that came to mind as they listened to the others. Invite them to share their drawings or fairy tales with the group if they would like to have them witnessed.

After each participant has had a chance to briefly share the experience, move into the formal supervision experience. Invite the first supervisee to share the experience she brings for supervision, paying attention to the ways the art process has deepened her understanding of her response to the supervision reflection questions several days prior. Allow several minutes for this exploration, giving space to honor the power of the arts to illuminate and deepen interior movements. As facilitators, offer reflections on what issues and feelings you noticed in the supervisee's sharing and on any questions that have been sparked for further exploration. Then open it up to the group members to offer their own insights. As facilitator, part of your role is to keep the sharing focused on the supervision process.

Reflection: One of the primary goals for an initial session is to build a sense of safety and trust among group members. Another goal is to offer an art exercise that is structured and accessible enough to be satisfying, even for participants with little experience engaging in forms of creative expression. Providing the experiences of drawing and writing will create a strong foundation for creative discovery and professional support in future sessions.

Finding Our Own Rhythm

Theme: This session explores the theme of rhythm. The focus is on building an awareness of how our rhythm or mood is affected by what is going on around us. The following exercise offers an opportunity for participants to keep their role as spiritual directors in mind and notice the times they are in rhythm with, or in disharmony from, the directee. Invite reflection on where the spiritual director tends to lead, follow, or co-create in the moment. A drum circle is a gentle and accessible art form which allows participants with little or no musical experience to engage meaningfully in an exploration of rhythm.

Materials Needed: A variety of percussion instruments such as hand drums, rattles, chimes, tambourines, and djembes. (If you do not have instruments, you can also use pots and pans, sticks, rocks, or other percussive objects.) Also have journals and pens on hand.

Exercise: Begin with an overview of the session and theme, an opening prayer, and some time for brief individual check-ins. Then invite the participants to the drum circle and gently remind them to keep their spiritual direction relationships in awareness throughout the exercise. Form a circle and take a few moments before beginning the drumming to invite the participants to become fully present to the moment and their internal experience. Ask them to place their hands over their hearts to connect to this primal rhythm before moving into drumming.

Round 1: Have participants drum with minimal instructions. Allow the experience to follow its own flow and come to a natural conclusion.

Take a few minutes to journal about the experience, reflecting on resistance, surrender, self-awareness, and group awareness.

Round 2: Let participants know you will be tapping them on the shoulder
at random and at that point they are to create dissonance. Drum again.
While participants are playing, tap individuals on the shoulder, instructing
them to start and stop with dissonant playing.

Journal following the experience: What is it like to have someone bring
you out of your rhythm? How quickly can you return to your beat?

Round 3: Drum again. Let the sound flow. Invite participants to consider
how to find their best rhythm to enhance the group.

Journal again taking note of what happened internally while playing.

One possibility for a next step, and a further example of communal
creativity, is to create a group poem. Invite each participant to select one
line from her journal writing which speaks of "harmony." Enter the lines
into the French Pantoum form and read the resulting poem together. (See
Chapter Nine.) One of our groups created the following Pantoum:

> Comfortable with silences
> I crave harmony
> Connecting enough while remaining distant
> Co-creating in the moment
>
> I crave harmony
> Delirious—Exhilarating—Boom Ba Da Bop
> Co-creating in the moment
> Harmony, it's totally boring
>
> Delirious—Exhilarating—Boom Ba Da Bop
> Connecting enough while remaining distant
> Harmony, it's totally boring
> Comfortable with silences.
> —*Supervision Group 3/19/2009*

Following the drumming and journaling, invite participants to share
a brief reflection on their experience. Then move into time for formal

supervision. Ask the first supervisee to share the experience he brings for supervision, paying attention to the ways the drumming has shifted and contributed to his understanding of how he responded to the supervision reflection questions several days prior. After this sharing, offer your own reflections to help break open the subject with him. Then open it up to the group members to offer their own insights.

Reflection: The pantoum poem above represents a lovely essence of spiritual direction's many rhythms. Group members may have a variety of responses to the rhythm exercise and this supervision process helps bring to mind our individual effect on others. Drumming can offer a potent metaphor for the experience of director with directee. This exercise can help to identify the limits of an individual director's personal levels of comfort, as well as each director's places of resistance and freedom.

Shadow and Light

Theme: Shadow and light are potent metaphors for our inner work and ministry with others. As spiritual directors, we may find our work with directees leaning in one direction or another (e.g. toward the light and away from darkness or conversely leaning into darkness and limiting focus on light). The focus of this supervision session is to move into greater balance, both personally, and in our role as spiritual directors. We employ the medium of photography to explore the interplay of shadow and light.

Materials Needed: Ask group members to bring a digital camera to supervision. (Please note, this exercise can be done as a contemplative walk without a camera.) Journal and pen are required.

Exercise: Begin the session with an opening prayer and a brief check-in from each participant. Then move into the expressive arts experience, reminding everyone to keep their roles as spiritual directors in focus.

Read the following excerpt on the role of shadow and light:

> When we stand in the light, we cast a shadow. Light and shade are to each other as breathing in is to breathing out. Some aspects of ourselves are in the light, visible to us and others. Other aspects, positive and neg-

ative, are in the shadow, unseen by us, even when seen by others. These are parts of ourselves that have been neglected, disowned, forgotten, judged, unrecognized or undeveloped.

Some of the ways we can glimpse what is in the psychological shade include noting what we idealize or denigrate in others; recognizing our uneasiness about others' perceptions about us (good and bad); and paying attention to our bodies, where shadow can sometimes reside as a physical symptom (an aching back, a pain in the stomach).

Our shadow is an infinite reservoir of energy. Learning to recognize and take responsibility for our shadow qualities gives us more choices in responding consciously and creatively to the possibilities life offers us.

> The shadow is anything we are sure we are not;
> it is part of us we do not know; sometimes do not want to know,
> most times do not want to know.
> We can hardly bear to look. Look.
> It may carry the best of the life we have not lived.
> —*Marion Woodman*[106]

Following the reading, prepare participants for their photographic journey as follows:

Close your eyes, and begin to center on your breath. Ponder both light and dark; image and shadow. You are invited to take a contemplative walk. As you walk, consider what you are drawn to: sizes, shapes, colors. Remember to consider how light and dark play into your views. Hold lightly image and shadow in relation to your compassionate listening relationships. Are there things you avoid? Take photos or use your imagination to capture images. Walk slowly. Breathe. Take in your surroundings holding the relationship of light and dark, image and shadow.

Invite participants to take a half hour for a contemplative walk with their cameras. When they return, move into a time of journaling with the following script as guide:

Close your eyes and center yourself again. Breathe.

Consider your walk. What were you drawn to? How did light and shadow influence your walk? Did you notice your own shadow? The shadow of trees? Buildings? Other things?

What about the light? How did it feel? Was it too bright? How did it interact with shadow?

Do you have opinions about darkness? About light? If so, have your opinions changed since this walk?

How did the quality of the light affect your photography? Did you need to make adjustments?

If you did take photos, review them for a few minutes and notice what feelings the images stir within you. (If participants did not bring cameras, invite them to call to mind specific images from their walk and notice what is stirred in response.)

Now consider your relationships with your directees or clients. Are you comfortable sitting with joy? With darkness? Do you rush to move from one to the other? Where are you drawn? Do you go toward the pain and darkness in sessions or push for light and clarity?

Can you rejoice with triumphs? Can you hold someone's dark place with them? Allow them to just be?

What have you discovered?

One of our supervision group participants describes her response to this experience:

One gentle morning, with camera and curiosity as companions, I set out in search of Shadow and Light. Drawn by the sound of children playing nearby, I noticed shadow in movement. A child leapt and her shadow leapt. A boy chased a ball and his shadow shape-shifted. A little one stood watching, and her shadow, twice her height, remained still. I began to wonder at the dynamic connection between Shadow and Light. I pondered my relationship with Shadow and Light within myself and within those whom I accompany.

> Shadow
> you draw me, as to hidden treasure.
> Sometimes afraid, I resist.
> Or run.
> Gently persistent, you wait.
> Longingly, fearfully,
> Watchful with hope

I ponder
Listening
Until you speak
Grace

Light
you invite me into delight!
Beauty. Abundance.
I stretch to embrace.
You penetrate, revealing more
Truths evoking grief.
Pain, loss
Too much to bear.
I flee into darkness
Hidden, I wait,
Until dawn breaks
Illuminating, healing
And I am
More
—*Maureen Fowler*

How do I engage Shadow/Light within myself? Within others? How do I allow my presence to the Shadow/Light in others lead me home to myself?

Close the art experience by asking each person to reflect on the insights from the photography and journaling. Invite participants to write a "Six-Word Memoir"[107] as a synopsis of their shadow and light journey. This is a very simple form that prompts us to consider the essence of an experience and articulate it in only six words. Similar to the structure of a haiku, the compactness and limitations of the form can encourage group members to focus their insights. Allow a few minutes for this experience and then invite sharing with the group. Here are two examples:

Pew, light, cross, shadow, opens, doors.
—*Paula McCutcheon*

Living in Paradox, Wholeness takes time.
—*Maureen Fowler*

Following the expressive arts experience allow a brief time for each group member to share any insights gleaned from the process. Then move into formal supervision and invite the supervisee to share the issues and concerns he brought for supervision, reminding him to keep in mind how this exercise has affected his awareness of the issues reflected on prior to the session.

Reflection: Playing with shadow and light through the lens of a camera (or their own awareness) gives participants the opportunity to consider the impact of shadow and light in their work with directees. The visual impact of photography helps to illuminate these issues in new ways.

One of our supervision group members offers a reflection here about the impact of working with the arts on her self-awareness as compassionate listener. Her process begins with our session on shadow and light and was developed further in the supervision session that followed, offering a window into the way themes from sessions can build on one another:

The client I chose to focus on in supervision was a man who had a very difficult childhood, and after being abandoned by both parents as a teenager, got in serious trouble with the law. Now, as a very driven successful businessman in his early thirties he is struggling to forgive himself for the things he did as a teenager and his parents for leaving him. I was frustrated that my efforts to help him see himself with compassion weren't succeeding.

Our first experience in supervision that day was a guided movement visualization where we reflected on previous groups and the moments of consolation we had received through the year . . . and then surprisingly, we were invited to reflect upon moments of desolation that had been part of our learning journey and think of them in terms of how we were blessed by them. As I allowed my body to move deeper into the meditation, an awareness of my client's struggles came to mind. I realized for the first time that my frustration about my own life and my unacknowledged childhood pain could become a gift to my clients in the form of greater compassion and my ability to see light in them and release my sense of judgment.

Later we did another exercise where we used improvisational singing. As I considered my own process as well as my client's, I realized what needed to happen was to welcome all of the parts of ourselves, even the parts of which

we are ashamed. I sang a playful whisper song to the group . . . "Welcome, welcome . . . all the parts of me . . . and welcome all of you!" I realized that I could
continue to welcome all of the shadow parts of my client as I continue to listen
to his frightening stories of prison life.

I began my supervisory sharing about my client with a prayer dance dedicated to him. I danced the sadness and anger that I felt because his parents
didn't nurture him appropriately, the compassion I felt for his feelings of bro-
kenness, my admiration for his courage to overcome his history, and my prayer
of blessing upon the desolation in his life that helped create his incredible ded-
ication to being an amazing father in spite of the extreme challenges of his childhood. My initial feelings of frustration and inadequacy were transformed into
compassion, and I experienced the truth that my presence could be a gift to
him without my having to "do" anything besides be really present to him with
an open heart. —*Sharie Bowman*

Additional Suggestions for Engaging the Arts in Supervision

Through collage-making, invite participants to explore the multiplicity of their inner selves in relation to their roles as spiritual directors.
(See Chapter Seven.) Exploring the ways their inner teachers, parents,
children, tricksters, and peace-makers (as examples) impact how they
are in relationship to their directees can be an illuminating process.

To focus even more deeply on aspects of their inner selves, invite participants into an exploration of their masculine and feminine energies.
Listening to music can be a powerful source of inspiration for a visual
art expression. First play a recording of the "Our Father" and then a
recording of the "Ave Maria."[108] After each song, invite participants into
a silent time of intuitive painting in response to their experience of the
music. Once both songs have been responded to visually, allow some
time for participants to gaze upon both paintings without judgment,
simply noticing the colors and images which have emerged, and engaging the images in dialogue with each other through journaling.

When you have come to the last session of a group process, it is important to have ways to bring closure to this shared experience. A simple

meditation is to lead participants in a modified version of the Examen prayer (see Chapter Eleven for an Examen with Movement). Begin the imaginative experience as a guided journey of remembering each of the sessions you have shared together. Then invite participants to reflect on what has been most life-giving in their experience of the group and what has been most life-draining or challenging. Follow with some time for journaling and sharing with one another. (See Chapter Fourteen for other suggestions for ways to bring closure to an experience.)

Conclusion

In this chapter we have offered some guidance in bringing the arts to a supervision context.

Art-centered supervision, like spiritual direction, requires a unique balance of being open to the Spirit and offering the arts as a container for listening. As supervisors, we create art experiences as a way of offering a safe space for participants to explore their inner process; at the same time we make room for the movements of the Spirit in our midst.

In other words, we tend to the "science" of supervision that Maureen Conroy refers to in the beginning of this chapter. When this is done successfully, space is created for new awareness to arise and opportunities to expand, resulting in spiritual directors who are healthier and better able to bring their directees to a place of depth and insight. We also tend to the "art" of supervision which allows enough freedom in the structure for openness to the movement of the Spirit and the spontaneous and surprising ways God can work with participants and facilitators alike.

Conclusion

Beauty will save the world.
—FYODOR DOSTOEVSKY

We've made it this far. Thanks for journeying with us through a land of plenty:

imagination and images,
songs and stories,
seasons and supervisions,
paints and processes,
dancing, dreams, and discernments.

We must admit, after this labor of love, we are energized and exhausted all at once! Such is the exhilaration from a creative project brought to birth. As is a custom in spiritual direction, we invite you to reflect with us a bit on the landscape we have traversed together.

There is a lot packed into these pages, and no one in his or her right mind would try to do it all. However, our hope is that you have been inspired to expand the possibilities of your own soul care ministry to include a bit of adventure, discovery, and creative spirit. We remind you, dear reader, as we remind ourselves, that in the hallowed space of spiritual direction, the art forms presented here are never meant to be employed as tricks or gimmicks. The purpose of the expressive arts process is not to

213

manufacture art. Rather, within the journey of spiritual direction, it is to discover our souls, discover the face of the Holy One, the Utterly Other residing within the sacred depths of our own humanity. Our intention throughout these pages has been to provide tools for you to allow the Creative Spirit to be awakened in you, and, by your outreach and invitation, in many others as well.

After reading these pages we hope you find yourself newly inspired to explore the arts in your own life and practice of spiritual direction. If you are completely new to any art form and the book feels a bit overwhelming, we suggest you notice where your curiosity is most alive; choose that chapter and begin experimenting with "Simple Ways to Engage the Arts." You may soon find yourself making more and more space for this expression in your life and ministry. As you grow in comfort, choose other modalities to explore and integrate over time. Additionally, our Resource Section offers a number of recommended books and music to encourage further steps on this journey.

Engaging the arts in community is a wonderful support for an ongoing commitment to artistry and integration. Consider inviting some fellow pilgrims to experiment with you regularly, exploring the arts for prayer and self-discovery, rotating leadership, and offering feedback to each other. We also recommend participating in workshops and classes when possible. Observing experienced facilitators at work is another doorway into developing your own craft and skill at making space for creativity and inviting others into the arts. Also, feel free to explore Awakening the Creative Spirit in its retreat format. We have been so delighted to connect with a growing community of creative souls who are exploring the arts in spiritual direction. We would love to get to know you in person and marvel at your own unique calling. Playing, praying, awakening, and creating together provide wonderful inspirations for us all—facilitators and participants alike.

We have invited you into a discovery of the arts, and explored a multitude of ways to embrace the arts as language of the soul. Before sending you off on your journey, we'd like to raise one more awareness of the unique position we find ourselves in as spiritual directors. We live in a commercialized culture where clearly not all images, songs, dances or stories bring us closer to the Divine. We are often bombarded by media expressions that promote over-consumption, objectification, or exploitation. As spiritual directors perhaps we can widen our calling to support our culture in reclaiming and re-centering the power of the arts as a doorway to the deep soul of our shared humanity. In our commitment and practice, we can constantly call ourselves and our directees back to the Spirit who awakens us, not only to our own creative journeys, but also to the innate belief that all on this earth are entitled to creative freedom; that none of us is alone in our creative struggle; and that even in the midst of struggle, art can be the gateway that sets us free.

Recall the story of the *Titanic:* As the ship was sinking, the band members offered their last life moments as a musical prayer, "Nearer my God to Thee." Following a mortar attack on a street in Sarajevo, which killed and maimed many, a local cellist played Albinoni's "Adagio in G Minor" at the site for the next twenty-two days in honor of the dead.[109] Likewise, music director Dr. Karl Paulnack recounts stories of how music and art have risen up in the most desperate of places—in the streets of Manhattan after September 11, as people lifted their voices in song, and even in concentration camps, where composer Olivier Messiaen was imprisoned and created one of the most profound musical compositions of all time, "Quartet for the End of Time." As Paulnack expresses it, "Art is one of the ways we say, 'I am alive and my life has meaning.'"[110]

In the midst of writing this book, I (Betsey) had my own reminders of the power of art to provide meaning and deep soul connection in the midst of life challenges. For a summer break, I had the occasion to visit my family and help out in caring for my memory-impaired ninety-three-year-old father. Dad doesn't smile much these days. Dad, of the gracious, unconditionally loving heart, can hardly crack a smile when his "Charming Princess" comes home. It breaks my heart. Until we find art.

After dinner, gathered with many of his grandchildren, we sing. He can't remember any of their names, but we sing, and all the words come pouring out: "Shine on Harvest Moon," "Oh Susannah," and "I've Been Working on the Railroad." Music buoyantly bridges the gaps in his mind. The next day, after an afternoon nap, we find poetry. All the poems he used to read to me jump off the pages of his beloved poetry book: "The Raven," "Stopping by Woods on a Snowy Evening," "Crossing the Bar." We are caught up together in sounds, rhythms, and images that have echoed in us since he read to me as a child. A few days later, when he asks me about my work, I hop up and begin dancing and describing my latest project, a performance of Mary Magdalene's story. She is crying at the tomb, crying for her beloved. (Now my dad is crying . . .) And then she sees the gardener. He is risen. He is risen! I am clamoring around the porch proclaiming good news. The scripture comes alive in our midst and we are laughing. We are laughing!

Indeed this experience remined me again that the arts connect us to our hearts, to each other, and to the power of Spirit. The arts are for life and spiritual direction is a deepening embrace of this abundant life.

So as we near the end of our book, we offer you one more story. This one takes us beyond the comfort zones of our offices and studios to the land behind bars. One of our colleagues and program participants shares her work with spirituality and the arts in jail. She reminds us that the art of creative prayer can help to free our spirits, no matter where we are.

◎ *Lectio Divina* and the Arts: Arts Behind Bars

As a jail chaplain, I see the transforming power of integrating the arts and imagination into spirituality on a daily basis. Far too often incarcerated individuals are lost in addiction, many of them navigating mental health challenges as well. In the long, bleak days of uncertainty, an opening for those incarcerated to reflect upon and discern their spirituality frequently arises. The invitation of jail chaplaincy becomes one of deep listening, attending to the holy in the hollows of concrete and lock down, anxiety and regret. In the midst of these constraints, I have found that weaving the arts of meditation, active imagination, dreamwork, and poetry into my one-with-one visits provides profound openings to honesty, healing, and hope.

In group settings, I find that music, drama, art, and meditation also serve as modalities through which the Holy Spirit finds expression. One of my favorite ways of integrating the arts into my group work is to use a modified form of *lectio divina*. (See Chapter Five.) With the first two readings, I inquire: what word, phrase, feeling or image arises? In the third reading I invite a staging or acting out the text. In the fourth reading, participants draw while listening to music. Spontaneous sharing arises as the symbols and feelings that have emerged are reflected upon, often unleashing tears of renewal and the awe of God's grace.

On an ongoing basis I am humbled and honored to witness the transforming wonder of the Holy Spirit, alive and active in the confines of the jail, continually inviting individuals to rebirth and to a deepening of their relationship with our Creator. What more wondrous way than through the creative process? *—Contributed by Ann Keller*

As we conclude our journey, we share a vision. We pray that the Creative Spirit be awakened in you through artistry, through spiritual direction, through life. We pray that this abundant Creative Spirit be free to reach out to all those you meet: your family, your friends, your directees, your communities, those in need, in prisons, churches, streets, and villages around the globe. We pray that in your shared awakenings, you are set free. We pray that one day, all shall be free.

Contributors

Several of our spiritual direction colleagues contributed exercises for inclusion in this book.

Sharie Bowman is the InterPlay Seattle regional coordinator, an Inter-Play/SpiritPlay leader and Life Practice Program teacher. She is also a mental health counselor who includes spirituality and expressive arts in her work with couples, individuals, and groups (www.InterPlay.org/Seattle).

Jane Comerford, CSJ is a spiritual director, retreat facilitator, pilgrimage designer, and adult educator in the field of spirituality. With an MA in Christian Spirituality, and a certificate in expressive art therapy she incorporates the expressive arts into most of her work. She is recognized for her innovative and imaginative programs and currently resides in Tucson, Arizona.

Trish Bruxvoort Colligan fancies a life rich with story, ritual, poetry, and beauty. A touring retreat leader/musician, her music is celebrated in diverse spiritual circles. She lives and frolics in Iowa alongside her beloved human and animal family (www.spirations.com and www.riversvoice.com).

Roy DeLeon, Oblate of St Benedict and spiritual director, teaches Blessed Movements, or praying with our whole beings. He authored *Praying with the Body: Bringing the Psalms to Life* (www.blessedmovements.com).

Carol Flake, PhD is a dreamworker, an anam cara, a photographer, a potter, and a retired professor. She holds a doctorate in human growth and development and a masters in religion and culture. Carol lives in Brevard, NC.

Marianne Hieb, RSM, D. Min directs the Wellness Spirituality Program at Lourdes Wellness Center. As artist, art-therapist and spiritual director, she utilizes Art-Journaling® in her retreat and creativity ministry.

Mary Lou Weaver Houser is a certified spiritual director, gardener, artist, teacher, parent of two adult children, and a grandmother. She and her husband Rod operate Herrbrook Farm Retreat, a facility for personal or small group spiritual renewal (www.herrbrook.com).

Kayce Stevens Hughlett, MA, LMHC maintains a private practice in Seattle, offering psychotherapy, spiritual discernment and exploration of the creative process as a tool for authentic living (www.diamondsinthesoul.com).

Ann Keller, MA is the Director of Catholic Detention Ministry at the King County Jail in Seattle, WA. Her ministry, based in compassionate listening, encompasses storytelling, art, meditation, dream work, and drama.

Pam McCauley works as a program coordinator at the Palisades Catholic Retreat Center in Federal Way, Washington. She is a fledgling poet and a joyful mother of five.

Debra McMaster is a spiritual director in Clearwater, Florida. She is a graduate of the Shalem Institute for Spiritual Formation and is a certified labyrinth facilitator.

Diana McKendree's passion for dream and image has led her to become a Jungian psychotherapist, international speaker, leader of women's pilgrimages, iconographer, and artist. An ordained interfaith minister, she is a senior faculty member of the Haden Institute, NC.

Sally O'Neil, RN, PhD is Clinical Professor of Nursing, University of Washington School of Nursing. She is a semi-retired counselor and spiritual director and author of *Spirit Called My Name*. She is also co-author of *And Then I Met This Woman* and *Pilgrimage of the Soul*.

Rachelle Oppenhuizen is an artist and spiritual director who lives in Holland, Michigan. She welcomes directees into her studio for their own exploration of inner work through the creative arts.

Eunice Schroeder, D. Min of Vancouver, WA, is a *Veriditas* Certified Labyrinth Facilitator, as well as a spiritual director in Vancouver and at the Interfaith Spiritual Center in Portland, OR (www.SacredJourneyMinistries.com).

April Sotura is a vocal coach and presentation consultant. She weaves her passion for vocally empowering individuals with her proficiency as teacher, artist, and yogini (www.VoicingSelf.com).

Maggie Yowell of Spirit Heart Journeys is a spiritual director who companions people as they tell their stories, process life transitions, and explore expressive arts and the spiritual life journey (www.spiritheartjourneys.com).

Jennifer Steil has a passion to use the creative process in the context of spiritual direction to help people grow spiritually by listening for God in their lives through their natural creativity. She weaves together the disciplines of prayer, scripture reading, meditation, contemplation and dreamwork, with various creative mediums.

Resource Section

Expressive Arts

Appalachian Expressive Arts Collective. *Expressive Arts Therapy: Creative Process in Art and Life.* Boone, NC: Parkway Publishers, 2002.

Diaz, Adriana. *Freeing the Creative Spirit: Drawing on the Power of Art to Tap the Magic and Wisdom Within.* New York: HarperSanFrancisco, 1992.

Farrelly-Hansen, Mimi, ed. *Spirituality and Art Therapy.* London: Jessica Kingsley Publishers, 2001.

Horovitz, Ellen. *Spiritual Art Therapy: An Alternate Path.* Springfield, IL: Charles C. Thomas Publisher, 2002.

Knill, Paolo, Ellen Levine, and Stephen Levine. *Principles and Practices of Expressive Arts Therapy.* Philadelphia, PA: Jessica Kingsley Publishers, 2005.

Levine, Stephen K. *Poiesis: The Language of Psychology and the Speech of the Soul.* London: Jessica Kingsley Publishers, 1997.

Levine, Stephen K. and Ellen G., eds. *Foundations of Expressive Arts Therapy.* Philadelphia, PA: Jessica Kingsley Publishers, 1999.

Malchiodi, Cathy A. *The Art Therapy Sourcebook.* Los Angeles, CA: Lowell House, 1998.

McNiff, Shaun. *Art as Medicine: Creating a Therapy of the Imagination.* Boston: Shambhala, 1992.

————. *Trust the Process: An Artist's Guide to Letting Go.* Boston: Shambhala, 1998.

Mellick, Jill. *The Art of Dreaming: Tools for Creative Dreamwork.* Berkeley, CA: Conari Press, 2001.

Rogers, J. Earl., ed. *The Art of Grief: The Use of Expressive Arts in a Grief Support Group.*
New York, NY: Routledge, 2007.

Rogers, Natalie. *The Creative Connection: Expressive Arts as Healing.* Palo Alto, CA: Science and Behavior Books, 1993.

Silverstone, Liesl. *Art Therapy: The Person-Centered Way.* Philadelphia, PA: Jessica Kingsley Publishers, 1997.

Creativity

Allen, Pat B. *Art as a Way of Knowing: A Guide to Self-Knowledge and Spiritual Fulfillment Through Creativity.* Boston: Shambhala, 1995.

———. *Art Is a Spiritual Path: Engaging the Sacred Through the Practice of Art and Writing.* Boston: Shambhala, 2005.

Arrien, Angeles. *The Four-Fold Way: Walking the Paths of the Warrior, Teacher, Healer and Visionary.* San Francisco: HarperCollins Publishers, 1993.

Azara, Nancy. *Spirit Taking Form: Making a Spiritual Practice of Making Art.* York Beach. ME: Red Wheel/Weiser, 2002.

Coffey, Kathy. *The Art of Faith.* New London, CT: Twenty-Third Publications, 2007.

Coleman, Earle J. *Creativity and Spirituality: Bonds between Art and Religion.* State University of New York Press, 1998.

Coupar, Regina. *The Art of Soul: An Artist's Guide to Spirituality.* Ottawa, Canada: St. Paul University Novalis Press, 2002.

Estés, Clarissa Pinkola. *The Creative Fire: Myths and Stories on the Cycles of Creativity.* Sounds True, 1991. CD.

Fox, Matthew. *Creativity: Where the Divine and Human Meet.* New York: Penguin Group, Inc., 2004.

London, Peter. *No More Secondhand Art: Awakening the Artist Within.* Boston: Shambhala, 1989.

Loori, John Daido. *Zen of Creativity: Cultivating Your Artistic Life.* New York: Ballantine Books, 2005.

Malchiodi, Cathy. *The Soul's Palette: Drawing on Art's Transformative Powers for Health and Well-Being.* Boston: Shambhala, 2002.

Nachmanovitch, Stephen. *Free Play: Improvisation in Life and Art.* Jeremy P, Tarcher, 1991.

Tharp, Twyla. *The Creative Habit: Learn it and Use it for Life.* New York: Simon & Schuster, 2003.

Trungpa, Chogyam. *True Perception: The Path of Dharma Art.* Boston: Shambhala Press, 2008.

Warner, Sally. *Making Room for Making Art: A Thoughtful Guide to Bringing the Pleasure of Artistic Expression Back Into Your Life*. Chicago, IL: Chicago Review Press, 1994.

Wuthnow, Robert. *Creative Spirituality: The Way of the Artist*. Berkeley: University of California Press, 2001.

Storytelling and Drama

Baldwin, Christina. *Storycatcher: Making Sense of Our Lives through the Power and Practice of Story*. Novato, CA: New World Library, 2005.

Beckman, Betsey. *The Dancing Word: Mary Magdalene*. Vision Video, 2010. DVD.

———. *The Dancing Word: Miriam and Mary*. Vision Video, 2000. DVD.

Gersie, Alida. *Storymaking in Bereavement: Dragons Fight in the Meadow*. London: Jessica Kingsley Publishers, 2000.

Krondorfer, Bjorn. *Body and Bible: Interpreting and Experiencing Biblical Narratives*. Philadelphia, PA: Trinity Press International, 1992.

Lipman, Doug. *Improving Your Storytelling: Beyond the Basics for all Who Tell Stories in Work or Play*. Atlanta: August House, Inc., 1999.

Maguire, Jack. *The Power of Personal Storytelling: Spinning Tales to Connect with Others*. New York: Putnam, 1998.

McKenna, Megan and Tony Cowan, *Keepers of the Story: Oral Traditions in Religion*. Maryknoll, NY: Orbis, 1997.

Mellon, Nancy. *Storytelling and the Art of Imagination*. Cambridge, MA: Yellow Moon Press, 2003.

——— and Ashley Ramsden. *Body Eloquence: The Power of Myth and Story to Awaken the Body's Energies*. Fulton, CA: Energy Psychology Press, 2008.

Pitzele, Peter. *Scripture Window: Toward a Practice of Bibliodrama*. Los Angeles, CA: Alef Design Group, 1997.

Rooks, Diane. *Spinning Gold Out of Straw: How Stories Heal*. Gainesville, GA: Salt Run Press, 2001.

Salas, Jo. *Improvising in Real Life: Personal Story in Playback Theater*. New Paltz, NY: Tusitala Publishing, 2007.

Sawyer, Ruth. *The Way of the Storyteller*. New York: Penguin Books, 1990.

Shea, John. *An Experience of Spirit: Spirituality and Storytelling*. Missouri: Liguori Publications, 2004.

Stone, Richard. *The Healing Art of Storytelling: A Sacred Journey of Personal Discovery*. Hyperion, 1996.

Contemplation and Imagination

Bohler, Carolyn Stahl. *Opening to God: Guided Imagery Meditation on Scripture.* Nashville, TN: Upper Room Books, 1996.

Fischer, Kathleen. *The Inner Rainbow: Imagination in Christian Life.* New York: Paulist Press, 1983.

Levine, Stephen. *Guided Meditations, Explorations and Healings.* New York: Doubleday, 1991.

———. *Unattended Sorrow: Recovering from Loss and Reviving the Heart.* Emmaus, PA: Rodale Publishing, 2005.

Linn, Dennis; Matthew Linn and Sheila Fabricant. *Praying With Another for Healing.* Mahwah, NJ: Paulist Press, 1984.

Paintner, Christine Valters and Lucy Wynkoop, OSB, *Lectio Divina: Contemplative Awakening and Awareness.* Mahwah, NJ: Paulist Press, 2008.

Samuels, Michael, MD. *Healing with the Mind's Eye: How to Use Guided Imagery and Visions to Heal Body, Mind, and Spirit.* Hoboken, NJ: John Wiley & Sons, 2003.

Schwartz, Andrew E. *Guided Imagery for Groups: Fifty Visualizations That Promote Relaxation, Problem-Solving, Creativity, and Well-Being.* Duluth, MN: Whole Person Associates, Inc., 1995

Vanek, Elizabeth-Anne. *Image Guidance: A Tool for Spiritual Direction.* Mahwah, NJ: Paulist Press, 1992.

Movement

Beckman, Betsey, Nina O'Connor and J. Michael Sparough, S.J. *A Retreat with Our Lady, Dominic and Ignatius: Praying with Our Bodies.* Cincinnati, OH: St. Anthony Messenger Press, 1997.

Chodorow, Joan. *Dance Therapy & Depth Psychology: The Moving Imagination.* London, Routledge, 2008.

DeLeon, Roy. *Praying with the Body: Bringing the Psalms to Life.* Boston: Paraclete Press, 2009.

DeSola, Carla. *Danceprayer.* Paulist Press. Video.

———. *The Spirit Moves: Handbook of Dance and Prayer.* Washington, D.C.: The Liturgical Conference, 1977.

——— and Thomas Kane. *Movement Meditations to the Songs of Taize.* Paulist Press. Video.

Halprin, Daria. *The Expressive Body in Life, Art, and Therapy.* Philadelphia, PA: Jessica Kingsley Publishers, 2003.

Levy, Fran. *Dance and Other Expressive Art Therapies: When Words Are Not Enough.* New York: Routledge, 1995.

Pallaro, Patrizia, ed. *Authentic Movement, Essays by Mary Starks Whitehouse, Janet Adler and Joan Chodorow*. London: Jessica Kinsley Publishers, 2000.

Phillips, Jan. *Divining the Body: Reclaim the Holiness of Your Physical Self*. Woodstock, VT: Skylight Paths Publishing, 2005.

Porter, Phil and Cynthia Winton-Henry. *Having It All: Body, Mind, Heart and Spirit Together Again at Last*. Oakland, CA: Wing It! Press, 1997.

Roth, Gabrielle. *Maps to Ecstasy: Teachings of an Urban Shaman*. San Rafael, CA: New World Library, 1989.

Roth, Nancy. *Spiritual Exercises: Joining Body and Spirit in Prayer*. New York: Seabury Books, 2005.

————. *An Invitation to Christian Yoga*. New York: Seabury Books, 2005.

Snowber, Celeste. *Embodied Prayer: Towards Wholeness of Body, Mind and Soul*. Kelowna, B.C., Canada: Northstone Publishing, Inc., 2004.

Stewart, Iris J. *Sacred Woman, Sacred Dance: Awakening Spirituality through Movement and Ritual*. Rochester, VT: Inner Traditions International, 2000.

Sweeney, Jon M. *Praying with Our Hands: 21 Practices of Embodied Prayer from the World's Spiritual Traditions*. Woodstock, VT: Skylight Path Publishing, 2002.

Tucker, JoAnne and Susan Freeman. *Torah in Motion*. Denver: A.R.E. Publishing, Inc. 1990.

Venard, Jane E. *Praying With Body and Soul: A Way to Intimacy with God*. Minneapolis, MN: Augsburg Fortress Publishers, 1998.

Winton-Henry, Cynthia. *Dance—the Sacred Art: The Joy of Movement as a Spiritual Practice*. Woodstock, VT: Skylight Paths Publishing, 2009.

———— with Phil Porter. *What the Body Wants*. Kelowna, B.C., Canada: Northstone, 2004.

Wuellner, Flora Slosson. *Prayer and Our Bodies*. Nashville, TN: Upper Room Books, 1987.

Young, Andi. *The Sacred Art of Bowing: Preparing to Practice*. Woodstock, VT: Skylight Paths Publishing, 2003.

Visual Arts

Bankson, Marjory Zoet. *The Soulwork of Clay: A Hands-On Approach to Spirituality*. Woodstock, VT: Skylights Paths Publishing, 2008.

Biggs, Emma. *Encyclopedia of Mosaic Techniques*. Philadelphia, PA: Running Press, 1996.

Cappachione, Lucia. *The Creative Journal*. North Hollywood: Newcastle Publishing Co., 1989.

Cassou, Michelle and Stewart Cubley. *Life, Paint, and Passion: Reclaiming the Magic of Spontaneous Expression*. New York: Jeremy P. Tarcher, 1995.

Ching, Elise Dirlam and Caleo Ching. *Faces of Your Soul: Rituals in Art, Maskmaking, and Guided Imagery with Ancestors, Spirit Guides, and Totem Animals.* Berkeley, CA: North Atlantic Books, 2006.

Fincher, Susanne. *Creating Mandalas: For Insight, Healing, and Self-Expression.* Boston: Shambhala, 1991.

Frost, Seena. *SoulCollage: An Intuitive Collage Process for Individuals and Groups.* Hanford Mead Publishers, 2001.

Ganim, Barbara and Susan Fox. *Visual Journaling: Going Deeper Than Words.* Wheaton, IL: Theosophical Publishing House, 1999.

Hieb, Marianne. *Inner Journeying Through Art Journaling: Learning to See and Record Your Life as a Work of Art.* London: Jessica Kingsley Publishers, 2005.

Koff-Chapin, Deborah. SoulCards 1 and 2 available at www.touchdrawing.com.

London, Peter. *Drawing Closer to Nature: Making Art in Dialogue with the Natural World.* Boston: Shambhala, 2003.

MacBeth, Sybil. *Praying in Color: Drawing a New Path to God.* Boston: Paraclete Press, 2007.

Owen, Carol. *Crafting Personal Shrines.* Lark Books, 2004.

Pearson, Paul. *A Brush With God: An Icon Workbook.* Harrisburg, PA: Morehouse, 2005.

Phillips, Jan. *God is at Eye Level: Photography as a Healing Art.* Wheaton, IL: Theosophical Publishing House, 2000.

Music and Voice

Bourgeault, Cynthia. *Singing the Psalms: How to Chant in the Christian Contemplative Tradition.* Boston, MA: Shambhala Publications, Inc., 2006. Book and CD.

Goodchild, Chloë. *Your Naked Voice: Sounding from the Source.* Sounds True, 2007. Instructional AudioBook / CD.

Hale, Susan Elizabeth. *Sacred Space, Sacred Sound: The Acoustic Mysteries of Holy Places.* Wheaton, IL: Quest Books, 2007.

Hernández, Ana. *The Sacred Art of Chant: Preparing to Practice.* Woodstock, VT: Skylight Paths Publishing, 2005.

Redmond, Layne. *When the Drummers Were Women: A Spiritual History of Rhythm.* New York: Three Rivers Press, 1997.

Mathieu, W. A. *The Musical Life: Reflections on What It Is and How to Live It.* Boston & London: Shambhala, 1994.

Newham, Paul. *The Healing Voice: How to use the Power of Your Voice to Bring Harmony into Your Life.* Boston: Element Books, Inc., 1999.

———. *Therapeutic Voicework: Principles and Practice for the Use of Singing as a Therapy.* London: Jessica Kingsley Publishers, 1998.

Sloan, Carolyn. *Finding Your Voice: A Practical and Spiritual Approach to Singing and Living.* New York: Hyperion, 1999.

Kalani. *Together in Rhythm: A Facilitator's Guide to Drum Circle Music.* Van Nuys, CA: Alfred Publishing Co, Inc., 2004.

Linn, Dennis, Sheila Fabricant Linn, and Matthew Linn. *What is My Song?* Mahwah, NJ: Paulist Press, 2005.

Audio Recordings

Ackerman, Will. *Pure Will Ackerman.* Windham Hill, 2006.

Berezan, Jennifer. *Returning.* Edge of Wonder, 2001.

Bommarito, Charlie. *Edge of Silence.* Bright Room Productions, 2005. (www.cdbaby.com)

Ciani, Suzanne. *Pianissimo II.* Musica International, 1996.

Colligan, Trish Bruxvoort. *Showings.* River's Voice (www.riversvoice.com).

———— and Richard Bruxvoort Colligan. *Unfolding.* River's Voice (www.riversvoice.com).

Darling, David. *Eight String Religion.* Wind Over the Earth, 2001.

Horn, Paul and R. Carlos Nakai. *Inside Canyon de Chelly.* Canyon Records Productions, 1997.

Koff-Chapin, Deborah and Anahata Moore. *Voices from the Deep.* SIGO Press, 1995.

Manose, Suskera. *Solo Bamboo Flute.* Garuda, 2002.

Nakai, R. Carlos, William Eaton and Will Clipman. *Feather, Stone and Light.* Canyon Records Productions, 1995.

Prayer for Peace. Various Artists. Silver Wave Records, 2000.

Redmond, Layne. *Chanting the Chakras: The Roots of Awakening.* Sounds True, 2001.

Roth, Gabrielle and the Mirrors. *Initiations.* Raven Recordings, 1984.

Tingstad, Eric, Nancy Rumbel and David Lanz. *Woodlands.* Narada Productions, Inc., 1987.

Watts, Trisha. *Deep Waters.* Willow Connection, PTY LTD, 1992.

Yanover, Gretchen. *Bow and Cello.* Gretchen Yanover, 2005.

Poetry

Barrows, Anita and Joanna Marie Macy, trans. *Rilke's Book of Hours: Love Poems to God.* New York: Riverhead Trade, 2005.

Bly, Robert, ed. *News of the Universe: Poems of Twofold Consciousness.* San Francisco: Sierra Club Books, 1995.

————. *The Soul is Here for its Own Joy: Sacred Poems from Many Cultures.* New York: Ecco, 1999.

————. *The Winged Energy of Delight: Poems from Europe, Asia, and the Americas.* New York: Harper Perennial, 2005.

————, James Hillman, and Michael Meade, eds. *The Rag and Bone Shop of the Heart: A Poetry Anthology.* New York: Harper Perennial, 1993.

Fideler, David and Sabrineh Fideler, trans. *Love's Alchemy: Poems from the Sufi Tradition.* Novato, CA: New World Library, 2006.

Gibson, Barbara. *Psalms for Troubled Times: Prayers of Hope and Challenge.* Olympia, WA: Crestline Press, 2003.

Hirshfield, Jane. *Nine Gates: Entering the Mind of Poetry.* New York: Harper Perennial, 1998.

Fox, John. *Finding What You Didn't Lose: Expressing Your Truth and Creativity Through Poem-Making.* New York: Jeremy P. Tarcher/Putnam, 1995.

Fox, John. *Poetic Medicine: The Healing Art of Poem-Making.* New York: Jeremy P. Tarcher/Putnam, 1997.

Ladinsky, Daniel, trans. *The Gift: Poems by Hafiz.* New York, Penguin, 1999.

————. *Love Poems From God: Twelve Sacred Voices from the East and West.* New York: Penguin, 2002.

Levertov, Denise. *The Stream and the Sapphire: Selected Poems on Religious Themes.* New York: New Directions, 1997.

McDowell, Robert. *Poetry as Spiritual Practice: Reading, Writing, and Using Poetry in Your Daily Rituals, Aspirations, and Intentions.* Free Press, 2008.

McGee, Margaret. *Haiku—The Sacred Art: A Spiritual Practice in Three Lines.* Woodstock, VT: Skylight Paths Publishing, 2009.

McGinnis, Ray. *Writing the Sacred: A Psalm-Inspired Path to Writing Sacred Poetry.* Kelowna, BC: Northstone, 2005.

Milosz, Czeslaw, ed. *A Book of Luminous Things: An International Anthology of Poetry.* Orlando, FL: Harvest Books, 1996.

O'Donohue, John. *To Bless the Space Between Us: A Book of Blessings.* New York: Doubleday, 2007.

Oliver, Mary. *New and Selected Poems: Volume One.* Boston: Beacon Press, 1992.

————. *New and Selected Poems: Volume Two.* Boston: Beacon Press, 2007.

Paintner, Christine Valters. *Sacred Poetry: An Invitation to Write.* Seattle, WA: Abbey of the Arts Press, 2009.

Roberts, Elizabeth and Elias Amidon, eds. *Life Prayers from Around the World.* New York: HarperOne, 1996.

Sewell, Marilyn, ed. *Claiming the Spirit Within: A Sourcebook of Women's Poetry.* Boston: Beacon Press, 2001.

————. *Cries of the Spirit.* Boston: Beacon Press, 2000.

Whyte, David. *River Flow: New and Selected Poems 1984–2007.* Langley, WA: Many Rivers Press, 2007.

Ritual

Bishops Committee on Liturgy. *Catholic Household Blessings and Prayers*. Washington,
  D.C.: United States Conference of Catholic Bishops, Inc., 1989, 2001.
Jensen, Jane Richardson and Patricia Harris-Watkins. *She Who Prays: A Woman's Inter-
  faith Prayer Book*. Harrisburg, PA: Morehouse Publishing, 2005.
Nelson, Gertrud Mueller. *To Dance with God: Family Ritual and Community Celebration*.
  Mahwah, NJ: Paulist Press, 1986.
Rupp, Joyce and Macrina Wiederkehr. *The Circle of Life: The Heart's Journey Through the
  Seasons*. Notre Dame, IN: Sorin Books, 2005.
Stein, Diane, ed. *The Goddess Celebrates: An Anthology of Women's Rituals*. Freedom, CA:
  The Crossing Press, 1991.

Recommended Websites

Abbey of the Arts (Christine Valters Paintner)—www.AbbeyoftheArts.com
Bibliodrama—www.bibliodrama.com
Bridge Building—www.bridgebuilding.com.
Free Song available from Trish Bruxvoort-Colligan at www.MusicForSpiritual
  Direction.com
Gabrielle Roth—The Five Rhythms—www.gabrielleroth.com
International Express Arts Therapy Association—www.ieata.org
InterPlay—www.interplay.org
Sacred Dance Guild—www.sacreddanceguild.org
SoulCollage—www.soulcollage.com
The Dancing Word (Betsey Beckman)—www.thedancingword.com
Touch Drawing—www.touchdrawing.com

Selected *Presence* Articles on Spiritual Direction and the Arts

Bough, Richard F. "Using the Creative Spirit in Spiritual Direction: A Personal
  Guide for Spiritual Directors." *Presence*, 12.3: 21–25.
Bryant, Cullene. "Creative Writing as a Way of Prayer." *Presence*, 10.2: 46–49.
Dean, Martin. "Imagination: A Route for the Journey." *Presence*, 5.3: 18–24.
Eibner, Ralph. "Gregory Palamas: The Body in Prayer and Spiritual Transforma-
  tion." *Presence*, 11.4:23–31.
Groff, Kent. "Using Howard Gardner's Multiple Intelligences in Spiritual Direc-
  tion." *Presence*, 4.2: 17–24.

Hieb, Marianne. "Art Journaling, Icon-Space, and Spiritual Direction." *Presence*, 2.2:19–28.

Mueller, Craig. "Dreams and Spiritual Direction." *Presence*, 4.3: 15–23.

Patterson, Rev. Deborah. "Poetry and Spiritual Direction" *Presence*, 10.1: 33–38.

Rankin, Terry. "Audio Divina: Introducing a Musical Aid for Spiritual Direction." *Presence*, 15.2: 37–42.

Roberts, Patricia. "The Dance of Life: *Lectio Divina*, Centering Prayer and Tai Ji." *Presence*, 11.3: 19–25.

Robertson, David, "The Art of Spiritual Direction as Improvisation." *Presence*, 13.2: 6–13.

Schank, Anne. "Spontaneous Images: Charms for Spiritual Growth." *Presence*, 7.2: 22–27.

Steinhauser, Jane. "Artprayer: a Dance with the Holy." *Presence*, 5.3: 8–20.

Notes

1. www.AbbeyoftheArts.com

2. www.thedancingword.com

3. Christine first heard the term "one-with-one" spiritual direction (as opposed to "one-on-one") from Willy Hernandez, a spiritual direction colleague in Southern California.

4. William Wordsworth, "Ode on Intimations of Immortality from Recollections of Early Childhood," in *The Norton Anthology of Poetry, Revised* (New York: W. W. Norton and Company, Inc., 1970), 601–605.

5. Claudine Roland, *Prehistory*, trans. Ann MacDonald-Plénacoste and Barbara Jachowicz-Davoust (Vic-en-Bigorre, France: MSM Publishing Service, 2006), 21.

6. Ellen Dissanayake, *Art and Intimacy: How the Arts Began* (Seattle & London: University of Washington Press, 2000), 7.

7. John O'Donohue, "Beauty is God," Recorded Workshop at Los Angeles Religious Education Congress, 2004 (Simi Valley, CA: CSC Digital Media, 2004).

8. Jill Bolte Taylor, *My Stroke of Insight: A Brain Scientist's Personal Journey* (New York: Penguin Group, 2006), 78.

9. Leonard Schlain, *The Alphabet Versus the Goddess: The Conflict Between Word and Image* (New York: Penguin Group, 1999), 17–27.

10. James Weldon Johnson, "The Creation" in *The Book of American Negro Poetry*, ed. James Weldon Johnson (New York: Harcourt, Brace and Co., 1922), 76–79.

11. Clarissa Pinkola Estés, *The Creative Fire*, CD Recording (Boulder, CO: Sounds True, 1991).

12. Ellen Horovitz, *Spiritual Art Therapy: An Alternate Path* (Springfield, IL: Charles C. Thomas Publisher, 2002), 25.

13. Howard Gardner, *Multiple Intelligences: New Horizons in Theory and Practice* (New York: Basic Books, 2006).

14. Stephen K. Levine, *Poiesis: The Language of Psychology and the Speech of the Soul* (London: Jessica Kingsley Publishers, 1997), 10.

15. Natalie Rogers, *The Creative Connection: Expressive Arts as Healing* (Science and Behavior Books, 1993), 43–45.

16. Jeremy Begbie, *Beholding the Glory: Incarnation Through the Arts* (Grand Rapids, MI: Baker Academic, 2001), xi.

17. Paolo Knill, "Soul Nourishment or the Intermodal Language of the Imagination." In *Foundations of Expressive Arts Therapy*, eds. Stephen K. and Ellen G Levine (Philadelphia, PA: Jessica Kingsley Publishers, 1999), 45.

18. Rumi, *The Essential Rumi*, Coleman Barks, trans (HarperSanFrancisco, 2004), 109.

19. Thomas Moore, *Care of the Soul* (New York: Harper, 1994), 4.

20. Ibid., 9.

21. Catherine Moon, "Prayer, Sacraments, Grace" in *Spirituality and Art Therapy*, ed. Mimi Farrelly-Hansen (London: Jessica Kingsley Publishers, 2001), 38.

22. Stephen K. Levine, *Poiesis*, 4.

23. Timothy Fry, *Rule of St. Benedict* (Collegeville, MN: Liturgical Press, 1982).

24. Ephesians 1:18.

25. Stephen K. Levine, *Poiesis*, 15.

26. Adriana Diaz, *Freeing the Creative Spirit: Drawing on the Power of Art to Tap the Magic and Wisdom Within* (HarperSanFrancisco, 1992), 92.

27. Shaun McNiff, *Art as Medicine: Creating a Therapy of the Imagination* (Boston: Shambhala, 1992), 99.

28. Pat Allen, *Art is a Way of Knowing* (Boston: Shambhala, 1995), 74.

29. Mary Caroline Richards, *Centering In Pottery, Poetry, and the Person* (Hanover, NH: Wesleyan University Press, 1989), 9.

30. Nancy Mellon, *Storytelling with Children* (Gloucestershire, UK: Hawthorn Press, 2000).

31. Christina Baldwin, *Storycatcher: Making Sense of our Lives through the Power and Practice of Story* (Novato, California: New World Library, 2005), 30.

32. Angeles Arrien, *The Fourfold Way* (San Francisco: HarperCollins Publishers, 1993), 54.

33. For information on InterPlay classes and "Untensives" worldwide, see www.interplay.org

34. Phil Porter with Cynthia Winton-Henry, *Having It All—Body, Mind, Heart & Spirit Together Again at Last* (Oakland, CA: Wing It! Press, 1997), 114.

35. Megan McKenna and Tony Cowan, *Keepers of the Story: Oral Traditions in Religion* (Maryknoll, NY: Orbis, 1997), 184.

36. Peter A. Pitzele, *Scripture Windows: Towards a Practice of Bibliodrama* (Los Angeles, CA: Alef Design Group, 1998), 11.

37. John Shea, *An Experience of Spirit: Spirituality and Storytelling* (Liguori, MO: Liguori Publications, 2005), 4.

38. Pitzele, 11. Also see www.bibliodrama.com.

39. Dennis Linn, Sheila Fabricant Linn and Matthew Linn, *What Is My Song?* (Mahwah, NJ: Paulist Press, 2005).

40. Bernie Siegel, *How to Never Grow Old,* audiotape (Boulder, CO: Sounds True, 1992).

41. Christina Baldwin, *Storycatcher.*

42. Jane Hirshfield, *Nine Gates: Entering the Mind of Poetry* (New York: Harper Perennial, 1998), 221.

43. Graham Wallas, "Stages in the Creative Process" in *The Creativity Question,* Albert Rothenberg and Carl R. Hausman, eds. (Durham, NC: Duke University Press, 1976), 69–73.

44. Earle Jerome Coleman, *Creativity and Spirituality: Bonds Between Art and Religion* (State University of New York Press, 1998), 171.

45. Roy DeLeon offers simple exercises like these on his website: www.blessedmovements.com. For further explorations, please see his book, *Praying with the Body: Bringing the Psalms to Life.* (Orleans, MA: Paraclete Press, 2009).

46. Reflective short pieces (3–4 mintues in length) are excellent for hand dances. Explore selections from Suzanne Ciani, *Pianissimo II,* Musica International, Inc., 1996.

47. To set a harmonious backdrop for warm-ups, consider *Woodlands* by Eric Tingstad, Nancy Rumbel and David Lanz. Narada Productions, Inc., 1987.

48. For an expressive range, experiment with selections from *Feather, Stone and Light* by R. Carlos Nakai, William Eaton and Will Clipman. Canyon Records Productions, 1994.

49. For exformations, music with a bit more percussion or emotional intensity can be helpful. See Gabrielle Roth and the Mirrors, *Initiations.* Raven Recordings, 1984.

50. Alice Walker, *A Poem Traveled Down my Arm: Poems and Drawings* (New York: Random House, 2003), 55.

51. For a beautiful selection of prayerful meditations, listen to *Prayer for Peace,* created by a collection of Native American Artists and published by Silver Wave Records, Inc., 2000.

52. Patrizia Pallaro, ed., *Authentic Movement: Essays by Mary Starks Whitehouse, Janet Adler and Joan Chodorow* (London and Philadelphia: Jessica Kingsley Publishers, 2000).

53. For the labyrinth, choose a long-playing ambient piece such as *Pure Will Ackerman* (Windham Hill, 2006); or Jennifer Berezan, *Returning* (Edge of Wonder, 2001); or Charlie Bommarito *Edge of Silence* (Bright Room Productions, 2005).

54. Romans 8:26, NRSV Translation.

55. Ginny Whitelaw and Betsy Wetzig, *Move to Greatness: Focusing the Four Essential Energies of a Whole and Balanced Leader* (Boston, MA: Nicholas Brealey International, 2008).

56. Ann Bedford Ulanov, *Religion and the Spiritual in Carl Jung* (New York: Paulist Press, 2000), 32.

57. SoulCards by Deborah Koff-Chapin come in two different sets and are available at www.touchdrawing.com.

58. www.bridgebuilding.com has a variety of contemporary icons available for purchase.

59. Marianne Hieb, *Inner Journeying Through Art Journaling: Learning to See and Record Your Life as a Work of Art* (London: Jessica Kingsley Publishers, 2005), 22.

60. Lauren Neergaard, "This is Your Brain on Jazz—It's Creative," *Detroit Free Press* 11 March 2008: 2.

61. Jalal Al-Din Rumi, from "Today Like Every Other Day" in *Rumi: The Book of Love: Poems of Ecstasy and Longing*, trans. Coleman Barks (New York, NY: HarperCollins Publishers, Inc., 2005), 123.

62. See the Resource Section for a list of recordings to support art-making, movement or prayer.

63. Margareta Wärja, "Music as Mother," *Foundations of Expressive Arts Therapy: Theoretical and Clinical Perspectives*, ed. Stephen K. Levine and Ellen G. Levine (London/Philadelphia: Jessica Kingsley Publishers Ltd., 1999), 172–175.

64. A piece of classical music could be chosen here. Or explore contemporary cello pieces from David Darling's *Eight String Religion*, 2001 or Gretchen Yanover's *Bow and Cello*, 2005.

65. Trish and Richard Bruxvoort Colligan, "Profession" and "Make Way," from *Pilgrim's to a New World* Audio CD, (The River's Voice Music, 2009). Due to Trish's generosity, you may download for free the songs referenced! Please visit: www.Music ForSpiritualDirection.com.

66. Deborah Koff-Chapin, For recordings and resources, visit www.Touch Drawing.com

67. Appalachian Expressive Arts Collective, *Expressive Arts Therapy: Creative Process in Art and Life* (Boone, NC: Parkway Publishers, 2002), 7.

68. Naomi Shihab Nye, *Words Under the Words: Selected Poems* (Portland, OR: Eighth Mountain Press, 1994), 36.

69. John Fox, *Finding What You Didn't Lose: Expressing Your Truth and Creativity Through Poem-Making* (New York: Jeremy P. Tarcher/Putnam, 1995), xiv–xv.

70. Jane Hirshfield, "Buddhism and Creativity" in *Women Practicing Buddhism: American Experiences*, Peter Gregory and Suzanne Mrozik, eds. (Somerville, MA: Wisdom Publications, 2008), 44.

71. Mary Oliver, *New and Selected Poems Volume 1* (Boston, MA: Beacon Press, 2004), 10.

72. David Whyte, *House of Belonging* (Langley, WA: Many Rivers Press, 1996), 26.

73. Edward Hirsch, *Lay Back the Darkness* (New York: Knopf, 2004), 3.

74. John Fox, *Finding What You Didn't Lose*, 78–80.

75. Christine Valters Paintner, *Sacred Poetry: An Invitation to Write*, available at www.AbbeyoftheArts.com.

76. Hadewijch of Antwerp in *Women in Praise of the Sacred: 43 Centuries of Spiritual Poetry by Women*, ed. Jane Hirshfield, tr. Oliver Davies (New York, NY: Harper-Collins Publishers, Inc., 1994), 99–100.

77. Dennis Linn, Sheila Fabricant Linn, Matthew Linn, *Good Goats: Healing Our Image of God* (Mahwah, NY: Paulist Press, 1994).

78. Joan Borysenko, *A Woman's Journey to God: Finding the Feminine Path* (Riverhead Books, New York, NY: 1999), 105.

79. J. B. Phillips, *Your God is Too Small: A Guide for Believers and Skeptics Alike* (New York: Touchstone, 1997), pp. 37–39.

80. For books and articles exploring the Universe story see:

Judy Cannato, *Radical Amazement* (Notre Dame; Sorin Books, 2006).

Thomas Berry and Brian Swimme, The *Universe Story* (San Francisco: Harper, 1992).

Moran, Terrence J., CSSR, "Spiritual Direction and the New Cosmology," *Presence* 15, (September 2009), 6–13.

81. Jan Phillips, "One" from *All the Way to Heaven: Songs of Courage and Comfort for the Creative Journey* (Jan Phillips, 2001).

82. Victor Turner, *Dramas, Fields, and Metaphors: Symbolic Action in Human Society* (Ithaca, NY: Cornell University Press, 1975), 51.

83. Rainer Maria Rilke, *Letters to a Young Poet* (New York: WW Norton, 1993), 35.

84. A beautiful children's version of this story is included in the following resource: Anita Ganeri, *Buddhist Stories: Traditional Religious Tales* (Minneapolis, MN: Picturewindow Books, 2006), 22–23.

85. Pema Chödrön, *When Things Fall Apart: Heart Advice for Difficult Times* (Boston, MA: Shambhala Publications, 1997), 88.

86. Psalm 42:7, Jerusalem Bible.

87. Stephen K. Levine, *Poiesis: The Language of Psychology and the Speech of the Soul* (London: Jessica Kingsley Publications, 1997), xvi.

88. Celeste Snowber, *Embodied Prayer: Towards Wholeness of Body, Mind, Soul* (Kelowna, Canada: Northstone, 2004), 52–154.

89. Elisabeth Kübler-Ross, *On Death and Dying* (New York: Scribner, 1997).

90. Snowber, *Embodied Prayer*, 152–154.

91. See the Resource Section for books on Mosaics.

92. Stephanie Kallos, *Broken for You* (New York: Grove Press, 2004).

93. Jill Mellick, *The Art of Dreaming: Tools for Creative Dreamwork* (Berkeley, CA: Conari Press, 2001), 4.

94. Ibid., 5.

95. Bill Plotkin, *Soulcraft: Crossing into the Mysteries of Nature and Psyche* (Novato, CA: New World Library, 2003).

96. Peter Mattheissen, *The Circle of Life: Rituals from the Human Family Album*, ed. David Cohen (San Francisco: HarperCollins, 1991), 230.

97. Ellen Dissanayake, *What is Art For?* (Seattle: University of Washington Press, 1990), 74–106.

98. Ellen Dissanayake, *Homo Aestheticus: Where Art Comes From and Why* (Seattle: University of Washington Press, 1999), 61–63.

99. Michael Joncas, "As Morning Breaks" from *O Joyful Light* (Portland, Oregon: OCP, 2004). Also available to purchase and download from iTunes (www.apple.com/itunes). Once there, search for "Michael Joncas—As".

100. The English translation of the Antiphon (adapted) from *The Liturgy of the Hours* © 1974, International Committee on English in the Liturgy, Inc. All rights reserved.

101. Kent Gustavson, "Prayer of Good Courage" from *Mountain Vespers* (Kent Gustavson Music).

102. For colorful scarves and dance resources, see www.dancingcolors.com.

103. Maureen Conroy, RSM, *Looking Into the Well: Supervision of Spiritual Directors* (Chicago: Loyola University Press, 1995) xx.

104. To see some helpful examples of reflection questions, refer to the Contemplative Reflection Forms in the excellent resource: *Supervision of Spiritual Directors: Engaging in Holy Mystery*, Mary Rose Bumpus and Rebecca Bradburn Langer, eds. (New York: Morehouse, 2005), 181–191.

105. For more information about how to work with the non-dominant hand and its benefits, see Lucia Cappichione's *The Power of Your Other Hand: A Course in Channeling the Inner Wisdom of Your Right Brain* (Franklin Lakes, NJ: New Page Books, 2001).

106. Marion Woodman, *Coming Home to Myself: Reflections for Nurturing a Woman's Body and Soul* (Conari Press, 2001).

107. The results were then compiled into a book. For examples, see Larry Smith and Rachel Fershleiser, *Not Quite What I Was Planning: Six-Word Memoirs by Writers Famous and Obscure* (New York: Harper, 2008).

108. These songs are suggestions as a starting place for engaging music in the service of spiritual direction and supervision. The "Our Father," sung by Rafe Perlman, comes from the album "Healing the Holy Land" (www.soundings .com/HTHL/index.html.) The "Ave Maria," sung by Ashana, is available on her album "All is Forgiven" (www.ashanamusic.com.)

109. This true story is retold in the novel by Steven Gallway entitled *The Cellist of Sarajevo* (New York, NY: Riverhead Books, 2008).

110. Karl Paulnack, from a Welcome Address entitled *The Power of Music* given to incoming students at the Boston Conservatory, September, 2004. (9 Sept. 2009.) http://www.bostonconservatory.edu/s/940/Bio.aspx?sid=940&gid= 1&pgid=1241

CPSIA information can be obtained at www.ICGtesting.com
Printed in the USA
LVOW11s1922021115

460557LV00007B/11/P